With best wishes,

W Graham Monteith

DECONSTRUCTING MIRACLES

DECONSTRUCTING MIRACLES

FROM THOUGHTLESS INDIFFERENCE TO HONOURING DISABLED PEOPLE

W GRAHAM MONTEITH

Published by
Covenanters Press
the joint imprint of
Zeticula
57 St Vincent Crescent
Glasgow
G3 8NQ
and
Scottish Christian Press
21 Young Street
Edinburgh
EH2 4HU

http://www.covenanters.co.uk
admin@covenanters.co.uk
Copyright © W Graham Monteith 2005

Paperback ISBN 1-905022-21-2
Hardback ISBN 1-905022-22-0
Large print ISBN 1-905022-23-9

Biblical quotations are from the *New International Version* (NIV) – International Bible Society, Copyright © 1973, 1978, 1984 by International Bible Society. They have been drawn from *Pradis* CD-ROM – Copyright © The Zondervan Corporation, 2002.

For my beloved wife
Edna Jean

μειςζονα δε; διςδωσιν χαςριν... διο; Λεςγει
: ὁ θεο; ὑπερηφαςνοι ἀντιταςσσεται,
ταπεινοι   δε; διςδωσιν χαςριν.

James 4: 6.

Contents

Acknowledgements

Many people have helped, either directly or indirectly, in the production of this book and in the formation of the ideas that it contains. Those who are mentioned by name have actually offered help with particular topics.

I have been convinced for a long time that an understanding of the healing miracles in the gospels are at the centre of any understanding of God's dealing with disability, and that disabled people's understanding of the gospels has often been compromised because of the insensitive way in which they are treated in a church which is relatively inexperienced about disability. Therefore, I should like to thank all members of congregations with whom I have lived and worked who have given me either positive thoughts or negative reactions by their insightful help or lack of understanding. For 22 years the Church accepted me as a minister and for those who were closely concerned there was a constant challenge of dealing with my disability, and I was also challenged by the response which I was forced to make. This sentence betrays a wealth of anecdotal material which I have disciplined myself to ignore in the writing of this text. But let no one forget the gratitude and, at times, the resentment which so many people have engendered in me over many years.

I have a habit of remembering sermons over a long period right back to the age of eight, and I was deeply struck by Professor Donald Macleod's sermon to the Episcopalian Theological College in Edinburgh, Coates Hall, in 1972 to which I refer in detail in Chapter 7. Although I seldom agree with them, sermons from the Free Church are amongst the most memorable.

In my PhD Thesis at one point I made great use of a passage from Sheila Woodcock's Masters Thesis on holistic medicine. The passage I quote is so full of feeling and so relevant to a holistic approach to patients that I am grateful that she has yet again allowed me to reprint an extract here. (On page 42)

I would like to thank members of the *Sea of Faith Network* in Edinburgh, which I convene, for listening to my ideas about quantum theory. As a result of a very intense evening of discussion several amendments were made and even more could have been added. Dr John Wilkinson came to my aid when I was looking for material for chapter six and he introduced me to the work of J Keir Howard, despite his disagreement with Howard's conclusions. Dr Wilkinson's work on the Church of Scotland's Committee on Healing in the 1980s helped me to understand many of the issues. It was a pleasure to be on the same committee and to learn from him and others who are mentioned in the text.

Dr Jean Morrison offered me advice on how to select important material in the chapter on counselling. She did so from a position of authority as an expert on the nocturnal dreams of people with disabilities.

Most of the material would not have been produced had it not been for my mother-in-law, Jean Little, who took it down to my dictation. This not only meant that it was done much more quickly but also more fluently because I tend to think with my tongue rather than my pen. When I am working on my own the only way I can succeed is to talk about what I am doing to others, and to all those who have been bored by such conversations, I offer my apologies.

My sincere thanks go to John Swinton, Professor in Practical Theology and Pastoral Care, School of Divinity, History and Philosophy, King's College, University of Aberdeen for his encouragement and advice. I should also like to place on record my appreciation of his pioneering and innovative course for divinity students on the theological issues surrounding people with disabilities.

Last but by no means least, I would thank my publisher and editor, Janet de Vigne and Simon Marlow, for their forbearance, patient listening and good advice.

Preface

When I am asked to describe what I study, I now say that my interest lies in religious discourse rather than theology. I do so not only because I believe that I have very little to add to the theological scene but also because I believe that the way people speak and write about religion produces more insight into present day problems than theology on its own. I am also perhaps expressing a hesitancy about my current beliefs. Religious discourse reveals what people believe, marks out their intentions and often reveals unintended consequences. Philosophers and theologians have written about miracles for many centuries and have inevitably linked them to disability or sickness. Most were uninhibited by modern sensitivities about disability and were only interested in the outcome of a miracle. What this book sets out to do is to consider how their language has discounted disability and made it almost incidental to both their writings and to the gospel message. By pointing this out we hope to redress the balance, not by rewriting theology but by showing that it can be more constructively used.

The converse of this method of working is to examine the discourse of disability. I have great difficulty in believing that there was any construct of disability during the time of Jesus' ministry, but as several authors have pointed out, we must hang our hermeneutic somewhere.

When it comes to discourse by disabled people or about disabled people, I am quite unapologetic about my use of secular studies and writings. There is not a wealth of religious material written by disabled people in the UK and the predominate discourse is written by people who are outwith, even antipathetic to, the Church. To ignore this literature would be to ignore the reality of Britain today and also to insult many people who have devoted much thought to disability. However, that does not mean that I always agree with the disability movement in the UK or in the models which they have produced. I basically reject the militancy of much of today's disabled movement and I do not much agree with the over-emphasis of a Marxist collectivism which pervades the descriptions of the social model of disability.

I hope that this book will present a righteous indignation about some of the treatment of disabled people without condemning the situation by an all-pervading ideology – which can become a dictatorship in itself. Christianity is an inclusive religion and inclusiveness without love is tokenism and is bound to lead to disappointment and patronization. To exclude is a sinful rejection of a major facet of the gospels.

The reader will have to judge my effort themselves. I pray that my shortcomings will be forgiven and that anything good will have a lasting effect on the way disabled people are discussed, both in the context of the healing miracles and welcomed generally within the Church, and that disabled people, in turn, may learn that theology is a beautiful discipline whose shortcomings should also be forgiven.

Edinburgh
November, 2004.

Introduction

The Healing Miracles and Disablist Language

The Forgotten Congregation

15 When one of those at the table with him heard this, he said to Jesus, "Blessed is the man who will eat at the feast in the kingdom of God."

16 Jesus replied: "A certain man was preparing a great banquet and invited many guests.

17 At the time of the banquet he sent his servant to tell those who had been invited, 'Come, for everything is now ready.'

18 "But they all alike began to make excuses. The first said, 'I have just bought a field, and I must go and see it. Please excuse me.'

19 "Another said, 'I have just bought five yoke of oxen, and I'm on my way to try them out. Please excuse me.'

20 "Still another said, 'I have just got married, so I can't come.'

21 "The servant came back and reported this to his master. Then the owner of the house became angry and ordered his servant, 'Go out quickly into the streets and alleys of the town and bring in the poor, the crippled, the blind and the lame.'

22 " 'Sir,' the servant said, 'what you ordered has been done, but there is still room.'

23 "Then the master told his servant, 'Go out to the roads and country lanes and make them come in, so that my house will be full.

Luke 14:15–23

Right at the heart of the teaching of Jesus is an exhortation to his followers to invite the 'crippled, the blind and the lame' to a banquet which had been spurned by busier, and wealthier, friends. The parable may be read today as a challenge to the Church to lay aside the chatter of its heavily involved and highly committed congregations and to urge them to reach out to those who are often regarded as different. Disabled people are manifestly absent from the Church's feasts, and congregations respond by meeting some criteria of physical access whilst often treating disabled people as outsiders in a psychological sense. Instead of being the central guests at the banquet, disabled people are marginalized as some abstract group who are characters in these parables and in the healing miracles. They are, in fact, central and our language and preaching about such biblical passages should reflect this. 'Different' was a word much favoured by the *World Council of Churches*. 'Differently abled' was the phrase chosen to describe disabled people – which was well-intentioned but masked the fact that the disabled are people with exactly the same needs and aspirations as everyone else. Yet, each individual comes with an identity formed over years of coming to terms with a body which has limitations, of interaction with others, and the disappointment or frustration caused by disablist discrimination. This book deals with the disablist legacy that is found in the Church's handling of the healing miracles.

The healing miracles of Jesus are central to all four gospels and should sound an evangelistic siren as loudly as do his sayings. Theologians have devoted books to giving rational explanation. Groups have sought to develop ministries of healing or sought to replicate them, whilst others have devalued them for diverse reasons. In the search for replication or illustration, disabled people have inevitably been understood to be the recipients of the mercy and power of Jesus as part a divine purpose. When regarded as instruments of a divine purpose, disabled people do not challenge the Church to include them as full and equal members but sideline them as both spectators and spectated. But, what if the healings of Jesus are subversive enough to offer disabled people a central place in both society and in the fellowship of believers? We shall look at the ways this question has been avoided and how an answer might be developed in a non-disablist hermeneutic. The answer will be multi-disciplinary, drawing on the insights of theology, philosophy and social scientific methods.

At the heart of this book are three central working principles, which demand that preachers pay more attention to the special sensitivities of disabled people when discussing New Testament miracles. First, miracles are related in stories about disabled people that arouse unexpected emotions in the ways we either relate to our own disabilities and illnesses or how people without disabilities respond after considering a miracle story in relation to disabled people. Second, there is no call for a new interpretation of the New Testament miracles but rather there is a need to consider how different theological and hermeneutic approaches impact on disabled people. Third, as the analysis progresses it will become obvious that the healing miracles are not narratives that stand apart but are complemented by Jesus' parabolic teaching and attitudes and *vice versa*.

It will be appropriate to dispose of a fourth principle which undergirds this book: disabled access to churches has been on the agenda of most denominations for at least the past two decades (See, for instance, Monteith, 1981; Part II), but the accessibility of theology and hermeneutics is a relatively new pursuit. Disabled people have sought for some time to appropriate, or embody, a theology which speaks directly to the situation in which they find themselves (Eiesland, 1994). However, our aim is to produce an understanding of miracles which will neither offend disabled people nor exclude them from a block of the New Testament which every faithful person must attempt to appreciate. In other words, we aim to produce a non-disablist hermeneutic rather than a new theology of miracles. If some of what is written is new to the reader, so be it; but this is not our primary aim.

An early aim of feminists was to make church language inclusive of both genders and to allow comfortable listening to theology and liturgy stripped of its male bias. In similar fashion, this book attempts to accommodate those disabled people who find that glib talk of the cure of impairments marginalizes them and leaves an uncomfortable aura of ambiguity surrounding their disabilities. This problem can be solved without re-inventing the wheel.

Who make up the forgotten congregation? Disabled people are not proportionately represented in the average congregation despite increased access. This is partly an outreach problem and is also in part one of perception. Unchurched disabled people simply are unaware that the local church is calling them, are unaware of gradual changes in access that have been taking place and are oblivious to efforts to bring disability to the heart of theological reflection. There is also a tendency throughout society to fail to recognize impairments associated with ageing as disabilities and therefore to discount elderly and infirm members of the congregation as members of the disabled community. They, in turn, seldom have a consciousness of disability.

Within the UK, the disability movement is characterized by a deep anti-clericalism at its centre. There is a tendency to compare this unfavourably with a contrasting situation in the United States, but the reality is that churches in both countries are still failing to attract disabled people. According to a 2002 survey conducted by the *National Organization of Disability*, '47 per cent of Americans with disabilities attend religious services at least once per month, compared with 65 percent of those without disabilities'" (Belkin, 2004); whilst no such statistics appear to be available for the UK.

In Britain, the mainstay of the disability movement is currently unduly influenced by a group of academics in about four universities who dominate the academic and voluntary training of disabled activists. Their courses have a distinct Marxist foundation and regard disabled people as an oppressed social group. With the current fashion for Foucault and critical discourse analysis, they find that society's knowledge structures are stacked against disabled people. (Monteith, 2001)

Church people and disabled people do make common cause on issues such as euthanasia, selective and elective abortions and increasingly in the field of genetic politics. The potential to eradicate and mitigate disability, which arises from our knowledge of genetics and our mapping of the genome, fills disabled academics with trepidation in an open way which the churches can and should respect. (See Kerr & Shakespeare with Varty [Illustrator], 2002) Such potential common interests and shared expertise offers new alliances and potential for broader understandings of both common issues and the appreciation of the treasured lifestyles which many disabled wish to retain. Put simply, many disabled people have no stomach for the eradication of their impairments and expect, nay demand, that society accept and value the otherness of disability. We will discuss later how thought about miracles has often resulted in a search for homogeneity and a fear of the variety in which the human body is manifested. (McFague, 1993)

Now, whilst this book is not about the disability movement, it is important to note at the outset that the language which the Church uses can be and is critically examined by radically motivated disabled people. This is not to say that such criticism is always theologically informed but the strength of feeling often is more persuasive than technical debate. Two examples will illustrate the power of language to cause distress in liturgy or the conduct of services.

First, take a verse from John Wesley's hymn, *O for a thousand tongues to sing*, which, when combined with several stirring tunes, remains a favourite. However, disabled people take exception to the fifth verse which should be cited along with the two previous:

> 3 He breaks the power of cancelled sin,
> He sets the prisoner free;
> His blood can make the foulest clean,
> His blood availed for me.
> 4 He speaks, and, listening to his voice,
> New life the dead receive,
> The mournful, broken hearts rejoice
> The humble poor believe.
> 5 Hear him, ye deaf; his praise, ye dumb,
> Your loosened tongues employ;
> Ye blind, behold your Saviour come;
> And leap, ye lame, for joy!

This verse is probably a reference to Luke 4:18–19 which records Jesus' response to Isaiah 61:1–2

> And [Jesus] stood up to read.
> 17 The scroll of the prophet Isaiah was handed to him.
> Unrolling it, he found the place were it is written:
> 18 "The Spirit of the Lord is on me,
> because he has anointed me
> to preach good news to the poor.
> He has sent me to proclaim freedom for the prisoners
> and recovery of sight for the blind,
> to release the oppressed,
> 19 to proclaim the year of the Lord's favour."
> 20 Then he rolled up the scroll, gave it back to the attendant
> and sat down. The eyes of everyone in the synagogue were
> fastened on him,
> 21 and he began by saying to them, "Today this scripture is
> fulfilled in your hearing."

The language of John Wesley's hymn can be analysed at three levels. At the most basic level verse five illustrates a use of politically incorrect language. An observer outwith the Church would object to words like 'dumb', 'lame' and maybe even to 'blind'. It is perfectly valid to argue that the hymn was written in the eighteenth century and that then no offence was apparent in the use of these words. However, the Church continues to use them today fully aware of their political incorrectness. Furthermore, it is totally ambiguous as to whether they are used literally or metaphorically. The hymn is given great exposure on BBC's *Songs of Praise* thus extending the offence to the very people who make up the core of the disability movement. The Church must ask itself whether its attachment to this favourite hymn is justified.

At the second level, the verse maybe understood as a celebration of the miraculous works of Jesus in healing the impairments which used to be signified by the words 'dumb', 'lame' and 'blind'. In every aesthetic way, the poetry and succinctness of this verse is masterful in praising the healing achievements of Jesus, yet the audience which objects to the verse is disabled by the triumphalism of its sentiments. Jesus, in this characterization, heals without any qualification and does so in broad categories. Is it little wonder that it causes offence to disabled worshippers? The dilemma posed by this analysis highlights a problem of this book: must we abandon such obvious poetic beauty in order to use language which is more inclusive and correct?

Third, the verse contains specific biblical references. It refers to both Luke and Isaiah and raises the whole question of prophecy. It is a fact that Isaiah expected these impairments to disappear in the perfect kingdom to be restored after the Exile. Jesus, in turn, interpreted this prophecy in terms of his own ministry, which did indeed bring relief not only to those who suffered impairments but also to the prisoner and the oppressed. This is a truth which cannot be evaded but perhaps must be restated in such a way that it does not cause offence. Such is the aim of this book as regards miracles.

Let us now turn to a second illustration of language which unintentionally causes offence. It is common for congregations to introduce rubrics into the liturgy which are designed to make visitors who are ill at ease in a church setting more comfortable. This is an example of political correctness which has gone wrong. The typical example is the rubric 'let all stand'. The boldness and brevity of this request is addressed to everyone and has no regard for wheelchair users or even for elderly people who are infirm. The problem here is that it is almost impossible to think of a rubric which can be included without being either clumsy or pedantic.

How does all this relate to the two governing principles on page 13 above? The politically incorrect language of this hymn affects not only the disabled, but interested observers and the committed alike. A stark choice faces lovers of this hymn: either it must be removed from our cannon or the language must be carefully explained both in its historical context and in its biblical and theological context. Such a solution is relatively simple, given the mountain of language feminists have already dealt with in a search for gender inclusiveness. But the fact remains that at the centre of the hymn lies a gospel passage which appears to present a 'manifesto' characterising Jesus' ministry.

The second assumption on page 14 above argues that theology and hermeneutics must be accessible to all, including disabled people. This implies that the biblical foundation which inspired John Wesley must have meaning beyond the triumphalism of the hymn. Jesus did not announce a flamboyant ministry but rather one of humility combined with a new vision of spiritual man. Jesus took the quotation from Isaiah and illustrated the nature of the spiritual revolution which his ministry was to bring about. Thus, following the argument of the most common exegesis, when he speaks of the blind receiving sight he is not addressing healing directly but talking of the emergence of a whole group of people from spiritual darkness. Later we will discuss whether it is useful to use blindness as a metaphor, but in this single instance Jesus is indeed talking about the darkness created by the outdated religious institutions of his time. In the same way neither Jesus nor Isaiah were looking for the freeing of prisoners but rather the liberation of all who have a legitimate right to expect freedom in 'in the year of the Lord's favour'. The picture is beginning to emerge of a ministry which is far from the triumphant picture of John Wesley and more in keeping with the humility of Jesus.

John Hull (2002) has examined the use of 'blindness' in a number of Victorian hymns which are still sung today. He does not totally disapprove of metaphor but does conclude that 'blindness' usually implies spiritual weakness, obstinate stupidity or heathen and satanic ignorance of Christianity. He concludes that deep-seated prejudice may be hidden in the thoughtless use of such metaphors.

> We must train ourselves to purify our language from
> unconscious traces of prejudice. The truth is that there
> is no such thing as spiritual blindness. There is spiritual
> insensitivity, stubbornness, ignorance and callousness, but

> when we refer to these qualities as being spiritual blindness
> we reinforce the prejudice, and collaborate in the continued
> marginalization of disabled people.
>
> (Hull, 2002; p 341)

Despite the reservation about the use of 'blindness', it becomes immediately possible to offer the offended disabled person a fresh insight into the intrinsic goodness behind the outdated language of Wesley. An explanation can take it further by putting compassion at the heart of the healing miracles of Jesus. It seems that he quoted Isaiah in order to stress the spiritual strength of his mission as one of compassion and liberation rather than to herald a great new religion.

> Do not think I have come to abolish the Law or the Prophets,
> I have not come to abolish them but to fulfil them.
>
> Matthew 5:17

If miracles are to be regarded as a major part of Jesus' ministry then they must be integrated into a wider perspective of religious reform rather than bracketed off into some strange theological department of their own. This is precisely what history has done to the miracles of Jesus. In modernity, David Hume commenced the trait of philosophers to discuss miracles in terms of the way they represent 'violations of natural law' rather than as social events which took place in the context of a compassionate human life of a historical healer and teacher with a visionary ministry. The aim of this study is to argue that the healings are social events with social consequences which do not depend upon preconceptions of natural law.

There are many different ways of examining miracles, each with a different agenda and outcome. Our aim is not to discredit these different approaches but to suggest that they have consistently failed to address the needs of disabled people who are at the centre of each healing miracle. It is not possible to compare the disabilities Jesus encountered with those of today nor is it possible to replicate his healings, but it is certainly possible to appropriate an understanding which might have been common to both eras. Given this very real difficulty, it has been easier to treat miracles as some kind of oddity which can be explained either to glorify God or to simplify the gospels. The former has led to metaphysical interpretations of 'violations of natural law' and to many protestant theologians finding it easier to put miracles aside by arguing that they only took place in the biblical period under a special dispensation. (Kelsey, 1995) The latter has been manifested in higher biblical criticism which dismisses miracles as simply stories told to boost the creditability of Jesus. In broad terms, preaching based on any of these ideas has stressed the glory of God which has been revealed in these events, or in their fabrication, but has forgotten both the humanity of Jesus and the person receiving healing. This is what must now be redressed by explaining how these philosophies and theories have erred and how we can move to a more human and social interpretation which offers hope and liberation to disabled people.

Hidden in most non-metaphysical theories of miracles are several underlying dichotomies which assume major importance because of their very personal nature. These dichotomies have directly and personally impacted on disabled people and their families and have heightened their sensitivities. They did so in New Testament times and many disabled people could tell stories about their influence today. Their significance is often not to be found directly in language but in the myths which are created about disability. Their structure could neatly be analysed by social anthropologists and linguists alike in terms of structuralist theory. (Barthes, 1977; Levi-Strauss, 1966, Saussure, 1916/1959) This will be explored in Chapter 5, pages 152ff where the contribution of medical anthropology is discussed as a tool for understanding the healing miracles and their relationship to disability. Barthes, Derrida and Foucault made a formidable trio in Europe with their emphasis on going beyond epistemology to hermeneutics, or the interpretation of meaning. Both Barthes and Foucault showed how semiosis and discourse reflect or cause power relations in society and perpetuate myths which are detrimental to groups within society. Derrida, on the other hand, showed how meaning is in the hands of its receptors and therefore indeterminate. (Derrida, 1988) The main feature to note in hermeneutics is that society reveals its structures by its choice of meanings. Mary Douglas is much more favoured by Anglo-Saxon writers probably because her English writing is much more accessible in America. She acknowledges that the European writers on semiotics have altered forever her understanding of the meaning of things. Meaning is now understood as being a multi-layered combination of the different perspectives of society, religion and many other institutions. Disability can now be understood to gain its symbolic significance from society rather than any written definition. (Douglas, 1999) Mary Douglas has successfully combined anthropology with theology in her studies of the Books of Numbers and Leviticus. The point to be noted in reference to this study is that by choosing to define disability in New Testament categories, those who have engaged in such a hermeneutic have failed to redefine disability in an inclusive and acceptable manner. Disabled people seek to define themselves dynamically with reference to the impact society has on their impairments and the constraints that arise from simplistic medical understandings. The Bible, on the other hand, defines disability in dichotomous terms which lead to stereotyping and facile characterizations of disability which were no doubt sufficient in the time of Jesus but are inadequate today. The indented dichotomies are usually specific to particular stories.

These dichotomies and their respective levels are set out thus:

Sinful ⟷ Forgiven
    Clean ⟷ Unclean
    Impaired ⟷ Unimpaired
    Blind ⟷ Sighted
    Light ⟷ Darkness
Faithful ⟷ Lacking faith
Possessed ⟷ Free

These dichotomies have become embedded in popular religious culture if not in the minds of serious theologians. At this point, we will not consider the accuracy of the translation of words like leprosy but will take English translations at their face value. Most of the healing miracles either deal with alleged sinfulness, or with demon possession which is not the result of sin. Thus disabled people, such as the lame and the blind, have often been accused of being guilty of sin or infected with sin through their families. Epilepsy, though, has traditionally been associated with demon possession, and this has led to many superstitious beliefs surrounding the illness and its associated fits. The fact that such episodes tend to be very frightening to the spectator has only increased the fires of superstition.

Leprosy has been labelled unclean and lepers throughout the ages have been subjected to a totally unnecessary quarantine which has ostracized them from mainstream society. The word 'unclean' was used in New Testament times to describe most gaping wounds and emissions of bodily fluid and this general belief has percolated into the Church's traditional beliefs about women and into society's general dislike of bodily functions.

Blindness is generally associated in the gospels with sin in the same way as lameness, but the stigma associated with it has been exacerbated by the general concern for light and darkness which is witnessed in the Bible from Genesis to the sayings of Jesus in John's Gospel. The metaphorical use and implications of blindness is an aggravation for people with sight impairments which causes vexation which must be relieved by fresh understanding:

> While I am in the world, I am the light of the world.
>
> John 9:5

It is not only that blind people are thought to live in the dark, but it is implied that the unfaithful also live in spiritual darkness. Such use of a metaphor is peculiarly common in the case of blindness and, despite great public sympathy for people with such impairment, there is an abiding ambiguity in the language used by the Church in talking of people who are blind.

What we have witnessed is language about disability offending disabled people with or without faith at two levels. First, the language, such as that of John Wesley, was considered to be inappropriate at the non-critical level of usage. Second, we find that the New Testament has woven a structure of understanding which has imbued disability with meanings which have defined the social standing of disabled people for many centuries.

The essence of structuralism is that phenomena are defined by their opposites, i.e. night and day. This means that in the discourse of the Bible, positive aspects of well-being define the negative aspects of dis-ease or disability. It is this cycle in our hermeneutic which must be broken. In the forthcoming chapters, an attempt will be made to seek ways of talking about miracles and disabilities that avoids the entanglement of these structures which for too long have defined disability and oppress disabled people rather than liberate them.

Plan of Analysis

We have discussed one example, only tenuously linked to miracles, which indicates that disablist language may be analysed in two ways.

Certain philosophical and theological approaches to miracles have paid scant attention to the human dimensions and concentrated on our knowledge of God's power and dominion over 'natural law'. In certain evangelical circles this has led to an over-emphasis on miracles being simply signs of his glory. In the same vein, but at the opposite end of the theological spectrum, those who have sought to demythologize the gospel or develop form criticism have objectified the miracles again at the expense of their humanity. One of the charges levelled at these two methods is that of reductionism – miracles are simply literary devices or remnants of an oral tradition. Another form of reductionism can be strict medical analyses which argue that the disabled person had such and such symptoms therefore the miracle is *only* an example the power of Jesus to heal this or that.

On the other hand, we will attempt to consider two ways in which language about miracles may be analysed positively allowing a non-disablist hermeneutic to develop. First, there is sufficient evidence to suggest that Jesus deliberately broke social conventions or norms to offer fuller lives to those who were disabled or stigmatized. Second, where language has become structuralized, there may well be a social pathology behind it. Constructive alternative modes of thought offer ways to escape the dichotomies and become liberated from the old language structures.

Third, an awareness of both the medical and the social models of disability must call into question whether people with disabilities can any longer be treated as objects either of investigation or as 'teaching aids' to help explain and glorify the ministry of Jesus. Christology must not rest upon the person of Jesus alone and on other people as *dramatis personae* in the background of an arid and manipulative life and service. The truth and the beauty of the revelation and glimpse of God which we find in Jesus must lie in the human complexity of all whom he met and whose lives he enriched and somehow made whole.

Figure 1

This table makes several suggestions as to how we might proceed by considering firstly the outer spectra, and the inner groups of explanations. Basically the top axis has been the staple of theological thought and preaching for many decades and beyond but because it lacks a fundamental concern for human process, it has not had to address disability issues. This is not to deny its hermeneutic value to many but to argue that a restatement of these basic tenets would cease to place a burden on disabled people. It will be shown that, by and large, these forms of argument, turn disabled people into instruments of a broader scheme.

The bottom axis offers a different perspective. It delineates disciplines which consider all the actors in a healing miracle and usually within its social context. There is little chance of linking a modern meaning of disability directly to New Testament understandings of illness, but there is every chance of discovering common themes and outcomes. Furthermore, the more the language structure of the healing miracles is compared to our contemporary hermeneutic, the greater the chance we have of discerning whether we are locked into a disablist mindset by challenging our over-dependence on the dichotomies outlined on page 10. The question will be asked: Do we need to think about disability and its theological connotations in dichotomous terms?

When we consider the nature of healing in the next chapter, we might pave the way to being able to discard the ultimate dichotomy

– unwell / cure – for a more productive and stimulating one – unwell / healed or made whole. This will involve defining healing and wholeness and looking at them in a historical context.

State of Current Literature

This book primarily uses secondary sources with the exception of some material in chapter seven relating to the Iona Community. It does not aim to be a text-book on the theology of miracles nor a source book on disability and religious practice. However, these two meritorious subjects come together in a study of how accessible to disabled people are emphases within the theology and hermeneutics of miracles. Therefore, the state of literature which deals with such a coalescence of interests should be reviewed after an explanation of the type of literature that is currently available on miracles in general.

Recent general surveys of miracles have tended to fall into three groups: those which deal with a very specific problem such as blindness or the influence of the contemporary culture of Jesus, (Hull, 1974; Eve, 2002) those which explain a certain approach, for example form criticism, process theology or philosophical critiques (to which chapters are devoted below), or general suggestions of meaning. Old examples of this genre would include the work of C. S. Lewis (1966) or Keller and Keller(1969), whilst a good modern example might be *The Meaning of Miracles* by Jeffrey John (2001). The reader would have to look to these for coverage of topics such as the allegorical understanding of miracles which is not discussed in this book. A second group of general texts concentrates on the power and role of Jesus in an openly evangelical way. These seem to share a common compulsion to finish by including 'questions for discussion', thus implying that miracles, but not Jesus, are debatable. (See Warrington, 2000; or parts of Tiffany & Ringe, 1996) When the philosophical texts of David Hume and the implications of quantum theory are discussed, we depart from any real Christo-centric discourse to one of theism or even a hypothetical god.

The major trend which must be recorded is the welcome move from a discourse about the access rights for disabled people to a discussion of the whole *accessibility* of theology and ecclesiastical practice for people with disabilities. The reviewable literature grows apace but here the review must ultimately be focused on the miracles of Jesus. This is a subject which is mentioned by nearly all, but is only one small item on a large agenda. These mentions of miracles are the chief concern here and not the larger agenda, except that to see it come to fruition would perhaps constitute the most longed-for miracle by faithful disabled people, their carers and the professionals committed to promoting such a transformation of church life.

In 1981 many churches were enthused by the publicity of the *International Year of Disabled People* (IYDP) but now it is the dead-line of the *Disabled Discrimination Act* (DDA) that has spurred them into action to make buildings accessible. From October 2004, this Act has made it illegal to have barriers that prevent disabled people from using goods and services. The Act includes churches as providers of goods and services, and organizations like *Through the Roof* have been offering advice and encouragement to churches. *Widening the Eye of the Needle* by John Penton is one of the best books on accessibility to have been recently published and is modelled on the classic text of the 1970s by Goldsmith. This book offers a very good guide to adapting historic churches, yet it fails to offer adaptations which would make ministry possible for disabled ordinands. It does however hint at its shortcomings and beckons us to examine literature which deals with the entire enjoyment of church practice by making theology and governance accessible as well.

> Only by making churches as accessible as possible is there any real prospect of generally achieving the inclusion of people with disabilities within our congregations. Whilst *access* to a church may be seen as gaining entry to it, the concept of *accessibility* embraces not only entry, but also enjoyment of the use of all the building's services and facilities.
>
> (Penton, 2001: p 2)

The issue of the accessibility of theology and ecclesiastical practice has rightly begun to dominate the agenda to such an extent that the *Ecumenical Disabilities Advocates Network* (EDAN) and the *Faith and Order Commission of the World Council of Churches* chose a definitive option not to deal with 'practicalities' and anecdotes in their latest report to Plenary Council in 2003 in an Interim Statement entitled 'A Church of All and for All'. The urgency to address theological matters swamps the practicalities:

> Those disabled people who share a Christian faith are united by their awareness of God's love and Jesus' compassion for

> sick and disabled people, and find strength in the care of
> Christ. However, many have found that the church's teaching
> on this truth has been too limited, and have looked for their
> own understanding. Each one's awareness of how long he/
> she might expect to live, and their own faith experience have
> affected how they accept their disabilities. They have relied
> upon certain theological tools to address their existential need
> to explain the mystery and paradox of love and suffering,
> coexisting and giving meaning to their lives.
>
> (WCC, 2003; §7)

This statement has now been reprinted in a book by two of its
authors, Arne Fritzson from Sweden and Samuel Kabue from Kenya.
Their book, *Interpreting Disability: A Church of All and For All* (2004),
has the merit of being written by two disabled people with different
impairments who devote space to issues within the developing world
which is welcomed by many Western commentators. It has been written
as part of the *Risk Series* to complement the statement which thus far
has been EDAN's greatest achievement. In the context of the developing
world the issue of sin is even more compounded with disability and
miracles.

To some extent the statement of WCC presents, in its entirety, a
standard by which others may be judged, but other books have different
readers and aims. These different aims are important in allowing the
literature to be subdivided by intent into those that seek to introduce
disability and non-disablist language to an uninformed audience, and
those which seek to address a theological readership. A second review
of the same books will show how they deal with the healing miracles
of Jesus. In fact, no books can be found within this genre which deal
exclusively with theology or homiletics and disability in the sole context
of the gospel healing miracles, although there are many titles dealing with
the 'miraculous' in the life of a disabled person. These books, whether of
an academic or inspirational nature, are outwith the scope of this study.
However, most of the texts mentioned do have chapters or passages
devoted to the healing miracles of Jesus. Nearly all of them are American
where the churches undoubtedly have a far greater number of pastors and
academics interested in a ministry to people with disabilities than can be
found in the UK. On the one hand, the paucity of texts entirely devoted
to healing miracles is surprising, because most references to people

with disabilities occur in the context of Jesus' healing miracles. On the other hand, disabled people have aspirations that go to the heart of the 'holy catholic and apostolic Church' which these books have perhaps a greater imperative to address. They also cannot assume a totally informed readership which, if it existed, would render their message redundant. There is an underlying polemic in practically all the literature which seeks to open churches to a welcoming frame of mind when inviting or offering acceptance to people with disabilities in their congregations. Titles like *Copious Hosting* by Jennie Block (2002) implies that Christians are called to serve at the banquet, whilst John Swinton's use of 'solicitous care' (2001a) reminds us not only of the personal qualities of Jesus but of parables like the Good Samaritan.

To eschew disablist language and mentalities is also to learn to welcome and accept the ministries of disabled people. One book published in the UK, *Making a World of Difference* (2002) by McCloughry and Morris, comprehensively introduces the various models of disability, touches on appropriate language and deals with the DDA. British authors seem to dwell more on the medical and the social models of disability than their American counterparts. They also seem to have a penchant for choosing puns and metaphors in their titles. One advisor to the EDAN Group suggested that *Copious Hosting* might have been a suitable model for their Statement but this was not well received because of the book's attention to the practical issues of language and disability awareness. Block carefully examines the history and current thinking of the American disability movement showing how community access has developed. The tenor betrays a tendency to objectivize people with disabilities and to a maternalistic Roman Catholic view of the pastoral care of disabled people. The Christian anthropology based on *Imago Dei* and Paul's doctrine of the Body of Christ is not dissimilar to that of EDAN and the WCC. However, their statement, 'A Church of All and for All', was composed by a group who were mostly disabled, or were related to people with disabilities, and who, therefore, had the right to ask the ultimate question about the multiplex gifts which add richness to the Body of Christ:

> … Is disability really something that shows the weaknesses in human life? Is that in itself a limiting and oppressive interpretation? Do we not have to take another, more radical step? Is disability really something that is limiting? Is the

> language of disability as a 'loss' an adequate one at all, despite
> it being a stage of the journey undertaken by persons with
> disabilities themselves? Is a language of plurality not more
> adequate? To live with a disability is to live with other abilities
> and limitations that others do not have? All human beings
> live with limitations. Is not disability something that God has
> created in order to build a plural, and richer, world? Is not
> disability a gift from God rather than a limiting condition
> with which some persons have to live?
>
> (WCC, 2003; §18)

This paragraph does not say that the suffering and deprivations that accompany disability are treasured gifts from God, but rather that the coping and transcendence can be so. The Statement reads more easily because it has been composed by people with disabilities and does not refer to the actual impairments but to the reliance needed to overcome them.

Kathy Black's *A Healing Homiletic* (1996) seeks successfully, within an American context, to explain the disabilities behind possible sermons about disabled people. One problem which occurs is that she devotes separate chapters to different functional impairments, thus dividing the solidarity of the disability movement. John Hull straddles the academic and popular genres in his reflections on blindness in the Bible from both personal experience and academic stature. His book *In the Beginning there was Darkness* (2001) shows how many passages may be read as seeming to be addressed to, or relevant to, blind people. He has a unique ability to relate matters biblical to his own situation without appearing inspirational or unduly autobiographical. Hull is also in the process of developing a more academic approach to these insights in 'Is Blindness A World? From Theology of Impairment to Theology of Disability' which is soon to be published as a contribution to a book centred around liberation theology. In this, he develops a phenomenological approach to the social model of disability which has thus far been poor in recognising the individual consciousness as part of its model. The inner spiritual experience of people with disabilities is as vital as the established generic models of disability.

Turning now to more academic texts, it is difficult to escape from Nancy Eiesland's *The Disabled God* (1994). The fundamental tenet of this book is criticized later, but what is more important is that it is largely, and more eloquently, prefigured in a little known paper by Alan Lewis, 'God as Cripple: Disability, Personhood and the Reign of God' (1982), which combines Eiesland's embodiment of Christ hanging on the cross with a profound understanding of how Jesus understood sin. What is new in Eiesland is her use of David Tracy, the originator of 'embodiment' as a way of expressing the consciousness of group identity. In 1998, Eisland and Saliers edited a book of contributions that aimed to reassess 'religious practice'. It expanded on embodiment and carefully developed a way in which liturgy and theology may be evolved to reflect the concerns of marginalized groups of disabled people, including those from the African-American community. Unlike the others mentioned here, there is a continued concern about ordination and ministry. The editors have added much more flesh to the skeleton ideas of *The Disabled God*. The writings of both Eiesland and Saliers, as in this book, are interspersed with reference to secular academic work, and the common thread could be that both Eiesland and this writer come from a social scientific background. The intention is to illustrate the application of the models of disability from the most relevant sources, which are invariably secular. In writing typical of the UK, McCloughry and Morris (2002) also reflect this style which is symptomatic of the fact that writers in this country probably have a smaller native religious corpus of literature on which to draw and a greater awareness of the dominance of the UK disability movement by social scientific analysis with less emphasis on the humanities. (See Corker & Shakespeare, 2002)

It is not surprising to find that almost all of this literature mentions the healing miracles. These are, after all, the passages where disability is most frequently featured, but no book is devoted entirely to the subject nor is there a great emphasis on the parables or eschatology. The healing miracles of Jesus figure prominently in most lectionaries and feature most often on 'ordinary' Sundays throughout the year. Some are deliberately inserted to highlight themes of faith or sometimes the sayings of Jesus or his power. Evangelical preachers often find 'proof texts' within them which are substantiated by the miracle – 'I am the resurrection and the life. He who believes in me will live, even though he dies; and whoever lives and believes in me will never die. Do you believe this?' (John 11: 25-26) Likewise, 'I believe: help my unbelief!', uttered by the father of the healed epileptic boy. (see page 124) From either perspective the requirement to preach about the healing miracles is compelling and the opportunities to understand or to abuse people with disabilities are manifold. It is usually the awareness of the pitfalls in such preaching that compels writers on the theology of disability to address these miracles in their books in such a way as to help readers to understand the humanity behind the oft perceived stigma of disability. Most authors also avoid the temptation to indulge in a reductionist approach to miracle, regarding them neither as improbable but useful narratives nor as accurate reports based on biblical inerrancy. Eiesland and Saliers (1998) offer chapters from other contributors on, amongst other subjects, cultic 'uncleanness' which is dealt with on page 203ff below; whilst Colleen Grant pleads for the honouring of disabled people, although the emphasis in exegeses of the healing miracles tends to be dominated by a Christological explanation. Simon Horne (1998) considers the concept and literary uses of disability throughout Hellenistic culture, allowing him to conclude that there has always been the presence of irony and paradox in language about people with disabilities which is not always negative, *vide* Hull (2001). Kathy Black's analysis of the healing miracles pursues some similar themes as this book but believes that in each type of impairment a healing homiletic will reveal how the lot of disabled people may be helped by the pulling down of the social barriers which define disability. She lays foundations for understanding concepts like 'heal' and 'cure' in terms that are not literalistic. One drawback which she shares with Block is a tendency to idealize disability. From a cursory survey of American newspapers, this seems to be a national trait which is not so pronounced in the UK. Whilst the development of ministries to people with disabilities is greatly to be welcomed, any idealization, or even 'idolization', of them should be avoided. McCloughry and Morris devote one chapter to healing and wholeness and their approach may be summed up in the following extract:

> Cure might be defined as 'restoring function', and 'healing'
> as 'promoting well-being'. Cure is medically defined; healing
> is defined in terms of every aspect of life.
> (McCloughry and Morris, 2002; p 102)

McCloughry and Morris raise a very important issue which echoes discussions around EDAN and the WCC. Can someone with Down's syndrome, for instance, be cured or healed when such an act would physically alter their entire being and remove the long-cherished personality traits? This problem will recur several times in this book. It may well be that writers in the UK have been much more focussed on rights than their American counterparts, which makes them less sentimental. Certainly, the DDA has concentrated ecclesiastical minds in ways, occasionally negative, which have forced them to consider disability in terms of rights.

... ...

Outline of Chapters

Chapter 1 will consider the nature of healing and its broad relationship to serious illness and disability. Part One will assess the usefulness of concepts like healing and wholeness. The second section seeks to examine how disabled people define themselves and shows how they have established both a secular identity and a theological thought similar to feminists and other minorities. The medical model of disability and the social model of disability will be introduced. If the reader requires detailed definitions and insights, there is a wealth of material to consult on the disability movement.

Chapter 2 will show how the legacy of David Hume has by-passed disabled people completely. However, the empirical philosophical approach has been made more flexible by the advent of quantum physics.

Chapter 3 will discuss a Church ill at ease with miracles. Strict Protestants have argued that miracles were performed by Jesus as a sign by dint of 'his own inherent might' showing God's revelation in his Son as a God of 'power and might' but also of compassion. These miracles were performed under a dispensation existent during the 'apostolic times'. Such a theology reinforces the medical model of disability by suggesting that disabled people are none other than the objects of God's beneficence and charity cases for Christians trying to emulate the 'unique' compassion of Jesus.

Continuing this theme, the next chapter will focus on the form criticism of Bultmann through to the radical stance of the Jesus Seminar under Robert Funk. Given the way miracles are dismissed, it is possible to examine how disabled people have been made 'invisible' in the name of scholarship.

Chapter 5 will consider the search for cures through medical explanations and the contribution of feminist theologians in encouraging us to embrace the body in all its manifestations. The overall argument will be that a medical model which looks for evidence of cures marginalizes disabled people whose social identity is often defined by their impairments in ways which are not entirely constructive. Just as the Church has had to learn to accept the social identity which comes with a female body, so it must learn to value the bodies of disabled people.

It will also show advances in our understanding of the cultural and anthropological significance of the healings of Jesus. Do these offer a key to the interpretation of the social model of disability or do they draw back from this? Some medical anthropologists have deliberately exploited the idea of dichotomous thinking (Pilch's (2000) shame/honour, for instance), whilst others have shown that the social construction of miracle is too complex for dichotomies.

Many people are inspired by the way in which Jesus appears to treat people as whole persons and that he never violates their wholeness even when correcting them. Counsellors have believed that Jesus' qualities must be translated into healing counselling for today. The problem which will be explored in Chapter 6 is whether such an approach devalues the healing of disabled people and goes on to consider whether people with disabilities actually benefit from counselling.

Chapter 7 will, finally, offer a way of thinking and preaching afresh about the healing miracles which does not marginalize disabled people but includes them in the whole Church's fascination with this aspect of the life of Jesus as one who was undoubtedly a healer who, in these acts, reflected the will of God. From the foregoing chapters, a list of issues to avoid will be developed and discussed before developing a method of exegesis which privileges disabled people in their social context. It will be suggested that the true nature of miracle lies in its message of the restoration of rights and status. So many disabled activists seek equality and respect for lives lived in faith and demand acceptance of impairments which would offer little obstacle to full lives if society lifted the physical, intellectual and, in this context, mythological barrier to full integration. The forgotten disabled people may be eventually included in our consideration of these wonderful stories of undoubtedly authentic acts.

Finally, why deconstruction? Deconstruction is not a subject, it is a process – a tool to be used to study the theology of miracles throughout this book. In a recent newspaper obituary written on Derrida's death, Professor Terry Eagleton wrote:

> Deconstruction, the philosophical method he promoted, means not destroying ideas, but pushing them to the point where they begin to come apart and expose their latent contradictions. It meant reading against the grain of supposedly self-evident truths, rather than taking them for granted.
>
> (Eagleton, 'Don't Deride Derrida',
> *Guardian, 15ᵗʰ October, 2004*)

Eagleton's words outline the intent of this book excellently. We neither intend to destroy belief in miracles nor rule out by criticism any particular theological perspective, but to tease out the unintended biases against people with disabilities. (See also Norris, 1987.) That having been said, all but the curious or fastidious may forget the concept.

The reader may find it useful to read the final conclusion at this stage. This offers an explanation of disability based on the foregoing chapters but in the process summarizes yet again some of the main arguments contained within them.

Chapter 1

The Insult of a Cure

Healing Ministries

Part I – Healing and wholeness

Exploring healing ministries immediately confronts us with a popular dichotomy which has for long beggared explanation:

Illness (dis-ease)$\longleftrightarrow$Cure

In modern thought and in the minds of many Christian healing ministries, from Lourdes –adjudged by the International Medical Committee – to the 'power healing' of the Vineyard Ministries, miracles deliver 'cures'. The secular mind looks to medicine to effect 'cures', and many a moderate prayer has thanked God 'for the miracle of modern medicine'. Yet, whenever medicine is critically examined little evidence of miraculous cures can be found. Nevertheless, ministers, theologians and medically informed laypeople have been, and remain committed to witnessing to the healing ministry of Jesus. In the first part of this chapter, there will be a review of how some have escaped the terminology of 'cure' and developed the concepts of healing and wholeness as non-dichotomous constructs.

Before devoting most of this section to healing and wholeness, the illness/cure dichotomy must be further unpacked. Invariably, when we talk of a 'cure', the alleviation or complete removal of symptoms is implied. Modern medicine typically deals with symptoms and can be described as either biomedicine or allopathic medicine. Allopathy is defined in *Webster's New Collegiate Dictionary* as 'a system of medical practice making use of all measures proved of value in treatment of disease', which implies that practitioners will systematically seek to treat symptoms with the best drugs or surgery available. However, it is wrong to assume that such treatment will always result in a cure.

Appendicitis$\longleftrightarrow$Appendectomy

Toothache $\longleftrightarrow$Extraction

Both these treatments effect a cure in the sense that both the pain and any danger is removed from a patient almost immediately and there will be no lasting and dramatic effect on their life thereafter.

However, such an account lacks obvious parallels with the common understanding of a miraculous cure. First, the *status quo* has been altered – the patient has either lost a tooth or an appendix. A miraculous cure is so judged by the restoration of the patient to the health enjoyed before the sickness. Second, many treatments mask symptoms rather than cure them although the effect appears to be a cure, for instance, paracetemol removes a headache but in fact it only alleviates the pain, leaving the underlying cause of the headache still active. Much of modern medicine has now been condemned for over-prescribing such 'cures' as antibiotics, tranquillizers and psychotropic drugs. Last, whenever the body is treated as a machine where parts can be repaired there is a process of reductionism, i.e., appendicitis is only a septic appendix which bears no relation to any reflection on the life-style or stress-levels of the patient. What emerges is that there is very little evidence that what we regard as miracle cures are in fact so.

It is necessary to distinguish between a commitment to promoting health in the name of Christ, and bearing a conviction that miraculous healings and cures are ever-present realities. Weekly intercessions for the sick, in general or by name, constitute a very formidable witness to the Church's commitment to a health promoting ministry, as do the numbers of Christian hospitals throughout history and the world. A calling to serve in a medical profession is a strong characteristic of many denominations. Both Christian hospitals and practitioners perhaps offer a greater emphasis on spiritual wellbeing as well as a high quality of medicine grounded on research of the highest academic standards. Mullin (1996; p 84ff) writes of the church's concern to open channels of prayer and action to promote 'providential health' which is witnessed in the Bible as a consistent desire of God for his creatures. Simply put, the gospels offer a view of salvation which involves healing and wholeness rather than a straightforward faith in miraculous cures.

The following pages show the importance of theories of healing and wholeness to the general commitment to health. The split between 'providential health' and miracles becomes evident to the extent that the disabling impairments which interest us are hardly mentioned. In fact, much of the subject matter lends itself to theories of counselling or pastoral concerns which bypass disability completely. The place of counselling will be discussed later.

In the medical profession there now exists a significant number of people who believe that allopathic medicine[1] fails to look after the needs of the whole person due to the development of an excessive medical specialism that has reduced the body to its different component parts serviced by their own consultants who never talk to one another. Schön (1992) writes of the demise of absolute trust in professional knowledge and the inflexibility of traditional medical training and pleads for a training which produces a 'reflective practitioner' who can respond to individual needs as a case develops. By learning to 'reflect-in-action' a doctor may attend to problems which would otherwise have gone unnoticed in the mechanistic treatment of a single disease symptom. Such an approach, he believed, would result in an enhanced role for the beleaguered professional. Such criticism has forced many practitioners into a more holistic medicine, which attempts to treat the patient as a whole person and whose symptoms may stem from other aspects of their life as well as the biomedical. For the sake of clarity it is vital to dispel the automatic association some readers will make with 'new age' thinking. Very often 'new age' treatments do claim to be holistic, but many Christian groups have claimed the same title when seeking to treat the whole person with traditional medicine and some well tried complementary remedies such as aromatherapy. It is a mistake to decry holistic medicine just because certain more extreme examples of 'new age' therapies also claim to be holistic. Christian groups have been set up to offer holistic medicine to patients who are disenchanted with the concentration on one symptom at the expense of all else. They have walked away from the idea that modern medicine can offer miracles and have sought healing and wholeness in such groups.

People in the medical profession who have heeded warnings like that of Schön have either shown their commitment in their praxis or in theorising, or both, and Christian practitioners have developed understandings of healing ministries which have gone far beyond the search for mechanistic models of illness or vain searches for cures. Why is Wimber's 'power healing' so contrary to their convictions? It may be that divine healing is inspired by motives other than those of healing and that wholeness may be far from the healer's intention. A powerful criticism of power healing comes from Percy (1992; p30) who argues firstly that healing in the context of Wimber's theology is a manifestation of the power of God to reveal himself in 'signs and wonders' which bring people to faith. Percy believes that a gospel is taught that lacks the essential quality of love which Jesus manifested in his healing where his concern was with the excluded and the weak rather than with an egocentric desire for self-amelioration on the part of the seeker or recipient of healing. Jesus healed at considerable personal cost and often with an awareness of the theological dangers in teaching onlookers truths about compassion and mercy – for instance when he healed on the Sabbath. Wimber has very little to say about the obedient relationship of Jesus as Son seeking his Father's will which was to reveal his love through his Son. Additionally, Percy suggests that power healing is manipulative: in so far as Wimber ceased to stress healing when the Toronto Blessing produced more successful results in building congregations. In his examination of the Church Growth Movement, Percy describes the rhetoric of evangelism which concentrates on power and identifies healing as one of the signs of powerful growth in congregations. Every writer whose views are examined here would eschew both the egotistical desire for miraculous healing leading to a 'cure' and the manipulative way in which it is offered.

After examining some anecdotal evidence of practice, we shall move on to theories of healing and wholeness which have underpinned some healing ministries in the latter half of the last century. In particular, we shall illustrate how holistic approaches can mitigate the excesses of technology, seek to find the 'reflective practitioner' and find evidence of holistic medical practices.

One of the things a hospital chaplain may do is mitigate the impersonal nature of technology by transcending it to the benefit of both patient and medical staff. In his pastoral role the chaplain may be able to humanize the effects of technology. Peter Speck (1988; p45f) relates how he was asked to visit a woman in the intensive care unit who simply grasped his hand for about an hour-and-a-half trying to overcome her sensory deprivation. The nurses were so busy handling the equipment that they had forgotten to touch and reassure the patient. Speck was able to point this out to them, resulting in better practice. (Speck, 1988; p45f) Technology, be it machines or drugs, can induce passivity and resignation in a patient. Complementary therapists give the impression of sparing more time for the 'whole person' and this is reinforced by the extent to which patients are willing to take responsibility for their own recovery. Penny Brohn spent years travelling the world, subjecting herself to horrendous 'cures' and offering, and gaining, support from fellow sufferers at the Bristol Cancer Care Centre working together in self-help groups. (Brohn, 1986) In its entirety this is an area of activity and very little passivity. The British Medical Association has made tentative moves in the direction of recognising and using certain complementary therapies, and accreditation processes are likely to continue for some time. (BMA, 1993) Technology can induce a resignation in a patient who is awaiting a 'miracle' in terms of technological progress in medicine. Christopher Reeve, star of *Superman*, who was paralysed in a riding accident has established the *Christopher Reeve Paralysis Foundation* which has a website with the following quote from its founder:

> I want to knock down the barriers to spinal cord injury research that our government erected last year. I want to tell more Americans that they can change their lives if they never give up hope. I realise these are some lofty goals. But if this year has taught us anything, it's that *nothing is impossible.*

The Foundation sponsors research on various techniques of regenerating and rehabilitating damaged tissue with a view to restoring lost function in the spinal cord. Such research requires more liberal legislation that permits the use of stem cell technology. This dependence on such technology may well conflict with the views of other disabled groups who are engaged in genetic politics. Shortly before Reeve's death from heart failure on 10th October 2004, his campaigning became an issue in the US Presidential election with John Kerry supporting his pleas for Federal research on the use of stem cell research and George Bush opposing it. What President Bush's ban on Federal funding does is to force stem cell research in America into privately funded institutions which are subject to less regulation. This confusion in his policy suggests a whiff of gesture politics. However, with the re-election of George Bush in November 2004, the matter may either stagnate over the next four years or be subject to even more conservative constraints. Christopher Reeve's death from heart failure illustrates an unfortunate fact that quite often medical complications, even ageing itself, can eventually be more devastating than the original impairment.

The second area of practice concerns 'the reflective practitioner' who seeks to offer a human face to biomedicine. The practice is often called humanistic practice. The following story is a good illustration:

> There was reported in the *Journal of American Medical Association* the case of a man with chest pains. He was admitted to hospital. The resident and student wanted to discharge him because they could find nothing organically wrong but the intern spent a long time with him – *listening*. She uncovered his biographical life from his happy European childhood to his experience in the concentration camps. The horrors he witnessed, the blame he took upon himself in his powerlessness and the constant guilt had taken its toll. He had come to America after the war and had believed that the Americans had done all they could to stop the mass extermination of the Jews and the pain was intolerable. Then the President visited Bitburg Cemetery and he felt totally alone with no-one to talk to or understand him. It had taken an intern who had struggled through college working part-time as a waitress, a nursing assistant and a taxi-driver because her immigrant parents could not afford to help her, who knew what struggle and hardship was. She listened and understood. She knew that Twentieth Century high-tech medicine was not the answer for this person and that a good doctor was more than a reader of laboratory reports and a prescriber of medicines. After his discharge he wrote to her saying that he possessed the only real peace he had known since childhood and was free from torment. He said, 'You have given me a piece of your heart'. It was a giving and receiving from a person to a person, a sharing, a deep personal relationship that briefly brought a Jewish gentleman *wholeness and healing* which gave him real peace to the end of his days.
>
> (Woodcock, 1989)

Sheila Woodcock paraphrased this story from the *Journal of American Medical Association*. It tells of the experience of a doctor called Sontag who sought to bring a human understanding in a situation which otherwise could have remained clinically cold and without humanity. Woodcock quotes other instances where interns have depended too much on technology rather than the human skill of diagnosis. Her stories do not undermine or underestimate the value of biomedical diagnosis but note the enhancement of the human ability to reflect upon the findings of tests and the proven properties of drugs and tests. To reflect is to recognize the innate gifts within the psyche of a practitioner. To develop these gifts is to restore reflection into practice.

The challenge of humanistic practice has forced us firstly to think about our dependence on technology, secondly, understand the need to reflect-in-action, and now thirdly, to value communities of practitioners who gather together to offer a humanistic practice. In the UK, Patrick Pietroni has pioneered holistic medical practice in London prior to becoming Professor of Community Care and Primary Health at Westminster University (Student BMJ, November 1998). His original holistic practice was located in the parish church which serves Harley Street in London. The St Marylebone Health Centre offers various therapies and the opportunity to partake of spiritual counselling and healing. Many such practices offer patients the opportunity to escape biomedicine and receive individual treatments like massage or aromatherapy. This not only provides variety but allows time for people to be treated as individuals rather than objects of prescribed drugs or specialist consultation.

Many doctors have felt the call to a ministry of healing as opposed to a profession of healing. A subsequent chapter will look at some doctors who have interpreted the miracles in the light of their medical knowledge but at present we are interested in those who have believed that the gospels provide healing in themselves. This healing comes not only from the example of Jesus but also from certain understandings of his saving grace. Evangelists like Martyn Lloyd-Jones abandoned promisingly brilliant medical careers to enter the ministry, believing that many people's medical symptoms in fact are indicators of spiritual problems. Other healers throughout history have offered remedies and 'cures' in an imitation of the miracles of Jesus. Whilst the Roman Catholic Church, charismatic groups and other non-mainstream protestant groups have looked for miraculous cures, many stricter presbyterian groups since the Reformation have avoided the whole issue of miracles by developing the doctrine of dispensational theology. This maintains that miracles were unique to biblical times and that we are the beneficiaries of the saving miracle of the resurrection through faith. Ferngren argues that the Church never really adopted healing as a central doctrine and that neither the early Church nor the Church of later ages chose to concentrate on this, although their prominence in producing and running hospitals increased its reputation for care considerably. Vaux (1984) likewise argues that a 'duty of care' in medicine is the basis of a Christian ethic. From a Lutheran perspective he discusses Pauline theology, human dignity, and compassion and care. He outlines the Christian's obligation to maintain high levels of nursing care at a time when more resources are devoted to clinical procedures and diagnosis and to see the patient as one who is vulnerable and for whom God has imposed on the professional carer an obligation to help.

Part of the explanation, Ferngern (1992) argues, may be that theologians could never come to grips with dispensational theology. Early theologians regarded the apostolic era as a special period of healing after Christ, which was not continued in future generations, and so they encouraged the Church to turn to caring, medicine and hospital provision Kelsey outlines how the Reformers spent little time dealing with healing and how the traditional neglect was carried on by liberal theologians such as Schleiermacher who devotes about twelve pages to miracles in *The Christian Faith* (Schleiermacher, 1928). Such undermining of Christ's healing ministry continued with the tradition of Bultmann and subsequent attempts to demythologize. Basically the Reformers rejected miracles because of their suspect position in the medieval church. (Kelsey, 1973; p 22ff) A theology of miracles sat uneasily upon Aquinas and others (Melinsky, 1968; p 42ff), who were trying to develop a neo-Platonic scientism, and their legacy spilled over into the philosophical arguments about the nature of miracles in the eighteenth and nineteenth centuries, in the philosophy of Hume and the English Deists (p 47ff).

This denial of the present relevance of the healing miracles will be dealt with later but it has become a characteristic of reformed theology that it looks at healing in terms of salvation rather than healing *per se*.

In the 1950s and '60s an interest in healing and wholeness developed in the theological department of Birmingham University which was inspired by theologians who had previously had a medical training. The understanding of healing and wholeness which they developed still retains a relevance today despite some cogent criticisms of their linguistic usage.

Healing and wholeness are yoked together by both tradition and subject matter as both are either linked by biblical usage or by some medical or ecological understanding, deriving from, in the former, hermeneutics, and in the latter, from an unintentional or deliberate adaptation of Smuts' definition of 'holism'.

> Holism .... comprises all wholes in the universe. It is thus both a concept and a factor: a concept as standing for all wholes, a factor because the wholes it denotes are the real factors in the universe. (Smuts, 1927; p 120)

Respect for the 'whole' has generated a host of literature in the three fields of biblical hermeneutics, medicine and ecology. From each, some guidelines must be drawn.

The principal area of theological discussion has lain in an understanding of the gospel miracles, although Lambourne also delves into social structures.

> So basic to the Hebrew thoughtform is 'total thinking', 'holism', 'corporate model concepts' or whatever we choose to call it, that it permeates the whole grammar and literary style of the Hebrew Old Testament.
>
> The Hebrew concept of a totality, which is neither just a summation of discrete particles nor a mass arbitrarily divisible into parts, but a living organism in which the parts co-inhere, both giving and receiving strength and purpose is nowhere better demonstrated than in the use of the word *mishpaha* (family) as a collective term not only for the human but all species. (Lambourne, 1963; p 26)

James Barr issues a cautionary note about the use of the word 'holy'. He argues that the Old Testament did not in fact offer any insight or understanding of wholeness, but rather the idea of holiness as a strictly religious term implying 'to be kept whole, not to be touched, inviolable'. (Barr, 1961; p 112) He goes on to talk about the 'English fallacy' which equates 'holy' with health or wholeness. Even if there are certain etymological links in the English words holy, health and wholeness, the equation of holiness with health bears no relation to the contextual occurrence of holy within the Bible (p 113ff). This is a particularly important point as the thrust of the argument is that the definitions of wholeness which have been offered, and which are mainly based upon this English fallacy, are weak and without foundation compared to conceptions of wholeness which are derived from experience or biographical factors.

Allen acknowledges the influence of Lambourne but avoids the criticisms which Barr makes concerning the 'English fallacy' of health and wholeness. Allen has a very simple yet far-reaching thesis: 'Semantics is praxis'. (Allen, 1995) He continues to argue that if there is a Christian obligation to treat the whole person as a committed practitioner, the semantics of body, mind and spirit structure the nature of one's practice by compelling attention on each facet of the individual. Allen has developed a holistic practice in America much as Patrick Pietroni has in London. His initial emphasis on praxis avoids the trap of making holism into a biblical obligation rather than a norm of choice. Praxis is his response to the need to witness as a Christian health-care worker with a commitment to whole-person treatment.

However, the main area of concern lies in the meaning behind the miracles of Jesus which are regarded as restoring wholeness and seeking wholeness in the individual. For instance, Sayword examines the healing of the woman with a haemorrhage and concentrates on the freedom she is granted from the constraining taboos surrounding menstruation. The author wishes to establish the wholeness of a woman from a feminist perspective. (Sayword, 1993) Similarly, Alan Lewis developed the idea of liberation from the disastrous effects of disability from the man lowered through the roof by his friends to meet Jesus. By offering to forgive his 'sins', Jesus not only took from him the stigma of brokenness but became 'the elephant man' himself. (Lewis, 1982) His declaration of forgiveness was made so that he might 'become a merciful and faithful high priest in service to God' as the writer to the Hebrews later reflected (Heb. 2: 17). There are many other types of hermeneutic but these two point to the flexibility of the concept of wholeness in biblical interpretation – a feature which will recur often.

Whenever a negative view of the fall or of creation is expounded, anything that appears different from the norm tends to become undervalued, or worse, tainted by original sin. For this reason, it is important to see all of God's creation as good and worthy to be celebrated. Matthew Fox offers a way of understanding incarnational theology and the celebration of creation without resorting to Greek mythology but rather to Christian mystics such as Hildegard of Bingen (1098-1179) on whom he has also written. (Fox, 1985) Hildegard recorded her religious experiences in a book entitled *Scivias*, which contains many references to cosmology and creation. She was also known as a healer, and writers such as Ulrich have exploited this in meditations.

(Ulrich, 1990) What is important is that she was probably a herbalist of some repute and developed medical theories of 'humours', which she tied in with the cosmos. Her two books on medicine were *Physica* and *Causae et Curae*,(Flanagan, 1989; p 80 – 91) which combined theology and medicine in a singular fashion that Fox regards as one of the precursors to creationist theology. His argument is that the created world is a blessing of God to be celebrated and affirmed. This cannot be achieved by placing guilt before the joy that lies in the Incarnation – Jesus becomes the ' ... "son of Adam, son of God" (Luke 3:38) [and] fully incarnates the Dahbar, the ever-flowing, cosmos-filling, creative energy of the Creator. Yet he becomes fully flesh as we are, pitching a tent in our midst.' (Fox, 1993; p 123) Jesus thus shares every aspect of nature both within our humanity and in our environment. This celebratory and salvific knowledge can lead us to understand both healing and wholeness. Fox explains thus:

> Salvation is about healing, and just as the cosmos itself can be ruptured and torn apart by injustice, so too it can be healed by all human efforts to bring justice, which is balance, back to human relationships to earth, air, fire, water, and one another. Just as dualism and subject/object living is sinful according to the Via Positiva, so too harmonious living and lifestyles of simplicity represent salvific action on humanity's part. The healing process of making whole and integrating also includes a return to one's origins, and the Via Positiva offers deep invitations to examine anew our pre-existence, both in the historical unfolding of the cosmos and in the Creator's heart. With this examination comes a greater reverence for our uniqueness, and therefore a greater reverence for that of God's other creatures. This reverence is itself salvific. (p 123)

Such an approach compels us to take geopolitical and green matters seriously and shows how incarnational theology has advanced with modern debate. The wider concern in liturgy for extending the idea of healing and wholeness into all social and political situations may be simply a reflection of the time. Similarly our last observation suggests a more precise and modern definition of wholeness than is encountered in the healing literature which is being examined.

Adrian Thatcher's interest in genetics reinforces the goodness of creation by showing how genetics affected the Incarnation and emphasizes the beauty of both the genetic makeup of Jesus and, by implication, of ourselves. Christians, it may be argued, have an obligation to respect the various genetic combinations which contribute to a variety of disabilities. Indeed, we should recognize the beauty inherent in these variations. Thatcher's concern is with a 'post-mythical Christ' and he seeks to allegorize in modern terms. He chooses to defend the virgin birth on the grounds that the early church fathers used the Chalcedonian doctrine of *Theotokos* to emphasize the uniqueness of the person of Christ. As an organic whole the man Jesus shared our DNA structure and all other life-forces which constitute our being. If there was a virgin birth, it is now obvious to science that the Y chromosome would be missing. Yet in his perfection he taught from his humanity the gift of unconditional love, forgiveness and reconciliation. These qualities were part of a unique whole with which mankind is invited to unite in the whole of the Body of Christ, the Church. According to this analogy, our wholeness is diminished when we fail to meet our human potentiality, when we waste the human matter which in Jesus was perfected (Thatcher, 1990; Chap. 9) This means that our sin breaks a perfection which could be achieved if we struggled zealously to be children of God.

Apart from the imprecise nature of 'wholeness' there are obvious dangers in its use, particularly when the debate drifts into the discussion of holism or holistic theories. Ash argues that it is inconsistent to conceive of the universe, or for that matter the personality, as a whole, then set another whole, God, outwith the system. (Ash, 1987; p 79ff) He argues for the suspension of belief in a being which cannot be subsumed into the whole. Incarnational theology on the other hand counters his argument by creating an interface between God and the world in the person of Christ. Thatcher writes: 'In the case of Jesus, God is the whole or centre. The Father does not replace the personal centre of Jesus; rather the integration of Jesus with himself .... and his integration with other persons .... presents a whole or unity which is also a unity between God himself and an open, perfect, human life.' (Thatcher; p 113)

Imago Dei, literally the image of God, is shorthand for the doctrine that God created mankind 'in His own image, in the image of God' (Genesis 1:27). Modern understanding of this doctrine suggests that every human being possesses the likeness of God. It is a radical doctrine to apply to disability because it speaks of equality in a way in which previous attempts of Christian anthropology related to disability have failed. It makes common cause with radical activists who have equality at the top of their agenda. We shall see later that it is being developed by the *World Council of Churches* amongst others. (See further discussion on page 71 and on page 139)

Last in this present discussion of wholeness, it is extremely simple to find authors who eschew discussion of holistic medicine or anything connected with 'new age' concepts of personal transformation. It must be recognized that there are valid moral objections to the worst abuses of holistic medicine, the lack of accreditation, incompetence and so on; and it is also undoubtedly true that many people have been misled to their cost by 'new age' practices upon which there are no moral checks. This kind of dilemma has led even 'moderate' writers to reject the whole debate in order not to risk the contamination of some spurious characteristics, such as the case of McGilvray who, in 1981, would not entertain the idea of holistic medicine except for some little known research by an American physician. (McGilvray 1981)

Part II – Wholeness

The words, wholeness and holistic, are used by academic and non-academic theologians alike and is of interest because their implied definitions are very often so imprecise; more often appearing to be implicit rather than explicit. Many of the writers who will be examined wrote between 1930 and 1960 and were probably unaware that to use the term was to invite entry into the much broader debate which was triggered by Smuts in 1926 and, independently, by gestalt theorists writing at about the same time.

It is surely a quirk of cultural history that Field-marshal Jan Christian Smuts, Prime Minister of South Africa in 1939, (Hancock, 1968; p 176ff) should bequeath to the English language the word 'holism' which has occupied so many minds in so many fields, not least in health care. Certainly, the majority of interested church people have been prepared to enter the debate during the past two decades. 'Holism' has been appropriated by many professionals, particularly those in health care, by practitioners of complementary therapies, by philosophers, and by proponents of a 'new age'. Because there has been so much expounded on 'holistic' medicine, which is drawn from other cultures and categories, there has been an inevitable clash with Christian values – a clash which has had many manifestations. Yet other Christians, including the writer, have found nothing but good as well as challenge in the entire debate. There are many approaches to 'wholeness' which are separated, almost to the point of antagonism, by language, categories and tradition. Religious discourse only serves to heighten the debate. In order to begin to establish common ground between religious groups which disagree, it will be necessary to show that many of the disagreements are based on a misunderstanding of language and of categories.

At the outset, it is best to quote one of Smuts' nine definitions of holism:

> Holism ... comprises all wholes in the universe. It is thus both a concept and a factor: a concept as standing for all wholes, a factor because the wholes it denotes are the real factors in the universe.

(Smuts, 1927; p 120)

There is a place for a mechanistic analysis of a component in a 'field', for instance in the examination of the constituent parts of a chemical suspension or the anatomical or physiological functions of parts of the body. However, the true nature of a whole cannot be encapsulated by such an analysis.

What has been discussed are wholes as factors or parts of universe. Holism, however, is also a concept which allows thinkers to form their own holistic theories around their chosen area of analysis. (Smuts; p 120)

Because Smuts offers an opportunity to admit creativity into any analysis, his theories open doors to more complex analyses by theorists adopting some or all of his positions. It is at this point that a degree of ambiguity enters which may or may not be of his making. One of his South African mentors, Monsignor Kolbe, attempts to be critical of his theory from a Catholic viewpoint. (Kolbe, 1928) Kolbe criticizes Smuts on three grounds, and then proceeds to adopt the theory for his own purposes. First, he argues that classical Catholic philosophy already deals with the evolution of forms in the Aristotelian sense. Second, he laments the passing of the Cartesian process of induction in scientific methodology, which will prove to be a recurring theme throughout this discussion.

Kolbe's third point illustrates, however, the difficulty of holism in general and that of Smuts in particular. Because he argues that the future of an evolving whole is charged with creativity, it becomes possible to build in one's own teleology; thereby slipping from description of some 'field' to one's construction. Such a path is taken, almost unnoticed, by Kolbe: 'The Holist would explain: "I do not need now to say whence matter got its creativeness. I see a continuous chain from Chaos to Spirituality."' Kolbe has turned a potentially hostile theory to his theological advantage by viewing the evolutionary path as one which is charged with spiritual speculation.

It is of interest to note that this creative aspect of holism has become its attractiveness to many green theorists. Lovelock, for instance, has written many influential books on the environmental crisis facing the world. Most of his analyses can probably stand up to scientific scrutiny, and yet, what makes his analysis almost cultic is his description of the world as a living whole, named Gaia by him, after the goddess of the Earth. (Lovelock, 1988) Lovelock can quote many academic antecedents to support the view that the Earth is a living whole, but is it logically justifiable? Furthermore, Lovelock became embroiled in theological controversy at an early stage and he later noted in response to his own questions that: 'Belief in God is an act of faith and will remain so. In the same way, it is otiose to try to prove that Gaia is alive. Instead, Gaia should be a way to view the Earth, ourselves, and our relationships with living things.' (p 207)

In several passages gestalt theory will be discussed, so at this stage it would be useful to outline the difference between the terms 'holistic' and 'wholistic'. 'Holistic' generally refers to the soma; whilst 'wholistic' refers to the psyche. Around the 1920s, gestalt theory was taking shape, and in the literature the word 'whole' was the preferred term when outlining the theory which could, in part, be popularly summed up as 'the whole is more than the sum of its parts'. 'Holism' was a neologism which suffered from the imprecision discussed above. Smuts offered nine definitions, all of which were different from gestalt theory.

Two central questions now arise which are germane to the aim of this thesis as it develops creationist theology. First, does holism allow analysts to admit new categories such as 'life' or 'spirituality'? Second, are such categories logically admissible or coherent? These questions are important because many Christians would wish to argue that such holistic theories as 'Gaia' are inadmissible because they admit concepts which have no place in their understanding of God's created wholes. To the former question, the answer must be that holism does allow it and Christians and others must accept it, aware that as others develop holistic theories, so, indeed, do Christians. The latter question, however, is much more complex and moves the argument to another type of analysis of wholes.

Holism is about three systems of thought. The ways in which they converge, part or by-pass each other, both in time and space, challenge us to accept fully the freedom of 'fields' to develop as they will.

Health and wholeness do have to go together; they are permanently yoked in the same way as say, health and fitness. Wholeness is qualitative, describing a desired state of well-being; or when used in another derivative, holistic, can describe the quality of the health care which is offered.

The standard definition of health offered by the World Health Organization is:

> a state of complete physical, mental and social well-being and
> not merely the absence of disease or infirmity.

> (WHO, 1948; p 1)

It is idealistic in many ways and full of the unfulfilled optimism that reflects the time when it was written – 1948. It is essentially qualitative and implies that the WHO was looking beyond the eradication of disease and towards societies free of the social injustices which have, in fact, increased and enveloped many more millions since 1948. The point to underline is that health is often linked to a qualifier and the subject matter here is that of wholeness.

Michael Wilson, along with Bob Lambourne, draws a distinction between 'cure', 'heal', and 'wholeness'. Both were trained in medicine and joined the staff of the Department of Theology at Birmingham University, where they concentrated on a theological model of counselling and healing, rather than a medical one. In their work 'cure' and 'heal' are not accorded the religious significance of 'wholeness'.

> Any conception of 'curing' is...embraced within the word
> 'heal', and given purpose. On the other hand, because
> physical health subserves the purpose of life – loving God,
> loving neighbour, loving self – it is legitimate to use the word
> 'healed' of someone who has been enabled to take up a life of
> self-giving, without having been cured physically.

> (Wilson, 1966; p 18)

In the context of Christian or Divine Healing, healing at wholeness nearly always go together. Wholeness represents a state healthy being which may not be the result of cure. Another example might be *Health and Healing: A Ministry to Wholeness* by Denis Duncan,[2] a minister distinguished by his ministry of healing and by his ability to communicate. His book outlines a ministry to the 'whole person' but either fails to define 'wholeness', or, in the context of the author's aims, chooses not to. He describes a cerebral palsied woman, Lin, who is also blind and outlines her adversities, her counselling, but most of all her success in life and her ability to help others through her writing and her own counselling skills. (Duncan, 1988; p 81f) Her success, seen as an outcome of her triumph over disability, becomes an illustrative narrative about wholeness. Wilson reserves a strictly religious definition for wholeness, which may ultimately be found in worship and the anticipation of the Kingdom of God.

> I deliberately use the verb 'wholing' rather than the noun 'wholeness' because wholeness is an ideal towards which we struggle and grow, a pointer towards the kingdom yet to be completed, now partly visible. Worship is an activity which helps us individually and corporately to grow towards wholeness.

> (Wilson, 1988; p 217)

To attempt to define wholeness would either involve a lengthy catalogue of recorded definitions, or would involve imposing one's own interpretation on the likes of the above. However, given that wholeness (or its derivatives) is usually part of the debate about healing, an attempt will be made to identify the ways by which theologians and others seek to present it, achieve it or advocate it.

Such an epistemological approach is justified when definitions are hard to come by, for instance, in the fields of medical discourse or that of prayer. Hufford (1993) seeks to offer an explanation for the persistent belief in prayers for the sick by offering two epistemological models of prayer rather than definitions. His paper presents two case studies, one of a Christian Scientist suffering terminally from breast cancer, and another of a man of a mainstream denomination with an acute hiatus hernia who attended a healing service and claimed to be healed. The first model used words and phrases like 'will cure', 'medical care is superfluous'; the second model used words like 'may cure', 'medical care is among God's ways of healing'. In the first model, failure is associated with the patient's own sin or lack of faith; in the second, God simply has other intentions. Thus, only a definition offering the common components of wholeness will be offered. There may indeed be ontological models which seek to clarify theories but these depend on a dogmatic approach. Take, for instance, Frank Lake's *Dynamic Cycle of Development* which overtly seeks to witness to Christian values and uses an understanding of Jesus Christ drawn from St John's Gospel. (Lake, 1986; p 33ff) A secular example might be transactional analysis with its emphasis on 'parent', 'adult' and 'child'. It is interesting that transactional analysis has been adopted by many religious groups, and Ian Davidson, the present director of *The Christian Fellowship of Healing (Scotland)* (Davidson, 1991; p 3) has Jesus intrude into the 'adult' where the devil or Satan often resides. This, together with his knowledge of transactional analysis constitutes the bedrock of his Christian gestalt.

The most notable common factor in any definition of wholeness as it relates to individuals is the universal desire to avoid reductionism, which may not always be feasible. (Foster, 1991) The individual must be treated and approached as a complete entity. Descartes placed all his emphasis on the mind and its ability to think. *Cogito, ergo sum* diminished the body and matter to dualistic objects of investigation and instigated the long-held belief that the body was little else than an intricately designed machine which had to be maintained and repaired. Such a view was enhanced by the 'design' theory of Newtonian physics. (Capra, 1982; Chap 10) A machine may be dismantled and small parts given undue importance. The significance of the holistic perspective is the fact that dualism is no longer admissible nor may the individual be reduced to various components.

Next, most would entertain the 'trinity' of body, mind (or soul) and spirit as being the three most important aspects of a 'whole person'. This formula may either constitute the basis of treatment, or serve as a bulwark against reductionism. More secular theorists tend to remain content with body and mind, *psyche* and *soma*. This is particularly so in discussions of psychosomatic illness. Griffiths makes a plea for a more 'fluid' approach to what he has dubbed the 'trinity' of the *British Holistic Medical Association* consisting of 'body', 'soul' and 'spirit'. (Griffiths, 1988, p 73ff) 'Concrete' thinkers tend to want to compartmentalize the different concepts, sometimes identifying something, for example as 'soul', which cannot really be identified. He cites Jungian analysis, Eastern thought and certain more radical theologians as more 'fluid'. (p 75) Most Christian theories which are holistic seem to reject dualism in so far as they recognize all the needs of men and women. The body is not simply irrelevant, as in a pure Cartesian system; and yet with very few exceptions their theories are dualistic because none are possible without a belief either in God or about his actions towards all men. (Kenny, 1970)

In the New Testament, many words centre on the healing acts of Jesus. R. A. Lambourne chooses words which translated from Greek mean 'heal', 'cure', 'cleanse', 'make whole' and 'save'. (Lambourne, 1963; Chap 8) If he introduces a word to be emphasized, it would be *sozein* in which he finds that 'the corporate aspect is strong and teaches us that "to be saved" or "to be made whole" is to enjoy a deliverance from defeat and destruction together with others.' (p 103) Other New Testament words may be chosen depending on an author's preference for the Gospels or the Epistles.

Reviewing the elements of holistic thought outlined in the last two pages, we have firstly wholistic therapies being pursued by gestalt counsellors. Second, there is the movement against reductionism. Third, we have witnessed the general consensus that a holistic approach to the person implies a 'trinity', variously described as 'body, soul and spirit' or 'body, mind and spirit'. Finally, there is the theological tendency of some to provide an holistic exegesis in biblical terms.

Part III – Healing Narratives

In the search for an alternative to 'cure', two main themes have emerged. First, doctors who are persuaded of the value of holistic practice have tried to escape from the mechanistic practices of biomedicine by developing techniques which address the whole person. Second, theologians have tried to develop the relevance of healing and wholeness as a theme running through the gospels and theology. Is it possible to draw a synthesis between these two? The concept of 'healing narrative' may well provide such a synthesis by showing how people experience healing and wholeness as a result of certain events in their lives.

Anthropologists have built many papers and studies around the ethno-medicine of various groups, which may provide a key to identifying the creativity linking the three elements mentioned in the preceding paragraph. Many of these studies have centred on Asian countries (some include Egypt) or are undertaken by medical sociologists who describe religious behaviour in terms which are suggestive of narrative. The attractiveness of Asian cultures lies in the pluralism of influences on medicine. Although we have concentrated on the narratives of healers, it is possible to learn from these studies. If there are health narratives, there must also be healing narratives describing the experience of healers as they have been exposed to the influences which have shaped their attitudes. A health narrative is the story of how the help of medicine or healers is sought by an individual; it is the story of his/her perception of progress and needs. A definition of such narratives has been developed by Early who suggests that the quest for health is episodic and may involve several ventures into different types of treatments – treatments which are appropriate to one's position and circumstance. Having made fundamental decisions about treatment the narrative continues to describe the search for the appropriate remedy and takes into account the feelings of peers. Early's studies have been about the gynaecological and child-care concerns of women in Cairo. (Early, 1982) These women are faced with the need to make decisions about their lifestyle in relation to Western values and decide whether to accept modern allopathic medicine or continue with the traditional beliefs and practices. She develops her definition of health narrative thus:

> A 'therapeutic narrative' is defined here as a commentary on
> illness progression, curative actions, and surrounding events
> – both relevant and irrelevant. (p 1,491)

The value of Early's work is that she insists that all narratives must 'provide a biographical context and experiential reference' (p 1,492) for the understanding of both disease and well-being. It is relevant in the context of this thesis, because practically all the people who have been examined have set their healing experiences in biographical stories. Again it must be stressed that the argument is that convictions about healing and wholeness arise out of experience and encounters.

The import of the former is in the model which is produced to provide a schema for examining therapeutic episodes in health narratives. However, by way of introduction reference might be made to *Therapy* by David Lodge who describes the life of a man who indulges his neuroticism about a pain in his knee by paying for many alternative therapies and

being willing to jump from one to another. Tubby Passmore, the central
character, is supposedly happily married but is known to be having a very
close, but platonic, relationship with another woman whenever he is in
his flat in London. She too is in therapy, seeking psychotherapy for her
lack of success in sexual relationships. When Passmore's marriage breaks
up he has a great urge to have sex with any woman he can remember from
the past. Interestingly, after a sordid weekend in Spain with his long-term
confidante, she dismisses her therapist because she realizes she actually
has no need of a man. Her healing narrative is completed by a random
experience. He is eventually cured by a combination of Kierkegaard,
with whose private life and resultant moral philosophy he becomes
obsessed, and an existential experience with an adolescent love – now
a mature woman on a pilgrimage in Spain.[3] The entire experience of
Tubby Passmore is an example of a therapeutic model in that he chooses
appropriate therapies at different times and eventually finds a cure almost
by serendipity when he joins the pilgrimage. Maureen had embarked on
this pilgrimage after the loss of her son, an aid worker murdered when in
Africa. Maureen had also had a mastectomy which caused her husband,
Bede, to reject her sexually, but she responded to Passmore's tenderness
in kissing the scars whilst making love. Once more, the healing narrative
has an unanticipated resolution. These few lines seem to sum up how
nebulous therapy, or healing, may actually be:

> "Damien was her favourite child. She was devastated. That's
> why she's gone off on this absurd pilgrimage."
> "You mean, as a kind of therapy?" I said.
> "It's as good a word as any, I suppose," said Bede.
>   (Lodge, 1993; p 277)

Lodge's novel is quoted because it is a perfect example of a health
narrative and an amusing look at the plethora of therapies available to
Passmore. It is also noteworthy that healing actually only occurred when
it was least expected, both in his case and in several other characters
– hence the nebulous definition offered above.

Alisdair MacIntyre, in a paper which is essentially a riposte to
Kuhn, describes the term 'epistemological crisis' to denote the way
individuals formulate their difficulties in coming to terms with a new
state of knowledge. (MacIntyre, 1977; also in Appleby *et al*, 1996) They
often do so in terms of dramatic narrative and MacIntyre argues that
the only study of this is in fact *Hamlet*. In the play, Hamlet returns to

Elsinore and has to come to terms with the death of his father, the new marital status of his mother and the rule of Claudius. He also had to relate to friends who were not familiar with the new ideas of Wittenburg, such as Rosencrantz and Guildenstern.

Now, the point that must be stressed here is that these narratives are manifestations of the subjective feelings and beliefs of people who must work out their positions with reference to their biographical and biological state at any given time. The narratives which people tell about their health are enriched by the various episodes which they undergo and by the choices which they make in the pursuit of health or a 'cure'.

The foregoing survey has suggested three ways in which people involved in medicine have sought to understand how we may talk of illness and disease, or dis-ease, in ways which recognize the limitations of talk about cure. These ways of mitigating the excesses of biomedicine have been the instruction of innovative practices, which have led to holistic treatments, to an academic exploration of healing and wholeness in the context of scripture, and to the search for identity in healing which is either received or offered.

Identity of Disabled People

Any attempt to describe the identity of disabled people in modern society will necessarily have to be selective. The disability movement offers certain inescapable definitions which it would be foolish to ignore, yet in the previous chapter it was made fairly clear that the movement in the UK, at least, is a very secular affair. Also it will become clear that people have to opt into the disability movement. This fact has tremendous implications for an ageing church because the population of old people present more and more impairments in their mobility, hearing and sight which they do not regard as disabilities in any political sense but as impairments associated with old age. Whilst disabled people are noticeably absent from our churches, these very churches are acutely acquainted with some of the impairments associated with disability. However, it is insufficient to simply tackle these impairments without understanding the modern meaning of disability. If disabled people are so absent from our churches we must remember that those who do attend have the potential to adopt a religious identity which will make them ask questions of sermons which others will not. This means that it will be necessary to consider the nature of their religious identity, or identities, and remember that the object of this book is to find ways of accommodating them when talking of miracles.

First, what are the salient features of disability which must be accommodated in our theology and hermeneutic? Most importantly, disability has become something one opts into by accepting that many of the limitations imposed upon a disabled person by his or her impairment are due to barriers erected by a society which has under-invested in barrier-free architecture and the elimination of attitudes of discrimination. To accept an apparently negative linguistic label, *dis*-abled, is a major choice in itself until people realize that this negativity is aimed at *society* and not at the *individual*. The point was made in the introduction that the churches have much to do to remove the barriers that this book is about, and in to change the attitudes which come directly out of the miracle stories or lie dormant in the subconscious of the Church. Once a disabled person has opted into the disability movement, he or she becomes acutely aware of these barriers to the extent that they become an assault on their identity. This is certainly so with physical barriers and almost as certain when it comes to attitudinal ones.

Unless a disabled theologian or preacher chooses to detach his or her thought completely from the reality of being disabled, it is highly likely that their thought and writings will reflect their attitudes towards disability. When a theology of disability is produced, its intrinsic worth is likely to judged by how it resonates within the disabled community and by its ability to inspire the 'outside' world to react in a positive way.

Thus secondly, Alister McGrath (1990) has argued that doctrine becomes part of a social identity or social demarcation. It will be argued that disabled people who are theologians have gradually built up an identity that has assumed the status of doctrine which challenges the churches to consider their attitudes in the light of current preaching. The doctrine which has emanated from the writings of Nancy Eiesland, particularly in *The Disabled God*, has provided both the means of finding an identity and the opportunity to adopt one which is already made. It will be argued that these identities have dangerous aspects theologically and that what we must really look for is a very well grounded theological cause to show respect for disabled people.

So, in order to describe disabled people in a way which is reasonable to theological discourse, it is necessary to take a two-pronged look at their situation. It would be easy to rehearse yet again the many descriptions of disabled people from a social policy point of view or a political standpoint, but rather than repeat such arguments we must distil the important characteristics which disabled people may bring to church. Once again, the churches must be reminded that their access is poor but this is not the subject of this book. Jennie Weiss Block has recently developed a theology of access in her book, *Copious Hosting: A Theology of Access for People with Disabilities* (2002), which puts a new perspective on the practical advice which has been published over the last two decades by many churches. Block very neatly and cogently points out that Jesus took infinite care over every person met. He 'hosted' their needs 'copiously' and eventually suffered because of his care. As followers of Jesus, we must begin to understand the long catalogue of access requirements not simply as troublesome features to be put in place, often at considerable cost, but as part of our 'copious hosting' of disabled people who seek to join our fellowship which, as the body of Christ, must be open to all who claim a part and have a gift to offer it. John Swinton (2000a) argues that our lack of understanding of schizophrenics and people with other such conditions makes them strangers – others – to the Christian community. In an eloquent use of Aristotelian concepts of virtue and friendship, we should approach such friendships in a deeply solicitous way. Advocating 'copious hosting' or 'solicitous care' in imitation of Christ are challenging theological insights which raise our legalistic attempts to provide access to a deeply spiritual level. Christian anthropology has become much more important in theological statements about disabled people, as we shall see. Block not only outlines the institutional changes which must occur to facilitate physical access but outlines the type of etiquette each copious host must observe when interacting with disabled people. (p 145ff) It should be noted that both Block and Swinton recommend behaviour *toward* disabled people by non-disabled people. It must not be assumed that the people with disabilities will always make the same suggestions and demands, but if a correlation between the writings of non-disabled people and their disabled counterparts can be achieved the resultant strength will enhance the solidarity of all who have concerns within the disabled community.

However, it would be remiss to ignore the ideology which results from the disabling effect of barriers and the aspirations of many disabled

people. Therefore, a brief résumé of the secular view of disability will
be developed. Second, attention will be paid to the theological tensions
which have arisen because Christian disabled people are demanding that
their identity be respected and integrated into theology.

No account of the disability movement or the developing
recognition of disabled people as a minority group within society can
begin without understanding the theory that undergirds it. Since the
Seventies this theory has been known as the 'social model of disability'.
An early definition reads:

> The disadvantage or restriction of activity caused by a
> *contemporary organization* which takes no or little account
> of people who have physical impairments and thus <u>excludes</u>
> them from participation in the mainstream of social activities.
> [Emphasis mine]

(UPIAS, 1976; p 14)

From such an early definition it is not difficult to see from the
emphasized words how easily a conspiracy theory could develop. Such
a statement contains the seeds which will ultimately define disabled
people as a minority, as with ethnic or minorities of differing sexual
orientation. But as Block points out, disabled people are not a unified
minority noted for one dominant characteristic, and membership of
the disability movement is often not confined to disabled people but
includes carers and interested friends and professionals.[4] To some extent
radical activists have sought to define members exclusively in terms of the
social model of disability and they seek to exclude all who do not have
an impairment by which they are disabled by society. In what follows,
the radical application of the social model of disability will be compared
with a generally accepted Christian application. Both have no difficulty
in accepting the Union of Physically Impaired Against Segregation
(UPIAS) definition but use it in different ways.

In the UK, the social model of disability is taught in many academic
settings and is built into the constitutions of many organization of
disabled people. The academics largely accepted a responsibility to serve
the ends of activists and to develop the powerhouse of the disability
movement in Britain, the British Council of Disabled People (BCODP).
(Campbell and Oliver, 1996) This combination has led to the disabled
movement in Britain possessing a strong conviction that a) the social
model is the foundational notion for any understanding of disability; b)

disabled people are oppressed or discriminated against because of their impairments; and c) there are powerful forces to be overcome before a 'barrier free' society can be created. McCloughry and Morris (2002; p 16ff) point out that Professor Michael Oliver, the leading academic in the UK disability movement, insists on exclusivity, i.e., one must have an impairment, have experienced discrimination and must consider oneself to be disabled by that experience. The inherent difficulty in such a position is that many disabled people do not subjectively experience discrimination and some would deny being disabled either for psychological reasons or because they cope so well with their impairment that they have little cause to regard themselves as disabled and to join the disability movement. The charge levelled at such people is that they suffer from 'false consciousness' in so far as they unable, or unwilling, to discern the social structures which theorists of disability social policy might consider 'oppressive'. Many disabled groups in the UK write the social model of disability into their constitutions as if the model was a religious tenet. Constitutions should be descriptive of the aims and objects of an organization without describing the means to achieving the same. The inclusion of the social model of disability neither adds nor subtracts from an organization's purpose. Such organizations seldom countenance the argument that the social model of disability may someday be superseded by a new paradigm of thinking about disability. The model as it is used in the UK is very materialistic and is either overtly Marxist or unwittingly so. Mike Oliver makes no secret of his Marxist leanings and is therefore part of a dying breed of academic sociology:

> I would go further and argue that the social theory that underpins Marxist political economy has far greater transformative potential in eradicating the oppression that disabled people face throughout the world than the interactionist and functionalist theories that underpin normalization ever can have.

(Oliver, 1999)

There is therefore a difference between the uses which Christians would make of the model and the uses made by materialists. Secular groups are often characterized by a lack of hope and a constructive relationship with the rest of society. The holistic hope of the Christian faith is not attractive to such people although they do recognize that the Church requires better access like any other institution. The most obvious characteristic of a Christian application of the social model of disability is that it not only relates to the whole of society but also to the inclusiveness of the body of Christ. (See below p 108ff) The medical model of disability is similarly rejected by Christians but for reasons which relate specifically to an understanding of miracles. They reject the idea that medicine may solve all problems of disability through corrective therapy and/or surgery and rehabilitation just as much as mainstream theologians would reject the idea of cures by miracles. Many writers suggest that we must resist the idea of a fix for disability. Disabled people are quite willing to live with their impairment if society can be improved as an accepting and enabling body.

Radical disabled activists and Christians share a common conviction that most problems facing disabled people must be solved politically and that there must a seismic change in the will of society to integrate them into all sectors on a basis of equality. Any activist or reformer looking in on the Church will justifiably see an institution in need of change; but a Christian reformer will see an institution in need of change in order to become its true self, obedient to its founder and head, Jesus Christ. This is a truth unique to the Church which comes of a spiritual understanding of the social model of disability. A revolution of legality and potential force may become one of love and inclusion.

Any social institution is governed by socially constructed norms and regulations that disable people by creating barriers in the ways first identified by the UPIAS (on page 59 above). For more than two decades churches have attempted to reduce these barriers mainly to physical access, but many in the UK have become obsessed with the legal requirement to conform with Part IV of the *1995 Disability Discrimination Act*, by 2004, and have sought to obey the law without reflecting theologically about the newly imposed obligations. In other words, many churches have tried to mimic secular organizations in their compliance and have forgotten that their first duty is to be the Church.

> From 1st October 2004, service providers will also have to take reasonable steps to remove or alter physical features of premises, which make it impossible or unreasonably difficult for disabled people to use a service, or to provide a reasonable means of avoiding the feature.
>
> (Disability Rights Commission website)

Access which is devoid of theological reflection is both barren and a negation of the nature of the Church which is an inclusive body – the body of Christ. This body is one and each disabled person is a gifted part of it. Churches have become tempted to believe that by making their building accessible under the law, they have addressed the needs of disabled people. Interestingly American churches are exempt from the provisions of the ADA and are therefore perhaps more strongly motivated by theological benchmarks rather than the civil ones. In the UK, the DDA comes with so many escape routes as to render it virtually meaningless in ecclesiastical structures which have been saddled with obstacles such as inflexible Victorian architecture. Service providers only have to make 'reasonable adjustments', and most architectural changes would be considered far from reasonable in the courts if they were subjects of test cases.

The UK has a long way to go before it catches up with American writings on the theology of disability. There are two reasons for this besides the obvious one that America has far larger churches and has developed a tradition of pastoral care for disabled people. The UK lags behind because, first, it has this staunchly secular and materialistic tradition, and second, the churches have resisted the idea of making disabled people a special case. Experience within the Church of Scotland suggests that to address the special issues of disability was considered discriminatory, rather than a means to end discrimination. This experience will be duplicated in other denominations. The one exception to the rule has been the long tradition of ministry to deaf people.

However, the neglect of disability issues is beginning to change with organizations like CHAD (Church Action on Disability) and 'Through the Roof'. There has also been the publication of *Making a World of Difference* by Roy McCloughry & Wayne Morris. The spill-over of ideas from America must not be underestimated and the influence of the concept of the 'Disabled God' has pervaded the preaching of many interested parties and crept on to many agendas for speakers. This means that we must now examine two aspects of the current scene, namely, the accommodation of disabled issues in the revision of theological practice and the self-definition of certain disabled people and their supporters by their use of Eiesland's development of the 'Disabled God'.

Most theologies of disability of recent years build on the foundation of Christian anthropology which emphasizes the giftedness of each (Pauline theology) and *Imago Dei*. Pauline theology stresses the importance of the Body of Christ as being made up of constituent parts which each have a unique gift to offer to the whole. Every disabled person has some gift which must be valued and nourished by the whole. This approach is typical of Block and is currently being developed by the *World Council of Churches*.

The WCC is also engaged in developing theology as a consequence of the study of *Imago Dei*. (Ecumenical Disability Advocates Network [EDAN], 2002; p 6) Such theology stresses that everyone is made in the image of God and that a disabled person, far from being imperfect, is part of that image. It is important to recognize that the traditional, mainly protestant, emphasis on imperfection has been part of our understanding of the nature of the world and of humankind for many centuries. The imperfection which is a characteristic of disability is a direct result of our fallen nature and of the sin of the world. Such a position is obviously dismissive of disabled people who neither consider themselves imperfect nor part of the imperfection caused by original sin. Luther's characterization of Adam is typical:

> Wherefore, when we now attempt to speak of that image, we speak of a thing unknown; an image which we not only have never experienced all our lives, and experience still. Of this image therefore all we now possess are mere terms – the image of God!.... But there was, in Adam, an illumined reason, a true knowledge of God and a will the most upright to love both God, and his neighbour.
>
> (Luther, quoted in Bornkamm, 1958; p 91)

Discussion that is centred on the fall normally results in another dichotomy which can easily debase disabled people.

Perfect relationship to God ←→ Imperfect (sinful) relationship to God

Such discourse debases disabled people and over many years has rendered them inferior to non-disabled people. The presence of disabled people reminds certain types of believers of the 'Fallen nature' of mankind. It also gives succour to the notion that the best treatment for disabilities is rehabilitation, to restore as much 'normality' as possible – in terms of 'miracle-workers' to effect a cure. The discourse is over-laden with notions of sin which will be discussed in a subsequent chapter. Moreover, there are two other flaws in arguments from the fall. First, perfection implies homogeneity and the whole force behind Pauline theology is that the body of Christ is characterized by a heterogeneity of gifts; and second, redeemed humanity which is a result of Christ's salvific incarnation is all-inclusive of those who are oppressed, but not defeated, by their differences which are seemingly in conflict with the perfect design. By contrast, redeemed humanity offers blessings in diversity.

This brings us neatly back to the work of Fox who argues that rather than looking at the fall we must begin to examine the implications of redemption of both humanity and ecology in the light of the saving incarnation of Jesus Christ. Disabled people become part of redeemed humanity by virtue of Christ's incarnation and as humans they become part of the body of Christ as well. It is impossible to conceive of redeemed humanity without including disabled people at its centre on a basis of equality with all others who are called to be part of the body of Christ. Furthermore, if we pursue the ideas of Adrian Thatcher we discover that all disabled people have in common the same genetic makeup as Jesus and this thought should guide our Christian attitudes towards genetic engineering, which were alluded to earlier in this chapter.

There are now overwhelming arguments for modifying our institutional behaviour towards disabled people simply in order to be obedient to the risen Christ and our consciousness of his body in our midst as the Church. This is why there have been so many efforts to modify Christian theology to accommodate disabled people. Yet, whilst we fully understand and accept the incarnational theology which we have been describing, there are good reasons for doubting the wisdom of some of these revisions. Previously we introduced the idea that doctrine was one way in which groups could mark their identity and found that disabled people were no exception. Eiesland argues very cogently that disabled people must embody their theology in an understanding of how their bodies relate to the life and death of Jesus and to his subsequent Church, and she developed the image of Jesus on the cross as a paralysed and wounded God taking on the nature of disability for our sake. The argument has similarities with those already advanced by Lewis whose seminal paper is inadequately acknowledged by Eiesland. The difference between Lewis and Eiesland is that Lewis sees the crucifixion as a price which had to be paid for the theological pronouncements of Jesus, whilst Eiesland actually considers that the crucifixion depicts the very nature of the disabled God. There is another problem, namely, that the nature of Jesus has traditionally been understood as the second part of the Trinity which depicts the nature of God but is not God Himself. It is therefore wrong to describe Jesus on the cross as a disabled God when in fact his suffering is a description of God's compassion for all who suffer, including disabled people. Whether Nancy Eiesland intentionally sought to imagine God as disabled is a point for discussion, but what is clear is that the concept of the 'disabled God' has become a rallying point for disabled Christians and a way in which they can uniquely appropriate God as one who cares for disabled people in a unique way. This has become an identity which goes beyond Christian anthropology and far beyond acceptance of a role in the body of Christ to an argument that God uniquely offered himself for the sake of disabled people. We must reject such a position whilst accepting the strength of the image of Jesus on the cross as sketched by Alan Lewis before his premature death from cancer. For those who hold the grammar of the Trinity to be important, the way in which disabled people have sought to mark out an identity is flawed.

So then, disabled people are missing from churches sometimes because the theology that is preached remains inaccessible in at least two ways. First, all theologies of disability, accessible or not, have a spiritual dimension which many disabled people would wish to ignore. If anyone harbours romantic ideas that disabled people must have a unique spirituality should disabuse themselves of this and seek another starting point. For those disabled people who do have a rich spirituality, they must be made comfortable by theological practices that address their sensitivities without corrupting hermeneutics for everyone else.

There follow two controversies which must be briefly introduced at this stage. The first concerns the status of disabled people in the Bible; the second asks whether Jesus really was a healer. This book will take a rather negative view of the first problem. It is not possible to project 21st century social constructs on to the characters and literary contents of the gospels. Disabled people have built a modern identity which was totally unknown in biblical times. Yes, there were Levitical proscriptions against imperfections in Priests but it is doubtful whether this is equivalent to prejudice as we now understand it. The proscriptions were specific to a class of people serving in the Temple and were not applied to Priests who became disabled later in life. Some authors have suggested that the proscriptions were not actually aimed at disabled people but rather were an attempt to maintain the purity of religion at a time when such purity was under threat. Much more relevantly, in a pastoral society based on small units, there would not be many associations of interest groups. There would be no disabled movement and probably no opportunity for disabled people of one locality to meet others belonging to another. Contrary to modern belief, disability was a catastrophe for both the person concerned and the family. Charity was likely to be the only relief to the visible tragedy which beset an individual. Politically incorrect words are deliberately being used to describe the situation of disabled people to emphasize the vast gulf in social thinking between biblical times and ours. It is thus perfectly in order to praise the compassion of Jesus in healing people with disabling impairments. What is unacceptable is to project the compassion of miraculous healing onto miracle healing of today.

The second problem queries the authenticity of the healing powers of Jesus. This book deals with the many ways in which the powers of Jesus are portrayed. Some argue that the miracles never happened; others say that they are highly formalized theological statements. The overall argument of this book is that Jesus must have been a healer of some kind. It would have been perfectly possible to make all the theological statements about him without mentioning healing – Paul almost did that. To hold such a position is almost fundamentalist in a book which proposes to be quite radical. What, therefore is the rationale behind this? Basically, the gospels give a place of honour to people with impairments and show that Jesus was concerned with such people. If theology tries to diminish this concern, it sells disabled people short. Those who cannot understand or appreciate this privileged position really have a problem with disability rather than with Jesus. This is why it is important to understand the traditional theology of miracles in order to bring disability back to the centre of our understanding of the gospels. The following chapters will unfold the way in which disabled people have been marginalized by the theological debate surrounding their healing.

Disabled people have the freedom to find wholeness in a variety of ways. The interpretations of the gospels which have been discussed offer an escape from the manifest impossibility of a cure, to finding healing and wholeness in their lives by coming to terms with impairments which can have devastating effects. Not all Christian disabled people will agree with the paths that have been taken and it is for this reason that the search must go on. Traditional theology may have valid truths about miracles but very often these fail to reach disabled people in a way which is welcoming and meaningful to them. The following chapters will begin to unpack some of these theologies, not with a view of showing their error, but to show how they could speak to disabled people if they were rephrased.

Chapter 2

What is Natural?

This chapter is going to look at four modes of thought which are interrelated by the nature and quality of their discourse and by their historical significance in the sense that quantum theory succeeded classical physics and the Enlightenment in particular. The modes of thought come in pairs: first, the philosophy of David Hume came at a time of certainty in the construction of the world and of doubts about religion. Proofs against miracles were on fairly sure ground because the analysis of them was based on factual statistics which seemed to disprove their existence. There was no experience which showed their regularity. As individual events, they stood isolated with no realistic proof of their existence other than faith which Hume had consigned to the 'flames' along with metaphysics. In similar vein, instances of disability were not necessarily rare but were certainly deviant from the norm of a healthy body. When healing miracles and the rarity of disability came together, philosophers like Hume had no difficulty in suggesting that they were freak violations of the laws of nature.

The next pair of modes of thought are those which have arisen out of quantum theory and out of a determination to observe disabled people as normal people who have special qualities and needs which define their disabilities. It is absolutely impossible to discuss the technical aspects of quantum, uncertainty and chaos theory in this text, but it is possible to point out that man's perception of science changed and became much less strong and dogmatic with these theories, and that many of its advocates have insisted that their influence extends to the way we look at society and order it, using metaphors and new creative ways of understanding our environment. The use of the word 'metaphor' is preferred by many, but in this context the word 'fluid' might be more appropriate. Since the 1940s, thinkers have been aware of their fallibility in investigative thinking and have developed interesting and innovative ways of describing social phenomena.

In this mode of thinking it is impossible to describe disability as something that is aberrant and which can be explained away as such. Rather, people with disabilities are now understood as complex social beings who have energies and skills which can be harnessed for the good of society as a whole. Although advocates of the social model of disability can be very dogmatic, the model does imply that no one group or profession has all the answers and that change depends on the co-operation of many people and the goodwill of all. Such an attitude shows strength in its collective approach but is weak compared to the dogmatism of Hume.

Part I – The Legacy of David Hume

One of the most embarrassing linguistic problems of disability surrounds the use of the word 'normal'. We often talk of disabled people being different from 'normal people'. We compare the gait of someone with cerebral palsy with a 'normal' gait and think of the 'Ministry of Funny Walks' portrayed by John Cleese in Monty Python's Flying Circus with ironic humour. A house-mother explained to a trainee in a special school for children with cerebral palsy in the 1950s, 'if it looks strange, it's spastic'.[5] Is there such a person as a normal person? Is disability always abnormal? The object of this chapter is to examine how theology has failed to contribute anything constructive to this issue.

The problem is essentially one of perception and Goffman, a sociologist, was foremost in the 1960s in attempting to describe how disabled people strove for normality by hiding their stigmas. He argued convincingly that disabled people managed their 'spoilt identities' by a variety of mechanisms to lessen the impact of their disability on normal society. (Goffman, 1968) With a prevalent emphasis on rehabilitation in post-war society, the onus was upon the disabled person to compensate for their disability, stigma, to make others at ease. The medical model of disability has never suggested that there is a burden on non-disabled people to assimilate the disability which was being disguised. It was as if the fault lay with the disabled person and that if medicine could not cure or ameliorate the condition, then the person with an impairment was obligated to put others at their ease. Such behaviour did occur and Goffman was not exaggerating his research findings. His earlier work on asylums had begun to explore the possibility that the environment actually has an effect on people's behaviour. (Goffman, 1961) A synthesis of the two books, *Stigma* and *Asylums*, might have created a sociological rationale for the social model of disability which was beginning to be developed in the same decade. This scene from the 60s illustrates the importance of examining theology which constantly refers to normality.

Fortunately, although many people experience a dilemma in finding suitable ways of distinguishing disabled people from non-disabled people there is a greater search for political correctness than in the 1960s when Goffman argued that individuals strove to conceal their stigma by over-compensating socially. When we move to discuss the theology of miracles, however, it is seldom possible to escape from a discussion of normality. Miracles by any definition are extraordinary events and in common parlance the word easily signifies a happy, unexpected event or outcome. Someone's life has been saved, a successful journey was made in adverse weather conditions. One may even joke about the miracle of finishing a book or a university course! The word miracle in other words is very positive but tends to emphasize deliverance from a very negative situation – death, illness and failure. In common parlance, the list of dichotomies is almost endless but in philosophical terms the dichotomy becomes formalized in terms of an opposition between normality and an abnormal occurrence. David Hume formulated his definition of miracle thus:

> A miracle is a violation of the laws of nature; and as a firm and unalterable experience has established these laws, the proof against a miracle, from the very nature of the fact, is as entire as any argument from experience can possibly be imagined.
> (Hume, 1777/1902; p 114)

The very first phrase of this definition sets up a dichotomy which has become ingrained in the theology of miracles. The miraculous is violent as opposed to the passivity of the laws of nature. Any deviation from the normal was defined by Hume in terms of perception. The Enlightenment permitted philosophers and scientists to escape from *a priori* truths and to map the world out by observation. Broadie makes the point that men like Hume found themselves fortunate to rejoice in a new '... perspective of the eighteenth century, [that] what previous ages suffered from was the dead hand of authority, especially political authority and even more especially religious authority'. (Broadie, 2001; p 16) They were searching for reasonable beliefs based on reasonable responsibilities. Right-wing critics of Hume tend to describe him as an atheist whereas he was a theist who was careful not to identify with disbelief. What he wanted, however, was to base his beliefs on reasonableness which came from observation. (Broadie, 2001a) The authority which guided thought in the Enlightenment was based on observation, not on scripture and tradition. The result was that laws of nature could only be identified after one was sure that the probability of a recurrence was indubitably established by observation. Such empiricism freed the mind to understand normality in human terms and to ask fresh questions about the odd, the abnormal and freakish behaviour.

It was on this intellectual foundation that Hume built his sceptical definition of miracles. Both normality and abnormality were based on the observation of patterns. That night follows day may be established as a 'natural law' by the frequency with which we observe the pattern. Normality is defined by the reliability that we find in everyday occurrences and in the circles of the Scottish Enlightenment, men like Adam Smith extended the establishment of such laws to the economy. During the Enlightenment not only was a more rigorous experimental science founded but also a new social science, and miracles could be explored not only theologically but from the perspective of an early and often crude social investigation. Natural laws are statistically based on the accumulation of observations which establishes that something occurs regularly. Universal laws are usually based on mathematics and are established by logic. (Swinburne, 1970) Newton's laws of mechanics and gravitation were established by mathematical deduction in Book III of *Principia* although they may have been prompted by the falling of an apple according to scientific folklore. The accumulation of observation is important because it suggests that observers are important. As regards miracles, it is assumed they are such irregular violations that they cannot either be replicated or established as laws by repeated observations. This means that they must either belong to God or be accounted for as some aberration of nature. Aquinas sets out the options for the Christian believer whilst Hume would argue that nothing short of observation on repeated instances could account for a miracle as a violation of nature. The two great fathers of the Church, St Augustine and St Thomas Aquinas, believed that our knowledge of nature or normality was incomplete. Aquinas sought to firmly establish that miracles were carried out by God not to disrupt the laws of nature but to further our knowledge of how nature works. He wrote:

> Furthermore, all creatures are related to God as art products
> are to an artist,... Consequently, the whole of nature is like
> an artefact of the divine mind. But it is not contrary to the
> essential character of an artist if he should work in a different
> way on his product, even after he has given it its first form.
> Neither then, is it against nature if God does something to
> natural things in a different way from that to which the course
> of nature is accustomed.
>
> (Aquinas, *Summa*; 3.100.6)

In a famous statement Augustine was even more succinct than
Aquinas:

> Miracles are not contrary to nature but only contrary to what
> we know about nature.
>
> Saint Augustine of Hippo (354-430)

It is apparent that there is a strong Christian tradition for defining
normality in terms of God's laws which Hume was unable to countenance
because in previous work he had consigned anything of a metaphysical
nature 'to the flames'. Yet much of the debate about normality hinges
upon his arguments. The observers, or witnesses, of miracles become of
great importance to Hume and to those philosophers who have sought
to build upon his argument. If miracles are divided into three categories:
1) Single events which are part of God's history, i.e. the resurrection; 2)
nature miracles; and 3) healing miracles – it is not difficult to imagine
that healing should have been traditionally the most easily attested by
witnesses. Actually in terms of the gospels there is one text which treats
witnesses in any kind of formal manner as germane to overall belief in
Jesus:

> [24] This is the disciple who testifies to these things and who
> wrote them down. We know that his testimony is true.
> [25] Jesus did many other things as well. If every one of them
> were written down, I suppose that even the whole world
> would not have room for the books that would be written.
>
> John 21:24-25

Luke also suggests that witnesses are part of the historical record in
the opening verses of Acts.

Flew (1961) argues that Hume greatly devalues the testimony of
witnesses as they appear in historical records such as the gospels. He

contrasts historical testimony with the empiricism which Hume advocates and appeals for scientific testimony to make the point. For example, one may witness only one eclipse in a lifetime and cannot expect to verify this experience by experiencing countless others but, despite this, no one would doubt the experience. Where empiricism fails, in this instance, is that it does not take account of the mathematical tables and calculations which predict and record past and present eclipses. When Burns comes to discuss testimony of miracles, he sums up the difficulties thus:

> The point is simply that, when Hume claims that a 'dead man coming to life ... has never been observed in any age or country,' and <u>therefore</u> (he implies) the several reports of this occurring (three in the New Testament alone) are obviously untrue, he is arguing in a circle; he has arrived at the premise from which he would derive the falsity of alleged resurrections by first deciding that the latter are false.
>
> (Burns, 1981; p 219)

The constrictions to which Hume's testimonies are subject have a great bearing on disabled people. Time after time, disabled people cause others to bear witness to all aspects of their lifestyles from a variety of motives ranging from objectivity to pity. Whilst most researchers in the field resist the temptation to give story-based accounts of the experiences of disabled people, there is a place for a story in contrast to overwhelming statistical evidence. Hume is correct in suggesting that experience confirms statistical probability, but the lives of disabled people must also be seen in the context of their individuality and their needs as very different personalities. Burns, in an appendix, quotes critics and supporters of Hume to show that their main motive is to find explanations of healing miracles in order to account for abnormality in a mechanistic world ruled by a beneficent God, and where the miracles of Jesus 'save' the world from such anomalies.

In subsequent chapters, it will be shown that the testimony of miracles is actually stronger than the theists of the eighteenth century where willing or able to contemplate. It is only actually a small minority of thinkers who seek to use miracles to restore a perfect world or perfect bodies, *vide* modern miracle workers and doctors who insist that miracles can be given a medical explanation. To escape this trap, it is necessary to consider other philosophical ways of understanding both miracles and disabled people. (*see part 2 of this chapter, page 80*)

Although Hume did dwell on healings in his discussion of miracles, he faced the same problem as every writer on miracles, which is the problem of discussing healing as opposed to the great miracles of God. Is there a justification in distinguishing between miraculous healing and the resurrection, the virgin birth or the parting of the waters of the Red Sea. In common with many previous writers this book distinguishes between healing and the other miraculous events which somehow mark the workings or economy of God. All the debates of the late nineteenth century centred on the virgin birth and the status of Old Testament miracles compared to those in the New Testament. Although they were reluctant to dismiss healing, many of the German schools were prepared to attack the virgin birth as an aberration and supported their arguments with reference to the primacy of Sᵗ Mark's Gospel which of course has no reference to it. The Oxford Movement, and particularly Pusey, defended its position as a principle miracle in God's plan.

Hume believed that miracles could not be proven because they failed the test of regularity when it came to the opportunity to observe them. Hume did not deny that there were witnesses to miracles and indeed offered contemporary examples of healing miracles. He was particularly fond of quoting French examples of limbs being regenerated after amputation and the like. What these witnesses failed to question was the probability of replication, which was likely to be very low. Jesus actually reprimanded his disciples for their inability to heal. Whilst the Enlightenment spawned a rigorous rationality, it was also a period of enormous irrationality. The philosophers spent a great deal of time discussing the nature of politics and of science, while most of the population of France and others countries were more interested in the popular sciences of mesmerism and ballooning. The most popular books at the time of Diderot and *L'Encyclopédie* were books on mesmerism or hot-air balloonists. The Revolution was low on the agenda of the small reading public.[6] (Darton, 1968; Leventhal, 1976; Thuillier, 1988)

With such irrationality there came fantastic stories of the healing of very abnormal conditions which Hume was prepared to take seriously enough to refute on the basis that the witnesses were unable to establish patterns of normality within them. He probably witnessed the near circus atmosphere when he visited Paris in 1734. (Graham, 2004: p 49f) These miracles had a crudity to them which the gospel miracles do not have, but for Hume's purposes they confirmed the futility of trying to establish the normality of miracles when they were subject to little corroboration.

Mackie argues that people who wish to regard miracles as violations of nature may in fact inhabit a closed world. Hume, he asserts, was neither for or against the occurrence of miracles but only that there were not convincing reasons for believing in them. In a closed world, it is assumed that everything works within a system and that the laws or design will eventually be found and documented. In this world there is no meaningful reason for accepting either the evidence for or testimony of miracles. Mackie argues that such a position is not tenable in a world whose system is not totally documented. (Mackie, 1982) The argument can be furthered by referring back to Augustine on page 71 above, where we note his argument that God's world had been far from totally discovered and that miracles may be part of that undiscovered order. In the discussion of Hume so far, it has been impossible to assume that any witness to a miracle has been a Christian, but now it is possible to insert faith into perception. In a recent book Eric Eve (2002) has argued that miracles are best understood as anomalies occurring within the normal course of events. Unlike Hume, he sets miracles within the Judeo-Christian tradition which allows him to make assumptions about the beliefs of witnesses.

> Miracles are, first, strikingly unexpected events that, secondly, are taken by believers to be, thirdly, acts of God.
>
> (Eve, 2002; p 25)

The first of Eve's conditions is obviously one which will be common to Hume and subject to the same criticisms concerning probability which Hume considered so important. However, the second firmly makes belief in miracles a matter of faith. It is not probability that either proves or disproves miracles, but that any reason for doubt is overcome by faith. In short, Augustine's adage becomes true because the witnesses have faith in an active God who they believe has brought the miracle to pass. With this argument we appear to move far from Hume; but do we?

There are several reasons for doubting the value of the religious perception of an anomaly. First, there is no indication that the dichotomy between normal and abnormal has disappeared. The healing miracles in the gospels do not address the question of how normality is achieved at this level of discussion. The disease or impairment is simply cured or removed and the witnesses are reported to have marvelled at the restoration to complete health and functionality. Accounts of miracles remain full of disablist language, in that conformity to the norm remains more desirable than the status quo. The perception which was described by Hume was one of calculation, that of Eve is one of acceptance of homogeneity. Second, compared to Hume, Eve's argument is tautologous. Hume doubted that an event was miraculous because it could not be observed repeatedly, whereas Eve appears to argue that an event is miraculous because it is believed to be miraculous. His tautology remains symptomatic of a closed system. Last, a miracle in his terms does not produce a hermeneutic which can break out of the dichotomous discourse and address real issues of disability, in short it remains in the mindset of the medical model of disability. This negative assessment of Eric Eve's contribution is only a beginning of what will eventually be a sympathetic review in a later chapter.

The reason why Hume's legacy is prominent in our investigation is because neither Hume nor most of the philosophers who have supported or criticized him have been particularly interested in biblical scholarship, but more the philosophical implications of rare and strangely witnessed events that are devoid of rational explanations. A miraculous event has a subject, an outcome involving that subject and some assumed intervention in what otherwise would be the norm. In the case of a healing miracle, Hume would argue that a person with an illness is cured as the result of divine intervention or some special gift possessed by someone. This, in a nutshell, is the mirror-image of what is considered to be the social model of disability. The concern of those wedded to this model is the removal of the impairment without an undue analysis of the intervening procedures. There are many cases of children with anything from cerebral palsy to spina bifida being offered horrendous surgery to help overcome some part of their impairment. Most of us learn to relate to disabled people by experience guided by common sense and we quickly learn that they are not aberrations of nature but part of our common humanity. To think that we can organize disabled people by neatly pigeon-holing them into general laws is a mistake which may have been common at the time of Hume but must be eschewed now. It is like our general perception of laws of nature. We know intuitively that apples fall to the ground – we have a phenomenological understanding of gravity but this does not imply that we immediately have an understanding of Newton's laws.

(Davies, 1999) People who are unfamiliar with disability often cannot trust their common sense understanding and seek for explanations which may not help to describe disability. Laws often provide explanations which are of little use to the outsider, just as theories about disability and cures cannot provide the reader with the experience which comes with personal encounter.

Part II – What about Quantum Theory and Chaos?

For some, quantum mechanics introduces boundless opportunities to explain irregularities in nature scientifically, as if Augustine's dictum on page **60** above could be fully justified and understood. Augustine's unseen aspects of nature appear to be in the process of being revealed and unravelled by an astonishingly rich new science. However, it is important to stress that quantum mechanics represents a precise statement of the limitations of measurement in the realm of particle physics with limited application to our subject. Whilst the new physics gives new understandings of nature, our main concern lies in the fresh openness of this new perception, as compared to the thought processes of the Enlightenment. Michael Frayn puts fictional words into the mouth of Neils Bohr in conversation with Werner Heisenberg in his play, *Copenhagen*:

> **Bohr:** It starts with Einstein. He shows that measurement depends – measurement is not an impersonal event that occurs with impartial universality. It's a human act, carried out from a specific point of view in time and space, from the one particular viewpoint of a possible observer.
>
> (Frayn, 1998; p 71)

The 'Copenhagen' debate brings together in our lay minds both the 'principle of uncertainty' and chaos theory, which progress us from classical physics to the multi-facetted scene of today. Whereas Enlightenment philosophers and scientists believed that their observations were objective; those working with quantum mechanics discovered that their observations and deductions were not only subject to the vagaries of human activity but also directly influenced the behaviour of what was being observed. Many popularists have argued that the 'principle of uncertainty' gave credence to the likelihood of miracles occurring as part of the order of nature as yet unexplained, as Augustine had implied. Yet the main shift has been in our acceptance of the limitations of our observations. A major leap had been made in our understanding of nature but not in nature itself. Einstein was reported to have said in conversation, 'God does not play dice with the world'. (Clarke, 1973; p 33) He offered this aphorism as if to underline his preceding argument which is summarized by Clark thus:

> God might pose difficult problems, but He never broke the rules by posing unanswerable ones. What is more, He never left the answers to blind chance ...

Einstein's viewpoint was perhaps informed and influenced by studying with theologians like Martin Buber. This was important because physicists like Rutherford harboured doubts which have been more vociferously aired by popular science. Physicists from the Enlightenment had always had some religious belief, and in the case of Newton the Church welcomed his insights as illustrations of God's grand design. In the same way, many of the 'new' physicists shared religious insights with theologians. However, it was the popularists who led the way in creating the impression that the new physics offered a completely different picture of God's creation and of the potentiality to discover God's hand at work in ways that hitherto had only been subject to speculation.

The fame of the uncertainty principle is really due to Werner Heisenberg who developed it as a small contribution to quantum theory, and to the debate which came to be known as the Copenhagen debate. The important thing to notice is that is not about the totality of nature but rather about the observation of certain parts of the natural world. It is not enunciating or describing a new natural law but recognising the limitations of our powers of perception. Cassidy, one of Heisenberg's biographers, sums up the principle succinctly in his own words and by quoting one sentence from Heisenberg's paper which was published in 1927:

> Because of this, Heisenberg noted, there seems to be a reciprocal relationship between the imprecisions, or uncertainties, with which one can simultaneously measure the velocity and the position of an electron at any given instant: 'The more precisely we determine the position, the more imprecise is the determination of velocity in this instant, and vice versa.' And this reciprocal relationship between uncertainties in measurement also holds for other conjugate pairs of variables, such as energy and time. This, in a few words, is Heisenberg's uncertainty principle.
>
> (Cassidy, 1991; p 228)

In other words, the more complicated and the more precise the observations of scientists become, the less reliable their observations actually are. Nuclear physicists were discovering the limitations of human observation. In a similar way theologians must recognize that the more they try to describe reality and its finer details, the less likely they are to be able to make precise observations either about nature or God.

Southgate (1999) insists that to have a quantum consciousness one must a) observe probabilities, b) adopt a holistic approach, c) recognize that statistics are not immediately available on any subject, and d) understand that calculations are no longer linear but have to incorporate random values as they occur. (p.114) First, quantum physics appeared to suggest a new understanding of natural law in ways which Einstein had warned against in his aphorism. Second, the reductionist characteristic of previous science, where everything could be reduced to the Greek understanding of the indivisible nature of the atom – atomism, in other words – led to a renewed search for holism. Third, with the advent of the atom bomb, popular imagination understood that the new physics was concerned with energy and this translated into a belief that energy affected everything to do with human beings. It developed many 'new age' applications but also affected Christian healers in positive ways which, when combined with the other two, offered the likelihood that science, theology and philosophy could begin to look at healing miracles in a non-dichotomous way.

We will now examine three ways in which these new perceptions have changed our understanding of reality. First, we now know that, whilst the reality of the created world has not changed, our ability to perceive and map what is going on has grown considerably. There has been a temptation to say that miracles have now been explained by the accounts we have of the irregular behaviour of atoms and the relativity of our observations; but, in fact, all that has changed is the sophistication of our measurements and observations. Never has it been more likely that St Augustine's understanding is correct that the laws of nature are incomplete and that miracles may lie within the realm of the undiscovered. God does not govern the world in whimsical and random ways, so there is no reason why miracles cannot be included in a broader understanding of the laws of nature rather than dismissed as violations. This has come about because of our new understanding that time is relative and that random occurrences can be accounted for in chaos theory as propounded by Feigenbaum. The common illustration of this theory involves a butterfly flapping its wings in Tokyo having an effect on the weather in New York. The chance that air turbulence around the butterfly can precipitate a chain of events that eventually affect the clouds over New York is remote, but – and this is the important point – possible. This means that it is no longer irrational to hold our minds open to thinking about miracles in terms of the same sort of possibility, even though the actual means of proof do not yet exist. Miracles are unique and often stunning events, and it is now possible to place them in the context of the wholeness of creation. Ward traces the work of several thinkers, not least Alfred North Whitehead, to develop the idea of 'emergent creativity' as a more adequate way of describing how God has created the world and continues to do so. He illustrates this by referring to the composition of a piece of music. Each note is unique and can be regarded as part of a creative plan by the composer. The uniqueness of each note is a small miracle in itself contributing to the whole, just as one miracle is a small incident in a greater plan within a divine mind. (Ward, 1996) The beauty of 'quantum thinking' is that the implications for perception gives us a much greater sense of reality than linear thinking about the laws of nature. Randomness in itself really proves nothing about miracles, but the broadening of our minds open us to enormous possibilities which will be explored as we continue.

Peacocke takes the issue of holistic thought a stage further. Within the world system, God exhibits a general providence and a special providence which would include miracles and the major events of Easter, the Exodus and the Incarnation. Peacocke encourages us not to localize 'special' events but rather to see them in the context of an unpredictable 'chaotic system' which is gradually becoming understood by both mathematicians and physicists who are developing non-linear calculus to describe and quantify micro-atomic events. We have mentioned Feigenbaum who popularized the illustration of butterfly wings and weather, but it was Poincarré who first identified the properties of chaos in 1915 when he used the behaviour of the balls on a billiard table to illustrate that certain complex natural phenomena could not be predicted with any accuracy. This means that we are obliged to consider miracles in the context of the whole rather than to see them as isolated instances of the violation of natural law. God has the ability to act in the world in any way which shows his omniscience within the parameters of logic. Peacocke describes his understanding of God's action in the world thus:

> The model is based on the recognition that an omniscient God uniquely knows, over all frameworks of reference of time and space, everything that is possible to know about the state(s) of the world-System, including the interconnectedness and interdependence of the world's entities, structures and processes. By analogy with the operation of whole-part influence in real systems, the suggestion is that, because the ontological gap between the world and God is located simply everywhere in space and time, *God could affect holistically the state of the world-System.* Thence, *mediated by the whole-part influences of the world-system on its constituents, God could cause particular patterns of events to occur which would express God's intentions.* These latter would not otherwise have happened had God not so specifically intended.

(Peacocke, 2001; p 109f [italics original])

Now, science cannot explain the divine purpose of God nor his mechanisms for achieving the same; but science can place on theologians and others the obligation to believe that everything is part of a whole and that if we had sufficient knowledge we could understand God's action in either causing miracles or allowing them to happen. This obligation was neither apparent nor logically required when David Hume wrote. Therefore our new awareness pushes the debate forward to a position where S¹ Augustine's dictum begins to make sense, as we humbly acknowledge that we understand the potential of God's actions. But as Peacocke points out we are faced with the same stillness which greeted Elijah as he sat in his cave contemplating fire, wind and earthquake, eventually finding God in the mystery of silence. Miracles now have a place in our perception whilst at the same time they pose a mystery as we contemplate the entire world-system in which we live and have our being.

Second, there is the question of holism which occupied much of our attention in the last chapter but is now of slightly less importance as we encounter the interest in energy. However, at the popular level of discussion, energy cannot be understood without reference to the holistic view, which is supposed to have come about with the new physics. David Bohm (1996) who taught physics in California and in London wrote a seminal book which was published in 1996 after his death three years earlier. In *Wholeness and the Implicate Order*, he contrasts the fragmentation of modern society, which still tends to use old models of physics, with the holistic approach of an implicit order which can be found in the more fluid approach of quantum physics or thought. God created an order in which everything is contingent, and this understandably led science to consider each phenomenon by itself. In the time of Newton and the earlier scientists who subscribed to atomism there was no real harm in considering objects in this way. But the modern mind has fragmented nature so much that we have lost sight of the whole. Bohm argues that a quantum understanding allows the detection of an implicit order in the whole which is a much more wholesome way of modelling the world. Coming from a different angle, Pannenberg and others argue that any theology of nature must now embrace models which respect the biblical understanding of contingency whilst recognising the interdependency of all aspects of the ecology. (Pannenberg *et al*, 1993; p 73ff) The pressures coming both from physics and from ecology to find new integrated theories of reality emphasize the new importance of holism. These pressures have also spawned a raft of popular works which pre-dates those authors but have given an impetus to the serious writing of Bohm and Pannenberg, to name but two.

Paul Davies, another distinguished physicist, is a populist who is concerned about holism in his book, *God and the New Physics*, which examines quantum theory but wanders into the far greater territory of biological science. He argues that 'quantum thought' represents a far greater revolution than a purist understanding of quantum mechanics. Davies argues that the atom is now to be understood as a multi-component unit with enormous potential for energy and configuration in contrast to the dead unit of physics before Einstein. Our understanding of the structure of DNA has shown us how atoms combine to produce life in a way which cannot be reduced to a single atom. He contrasts the ancient understanding of life as being the will of God in bringing together living organisms (vitalism) with the modern understanding of combinations of atoms evolving into living material. (p 60) Examining a living unit now involves looking at the whole structure and the activities of that unit in ways which encourage and liberate the mind to consider the wonderful complexity of God's creation, rather than reduce it to small and dead component parts. Such a perception represents a considerable revolution in man's thinking. When combined with the concept of energy it becomes even more potent and will eventually lead scientists away from the medical model of disability to the social model of disability as they learn to respect the energy and potential in each disabled person rather than regarding them as an irresolvable problem.

Third, Fritjof Capra wrote a series of books beginning in 1975 on the implications of the new physics for man's thinking in general and medicine in particular. His influence as a popularist is worthy of note and his effect upon the healing movement was considerable. Capra's *The Tao of Physics* describes the atom as a focus of the vibrating energy which permeates the whole universe and which we may tap into with the heightened awareness of our unity with nature. His later books expand his thesis on the Cartesian dualism which exists in medicine. He is basically arguing that, from the Greek atomists to Newton, particles were regarded as solid and irreducible. They were thus objects in a mechanical universe which were observed by a different order, i.e. man. From La Plank onwards the atom became spatial and subsequent scientists developed quantum mechanics to help understand the nucleus and the orbits of electrons. (Capra, 1975) The research by Bohr, Rutherford and Heisenberg added to our knowledge of the energy contained within the active atom. Heisenberg is most frequently quoted because his 'uncertainty principle' is seen as a breaking down of the barriers between precise science and speculation, when in fact it is a rather precise description of the relationship between an electron's momentum and position.

In combination with chaos theory, the impact of this principle on mysticism has been noted by many. Capra was able to argue that dualism had disappeared and that humans were at last united with nature. With Capra's emphasis on energy, and mankind's potential to harness and use it as a source of power, the talents of the healer came into their own. In the last chapter, we saw how doctors such as Patrick Pietroni developed holistic practices of medicine and hinted at how this affected 'new age' healers. In Scotland, one such practitioner, Bruce MacManaway, built a whole theory of healing around the concept of energy. He was active for many years in Iona and Fife. He appears to have been a gifted healer who accepted that healing is of God and gave praise for his gifts, but his book never strays far from Spiritualism or from the conviction that there are cosmic energies into which we can all tune and thus become much more complete people. (MacManaway & Turcan, 1983) Wallis, a lecturer in Social Anthropology at the University of Edinburgh, recounts how he attended one of MacManaway's courses in Fife and, being asked to take part in the laying on of hands for the first time, was impressed by the discovery of his own talents as a healer (1992).

It is indeed debatable whether the new system of thought generated by the ideas of random intervention, holism and energy is justified, let alone scientific, but it now exists both within the Church and without and has, for many, replaced the primitive empiricism of pre-Einsteinian physics. It represents a shift in perception which allows the potential to look at disabled people in terms of miracles in a much more fluid way. The key to this thinking goes back to the perception of the atom – be that the atom of physics or the atom of any system. Quantum physics stated for the first time that an atom is not a unit of dead matter but is characterized by energy and flux in every moment of existence. We can see the value of such thinking if we extend the idea to disabled people.

The medical model of disability is a modern example of atomism. It regards a disabled person as a non-energetic unit that remains malleable in the hands of medical personnel in so far as they seek to cure, or at best, to rectify whatever impairment is manifested. Modern medicine has become so specialized that physicians treat smaller and smaller parts of the body and depend on more specialized diagnosis in the treatment of that part. It also treats a disabled person as a single unit with an identifiable disability that can be rectified by specialist treatment or methods of rehabilitation. The disabled person becomes an object to be observed and acted upon and is not viewed as part of a social unit or group. There is a danger that the healing miracles of Jesus can be viewed in a similar way. Each miracle addresses one individual with one symptom which Jesus can cure. Whilst this is undoubtedly how the gospels read, such a reading does not encourage any exploration into the true nature of the miracles.

The social model of disability, on the other hand, implies a collectivity of different kinds of disabled people with common social goals which is alien to the mind of someone who is a prisoner of the medical model of disability. It offers the possibility of recognizing the energy which powers a disabled person to find ways of both challenging themselves and society to overcome their disability. Defining this energy is a difficult and dangerous exercise because it can potentially be immensely patronising. Davidson (1977) offered a definition in a study of adults in Scotland with cerebral palsy when she chose to use the word 'resilience' as way of characterising the energy which they brought to life. Carolyn Thompson, a theologian and disabled rights worker from Boston, suggested another definition to a seminar in Geneva for the *World Council of Churches* in November 2002 as part of the preparation of the WCC's 2003 *Interim Statement*. She recalled a remark made by a survivor of 9/11 who refused to be labelled as a victim but rather as a survivor who had become 'a reluctant expert' in all the aspects of life which faced survivors of that terrible event, such as life insurance, job hunting and mutual bereavement counselling. Carolyn Thompson applied this remark to disabled people by listing the number of issues which a successful disabled person must master. All disabled people must master their impairments by learning new skills with parts of their bodies to compensate for others which do not work; they must learn about the benefit system; they must overcome discrimination and find ways of interacting with non-disabled people which are fulfilling rather than a chore and necessary politeness. The social model of disability also implies activity rather than passivity and this translates into political activity and a search for social remedies which go far beyond rehabilitation and betterment. (McCloughry & Morris, 2002; chap. 2) This awareness of the energy which can be pent up in disabled people not only demands that we take regard of the whole person but that we develop a profound scepticism for any theory which simply perceives disability as a problem requiring a medical solution.

In terms of hermeneutics, the choices facing someone who wishes to preach about miracles become very stark. Do they understand the healing miracles as violations of the laws of nature? Do they see the disabled person as an instrument of the miraculous drama which is unfolding in the gospel and as the recipient of a power which is truly supernatural in the sense that it becomes from beyond nature? Or do they believe that the disabled person at the heart of the miracle is the source of at least some of the energy in changing his or her life? Could it be that when a healing miracle occurs in the gospels, it is not the laws of nature that are being violated but rather the norms of society. If this is so we can move away from the dichotomy of normality/abnormality. We can begin to recognize that the uniqueness of each disabled person actually makes it impossible to maintain such a dichotomy because disability represents a normality within society that is only made abnormal by the adverse reactions of parts of society to it. The philosophers and scientists which have been examined here have sought to stress disability as an abnormality which may be only fixed by divine intervention. The introduction of quantum thinking has certainly opened up the possibility of recognizing the social dynamic of disability, but it could be argued that if philosophers had been willing to listen to St Augustine many thinkers before the quantum age might have escaped from the trap of the normality/abnormality dichotomy.

Science and religion can often make good bed-fellows – although marriage is less promising. Whilst there are scientists and populists who argue that quantum theory does explain miracles, a more reasonable approach would suggest that science now supports a more rounded holistic view of miracles rather than their compartmentalization into this or that little theory. If we accept such a view we can begin to look in the next chapters at the ways in which we can regard miracles as part of God's providence and the reality of Jesus' ministry. In addition, the conclusion of this chapter will ultimately give us permission to declare in the final remarks that disability is both natural and normal. (See page 201ff)

Chapter 3

The Trouble with Christology

The Subordination of Disabled People?

The problem to be addressed in this chapter is probably the most difficult in the book. Throughout it has been argued that disabled people should be honoured in any hermeneutic surrounding miracles, whereas Christology demands that we honour Jesus Christ over everything. Furthermore, if Christ is the fulfilment of biblical history, we must see how this fulfilment has come about and its implications. Many theologians honour Christ in their studies at the expense of disabled people and, by describing the love of God as recorded in the Bible, paint a picture of disabled people as objects and recipients of God's love or charity. This, of necessity, leads to an assumption that to reach our true humanity, we must imitate the love of God and of Jesus Christ in a charitable concern for disabled people in all aspects of their lives. This charitable form of religion is often despised by disabled people and their desire to be recognized as truly human often inspires them to oppose anything which smacks of a charitable theology. Also, if such a beneficent attitude is sought from the churches, it is all too easy to criticize their short-fallings. We will first look at the Bible as a record of God's love in terms of healing, and then examine the full implications of Christology.

God's Care of the Distressed

Throughout the Bible there are many stories of God's care of the distressed. Such care can be seen as a sign of his love and of the broadness of his desire to heal the sufferings of many. Central to the Old Testament is the story of the Exodus – God saw the sufferings of the Israelites at the hands of the Pharaoh and acted upon it. You then have the ambivalence of Moses healing the plagues which God had visited upon the Egyptians. In a sense the Exodus is about the restoration of health to an oppressed race who had been deprived of all their social rights and rites of worship and kinship. Remus takes up the theme of the New Testament description of love as embracing not only providence but teaching and the healing miracles:-

Even as God fed the birds of the air and clothed the lilies of the field (Matt.6.25-33) and caused the sun to shine and rain to fall on the just and unjust alike (5.45), so God's gift of healing was gratis. Jesus' calls to discipleship (the subject of another book in this series) were invitations to others to live in a way that would demonstrate God's compassion and care, also to those outside Jesus' immediate following. The Good Samaritan in the well-known parable (Luke 10:29-37) exemplifies this: he crosses social boundaries in order to tend the injured man's wounds and then even to provide care during his period of recuperation.

(Remus, 1997; p 116)

Remus argues that not only did Jesus perform healing miracles but that he consciously portrayed the love of the Good Samaritan as an act of healing which demonstrated the true imitation of God's love by a neighbour to a neighbour. Funk (1996, Chapter Ten) argues very strongly that the parable of the Good Samaritan illustrates Jesus' intention to preach to the marginalized and underprivileged rather than to the establishment of Israel. The Samaritan was not expected to help a Jew and the priest lived up to expectations by refusing to break the cleanliness laws in order to assist the wounded, possibly dead, man. The problem with Funk is that, whilst he accepts that the parable sets out a manifesto of preaching and assistance to the dispossessed, he devotes little or no space for the miracles which were addressed to helping these very people. Some commentators go further and argue that Jesus' feeding of the 5,000 was in a sense a healing act rather than a nature miracle in that their collective distress caused by hunger had been alleviated.

Some authors trace the development of concepts of health through the Old Testament arguing that Jesus brought the true understanding of health in his teaching and practice rather than simply reiterate the Old Testament teaching. His understanding was one of fulfilment and the implied a command to the Church to concern itself with health and healing in a way which had not been specifically demanded by the Old Testament statutes and prophecies. (Brown, 1995) The debate about health was a developmental one and produced several different themes rather than the consistent one of love which Jesus taught and exemplified. Three examples can be considered.

First, there is the idea of good health and long life as a blessing rather than a curse. This is expressed well in Deuteronomy 30:19:

> This day I call heaven and earth as witnesses against you, that
> I have set before you life and death, blessings and the curses.
> Now choose life, so that you and your children may live…

The writer of Deuteronomy presents a clear case that God expects his statutes to be obeyed and that a full life is the reward for such good living. In a sense, the idea that sin is associated with illness, disability and misfortune in general emanates from this clear statement of choice which God presents to his people.

The second example introduces a real debate about health and God's providence. The Wisdom literature coincided with a turbulent time in Israel's history when the nation's enemies appeared to have the upper hand and vast swathes of the population were made to suffer in exile and degradation. Psalm 137 illustrates the loss and confusion felt by a population which was deprived of its religious institutions in exile. 'How can we sing Yahweh's song in a foreign land?' asked the bewildered psalmist who was not used to individual suffering as part of God's plan. The book of Job, and to a lesser extent Ecclesiastes, begins a dialogue about how individual suffering can be related to God's love. Job's afflictions were totally unmerited yet his comforters were unable to detract from his faith in the goodness of God and in his providence. At the end of the torment Job is still able to affirm the goodness of God and to enjoy a long and righteous life. The theme of individualism becomes much more apparent in many of the Old Testament books. The story of Jonah is basically an account of the misfortunes of a servant of God who was disobedient in his mission, yet eventually lived to righteousness in his mission to Nineveh. Evangelicals make much of this individualism which culminates in the sinner being called to repentance and conversion to Christ. Again the implications of sin being associated with illness is never far away.

Third, a prophecy of Isaiah enabled Jesus to place his ministry in the eschatological tradition of the prophet, when he quoted him in the synagogue (Luke 4:14-21). Isaiah prophesied a world where the blight of common disabilities would disappear and Jesus very deliberately took this to himself not only in his teaching but in the type of healings which he chose to perform – healings which addressed the very issues about which Isaiah had written. Of all the Old Testament discussions on health this is the one which most uniquely characterizes the work of Jesus.

Writers on Christology tend to look at the miracles as indicators of Jesus' messiahship. As such they take on the significance of signs and of power rather than simply being stories about restoring people with illness or disability to health. Most authors actually devote very little space to the miracles and even less to the ones concerned with healing. In these, writers tend to look for the sayings which demonstrate Jesus' status as Messiah. Thus, in the healing of Lazarus the important point is Jesus' declaration that, 'I am the Resurrection, and the Life'; and in the feeding of the 5,000 the focus is on him saying, 'I am the Bread of Life'. Many writers dwell on Jesus' power to forgive sin, and on the question of faith in the situation of a healing. These are both major stumbling blocks to disabled people. People with disabilities may often feel the pressure to have faith and to believe simply to escape the psychological tyranny of a religion which has a propensity to make people feel guilty when they appear to fall short of its standards, and which makes Jesus so removed from humanity that his power to touch is too rarefied to meet the basic needs of a disabled person. Jesus' healing miracles have nothing to say to the disabled because they have become divorced from life today and exist only as historical curiosities.

There are three, or possibly four, interesting periods in Christology beginning with the Patristic period which may be considered to extend into the medieval period, particularly in the writings of Aquinas. During this period the main concern was the humanity of Jesus and his relationship in the Trinity. There were heresies which stressed the alleged non-humanity of Jesus, i.e. he was simply a spirit, whilst others maintained that he was purely a human being who was adopted by God. The great advance of the period which extended into the writing of Aquinas was the renewed understanding of Platonism which allowed the development of a coherent philosophical account of the two natures of Christ as both human and divine. (McGrath, 1998; p 41ff) This theology neither added to or detracted from our awareness of disabled people except, possibly, that it paved the way to allow Eiesland to suggest that Jesus was a disabled God. The fact that disability is now understood as a social and human problem made it much easier for her to concentrate on the human body frailly hanging on the cross.

Reformation theology is the next formative period, but it did not advance the cause of disabled people as much as might have been desired. The main reason for this is that much evangelical theology emanated from this period and whilst their arguments have a validity they are concerned with faith and faith alone which does not allow much consideration of the object of a miracle. Warrington has put this point of view quite succinctly:

> The demonstration of the authority of Jesus via his healings and exorcisms is not to be understood as an end in itself, but as a means to an end. His authority functions as a spring-board, to aid the leap of faith that may result in a lasting relationship. However, while many welcomed Jesus' authority over sickness and demons, few recognized their potential to develop beyond this. It was particularly important to establish the authority of Jesus in order to demonstrate his supreme ability to achieve his mission, a mission to reinstate the outcast, to initiate the Kingdom and to forgive sins.
>
> (Warrington, 2000; p 3)

Warrington makes it quite clear that the chief purpose of miracles was to elicit faith, usually from the onlookers, and to demonstrate Jesus' power both in his general mission and specifically over miscellaneous spirits and demons. The Reformers, notably Calvin, stressed two words, 'sign' and 'power' or *semeion* and *dunamis* in the original Greek, which they considered to have great meaning and importance. Calvin maintained that the miracles and signs were demonstrations of God's power coming through Jesus. Such power glorified God. The greatest sign of all was the resurrection, and Calvinists have since consistently argued that the resurrection is the only miracle that matters because without it there would be no salvation. All the other miracles were simply signs pointing towards the divinity of Jesus, and as such were so relatively unimportant that their significance tended to become lost with the Pauline focus on the cross. This trend was exacerbated by catholicism's over-emphasis on miracles throughout the middle ages and on into modern times, and further strengthened by the belief that miracles emanated from saints. Indeed, a list of accredited miracles often was and still is a path to canonization.

The development of a 'sign' theology of miracles has led many churchmen and women away from a consideration of healing to a preaching of Jesus which stresses only the faith which can come out of miracles. This has led many disabled people to feel guilty at their apparent lack of faith when healing becomes impossible to achieve. Kathy Black says that she only wrote her book, *A Healing Homiletic* (1996), after the death of a young man with epilepsy who tried to show his faith by coming off his life-sustaining drugs to prove the point. If Jesus healed simply as a sign, it has led certain authors to query the reason behind it. Tiffany and Ringe ask:

> Why is such a premium placed on able-bodiedness? Why is the 'good news' not expressed as a world made accessible to and accepting of persons of all physical, mental, and psychological circumstances, rather than as persons changed to conform to the world's norms?
>
> (Tiffany & Ringe, 1996; p 183)

In other words, why are disabled people used as signs and, if indeed they are signs, why does the Church not look beyond the world of faith to the world of acceptance in faith? There is an answer to such questions which does not contradict the priorities of evangelical theology but complements its thrust towards faith and conversion. When the eschatological dimension of Christology is discussed, it will become obvious that disabled people can be honoured in an evangelical context. It is only when the miracles are understood in the wrong way that disabled people become offended by the idea that their main aim is to restore a disabled person's body to the perfection of God's 'original' creation and restore them to the functional ability to have dominion over his creation. It sometimes appears as if American theologians are, however, over-sensitive about the culture of perfection and achievement in the world beyond their shores. Experience shows how robustly people with disabilities can come to terms with such cultural barriers.

Modern Christology displays little concern for disabled people and not much more for healing miracles, but rather is focussed on form criticism. In the work of Hans Küng and Karl Rahner, for example, the sayings of Jesus are seen as being reinforced by his healing miracles and by what most of these theologians call the 'heroic' nature miracles and those surrounding his birth and resurrection. They seem to argue that the messianic mission of Jesus was reinforced by the miracle stories, arguing in the same way as the Reformers did, but lacking their conviction that the miracle stories are historically correct. Such a position undermines the entire life and purpose of Jesus for many but can add colour and substance to the spirit of his ministry for others. Mackey, for instance, places the miracle stories at the heart of the gospel writers determination to record and describe the work of their Messiah. He writes:

> If we follow with any fidelity these clues scattered so liberally throughout the New Testament it must become clear to us that the so-called miracle stories, as well as their conventional function, and in addition to their function as symbol and myth, have also the more important purpose of emphasizing that the experience of the reign of God is, in one most essential aspect, an experience of a power or spirit in our lives that makes us heal the ills of our fellows and see to their needs (it is not only Jesus who heals, any more than it is only Jesus who experiences the reign of God; see Luke 10:17, 9:50) What is important at this level is not that the feeding or healing is miraculous; the real 'miracle' when people are hungry is that anyone should feel favoured enough to feed them
>
> (Mackey, 1979; p 158)

Like the others mentioned, Mackey captures the spirit of Jesus but leaves us with what many would regard as a skeleton which requires the flesh of a more literal understanding of some of his ministry to give adequate grounds for a belief, nay a faith, in Jesus of Nazareth as one who deals with illness and disability with the assuredness described in the Gospels. The next chapter will show how inadequately form criticism actually addresses the needs of real disabled people searching the Gospels for some understanding of Jesus' purpose.

A more recent approach to Christology mitigates some of the problems associated with a deliberate diminution of the role of disabled people by combining Christology with an understanding of social science. McGrath (2001) considers the sayings and deeds of Jesus as recorded in the Gospel of St John as a form of legitimation of how the community around John regarded Jesus. Christology is, in other words, the sum total of the community's belief in Jesus and the way in which it was expressed in the writing of the Gospel in the face of challenges from opponents and contemporary critics. Such a methodology will tie in with our later discussion of medicine and medical anthropology where we will see that the work of Jesus was always performed in the context of the beliefs of the community, both religious and social. To argue, as McGrath does, that the community legitimized the ministry of Jesus by recognising that its spirit transcended all previous ministries, and distilling this so as to defend it against Jewish critics, offers us an understanding of the Messiah that may be a liberating departure from the desire of earlier theologians to constrict the messiahship of Jesus by dwelling only on the form of the material written about him. The Gospel of St John was written at a time when more reflective opposition by the Jews was developing and thus the Johannine community was much more aggressive in its defence of the status of Jesus compared to the Synoptic Gospels.[7] (p 34ff) This more recent approach has the potential of understanding disabled people within the context of the ministry, rather than as objects of the ministry of Jesus. Of course, this is not the purpose of McGrath's study but we can point out one of its potentials.

In each era of Christology, theologians have pointed towards the spirit of Jesus and the substance of his claim to be Messiah. This is the foundation of any understanding of Jesus as the Christ, but such study lacks the building blocks out of which the edifice of the dominance of the ministry of Jesus is made. All who write about Christology identify the individual characteristics of his ministry and the way in which they relate to the healing miracles. From this emerge the dichotomies which have so plagued disabled people but which cannot be avoided if flesh is to be added to the spiritual portrayal of his ministry. Jesus demonstrated the reign of God by mastering demons and evil spirits; he took upon himself directly from his Father the ability to forgive sins; he glorified his Father by bringing people to faith; and he offered hope to the lost sheep of Israel as opposed to the privileged classes of the Pharisees and Sadducees. Each of these will be examined in the context of the healing miracles and it will be shown how the dichotomies have resulted from an over simplistic understanding of Jesus' purpose in consorting with outsiders who not only included tax collectors and women of loose morals but also those who were stigmatized by deformity and impairment.

The healing miracles will be examined in the light of the above from the point of view of all types of conservative theology and then we can begin to build a way forward which will avoid the dichotomies of the past. Certain powers or authorities were ascribed to Jesus in the light of his messiahship which colour the way in which the healing miracles are used in Christ-centred preaching. 1) Jesus demonstrates through the miracles the power of God in the face of spirits and demons. 2) These miracles engender faith which arguably is a justification of all the other associated outcomes of miracles. 3) The ability to forgive sins negates all previous understanding of the relationship between disease and sin. 4) Jesus announces the kingdom or reign of God by defeating the powers of demons and heralds the kingdom by his deeds. Last, and 5) Jesus proclaims the last days and in so doing offers us a new interpretation of the Old Testament prophecies.

The verses which are listed in the following five sections are taken from Nave's categorization in his *Topical Bible*[8] which illustrates an evangelical structural predisposition for the primacy of Christology. (c1979)

Power

> How clearly and transparently does this appear in his miracles? I admit that similar and equal miracles were performed by the prophets and apostles; but there is this very essential difference, that they dispensed the gifts of God as his ministers, whereas he exerted his own inherent might. Sometimes, indeed, he used prayer, that he might ascribe glory to the Father, but we see that for the most part his own proper power is displayed.
> (Calvin, Institutes, Book I, chap.-XIII; §13)

In the eyes of the Reformers, all the miracles, including those involving healing, demonstrated the power of Jesus to glorify His Father by acting uniquely in obedience to his will. The most important miracle was the resurrection and the healing miracles were not only secondary but were not to be repeated outside the apostolic period. In the healing of the man born blind in John 9, one of the most puzzling and perplexing passages is contained in verses 3 & 4:

> 'Neither this man nor his parents sinned,' said Jesus, 'but this happened so that the work of God might be displayed in his life. As long as it is day, we must do the work of him who sent me…'

Let us leave aside the question of sin at the moment and concentrate on 'the work of God might be displayed'. There is a lot of literature written by disabled people which attempts to demonstrate that the disability was caused by a purpose which is God's. The early work of Joni Eareckson illustrates this well. (Eareckson, 1991) Joni convinces us that God had a purpose in her diving accident in 1967 and that her subsequent battle with illness and disability illustrated the power of God to manifest itself in a life struck down by misfortune. She is almost writing a modern Book of Job. It is a theme taken up by so many others and usually seeks to illustrate that a serenity can be attained by the acceptance and willingness to display God's will through the life of a disabled person. Certainly her thirty books and the many honours she has received makes one wonder whether it is indeed not the case that God is being glorified by her disability. The alternative is to believe that God should be totally rejected, nay, even blasphemed against, because his power has not spared someone from disease or disability. Many of the psalms embody such a theme and it is perhaps most vividly illustrated in the words of the crucified Jesus quoting psalm 22: '*Eloi, Eloi, lama sabachthani?*' – which means 'My God, my God, why have you forsaken me?'(Mark 15: 33-34) In the context of the weakness in which Jesus uttered these words, Eiesland can find profound meaning in the idea of a disabled God being bereft of God's presence in the depth of his personal crisis. Illness and disease always constitute personal crises and it is therefore not surprising to find narrative theologians like Hauerwas showing how individuals build stories and narratives around their illnesses which often conflict with narratives of others. For instance, in *The Naming of Silences* (1990), Hauerwas shows how children in a cancer ward built a complete understanding of both the treatment and he prognosis of death whilst their parents went to considerable lengths to try and 'protect' them from the harsh truth of their situation. Hauerwas recounts one father's angry outburst against God for his failure to intervene in the misfortune of illness and disability. In his autobiography (1987), Christy Nolan recalls the occasion when he was wheeled into a church and let out a torrent of blasphemies at the crucifix in the centre of the altar in his local Roman Catholic Church. It is often said that until you are angry with God it is impossible to come to terms with disability.

The following verses suggest that the primary purpose of a miracle is to use the demonstration of God's power through Jesus is to encourage faith. They can be grouped in three ways:

1) Performing miracles – Matthew 8:27; Luke 5:26

These verses illustrate a common device in the synoptic Gospels where the amazement of the crowd and the awe and wonder at the power of Jesus become the highlight of the miracle story.

2) Enabling others to work miracles – Matthew 10:1; Mark 16: 17,18; Luke 10:17

This second group shows that the power to heal was passed from

Jesus to the disciples, to the seventy and then to the apostles, as it is recorded in Acts and in the Epistle of St James in particular. There is a vast debate as to whether the power was passed to the Church as a whole, but that debate is not relevant at this point. Again it is an occasion for triumphant sermons asserting that the power Jesus had through His father was continued by Peter and John most notably in Acts 3, thus showing a continuity in the Gospel after the resurrection and ascension of Jesus.

3) Establishing the supreme authority of God in Christ – Luke 11:20

This verse is worth quoting in full for both positive and negative reasons:

> But if I drive out demons by the finger of God, then the
> kingdom of God has come to you.

From a positive point of view, this verse clearly shows Jesus' healing but only through the power of God and giving him all the glory. Negatively, Hull and others have suggested that this is a traditional magic formula. (See page 121 below)

In the context of miracles the word 'sign' is almost interchangeable with 'power'. However there are instances in the Bible where a sign from God appears after a long period of inactivity on the part of God. Moses was equipped to perform signs before the Pharaoh and in 1 Samuel, we are told that there had been an absence of signs prior to God speaking to Samuel (verse 1) and relating his experience to the old priest Eli. (1 Samuel 3). In the New Testament the story of the wedding at Cana in Galilee traditionally is regarded as the first miracle of Jesus and is sometimes read at Epiphany as an alternative to the story of the three Wise Men. In the other verses quoted below 'sign' does not have the same very specific meaning which is to be found in the story of the wedding at Cana in Galilee in John 2.

Matthew 12:38; 16:4; 24:3,30; Mark 8:11,12; 13:4; John 2:11; 3:2; 4:48

In these examples the signs are demanded by either the opponents of Jesus or by his disciples and Matthew 12:38 ties the need for a sign to miraculous events:

Then some of the Pharisees and teachers of the law said to him, 'Teacher we want to see a miraculous sign from you'.

Jesus was characteristically opposed to offering signs of his sonship or divinity. He opposed the whole idea of spectacular signs at the time of his temptation in the wilderness. Recent scholarship emphasizes that Jesus was very secretive in the way he performed miracles, particularly as described by St Mark. Such secrecy might be alien to our modern media culture where people have an insatiable appetite for happy or successful medical stories, or for stories about overcoming disability usually with modern technology. A recent chat show devoted a considerable time to showing that botox can not only be used by vain people wanting to get rid of their wrinkles but that it can also be used to reduce the spasms caused by cerebral palsy in children. The appeal of such stories lies in the contrasting symbolism of the trivial and the profoundly useful. The spectacular, the happy and, in the last instance, the paradoxical have become the staple diet of journalism both in popular newspapers and on television. In the time of Jesus, as now, the key is in the telling.

To sum up, the gospels use the miracles to demonstrate the power of Jesus and to hold them up as signs of his power which he shares and derives from the Father. This use of the miraculous to define the messiahship of Jesus does not have to dwell on the recipients of healing but only has to record the fact that something spectacular had happened at the hands of Jesus.

Faith

We have already seen how theologians such as Warrington regard the faith which is engendered is of prime importance in understanding Jesus' purpose and the reason for recording the miracles in the gospels. Warrington is quite clear that Jesus never demanded faith as a prerequisite to a cure. When Jesus comments on faith in the context of a healing miracle He is either commenting on the faith of friends, as in the case of the man let down through the roof, of relatives and friends, as in the case of Jairus or the Roman Centurion, or chastising his disciples for their lack of faith. Just as faith created the possibility of a miracle so lack of faith diminished the effectiveness of the ministry of the disciples. The miracles where faith is mentioned can be listed below:

The woman with the issue of blood – Matthew 9:21,22
Jairus, for the healing of his daughter – Matthew 9:18,23-25
Two blind men – Matthew 9:29,30
Blind Bartimaeus and a fellow blind man – Matthew 20:30-34;

Mark 10:46-52; Luke 18:35-42

    The Samaritan leper – Luke 17:11-19

    The sick people of Gennesaret – Matthew 14:36; Mark 3:10; 6: 54-56

        Those who brought the paralyzed man to Jesus – Luke 5:18-20

        The Syrophoenician woman – Matthew 15:22-28; Mark 7:25-30

        The paralytic man – Matthew 9:2

Jesus was almost always sought out by people seeking healing or a cure. He did not offer himself as a healer indiscriminately and on occasions felt the need to escape from the crowds. Faith was invariably evoked by coming near to Jesus and was portrayed as the perception of either his power or as a sign of his power. The healing itself was not dependent either on faith or belief but was shown through it. When miracle workers perform miracles today, faith is the key to the cure rather than a consequence of witnessing the work of Jesus. Jesus healed out of compassion; he never healed to amaze. This is what makes the power healing of Wimber and others so contrary to the spirit of Jesus, who met people with compassion and turned potential pity into something dynamic.

Keith Warrington devotes his entire book, *Jesus the Healer*, to showing the relevance of faith in the narratives of the healing miracles. His main contention is that Jesus was a pedagogic healer in so far as he used his healings as an opportunity to teach about faith and to demonstrate the power of God. This highlights a tension which will become apparent in chapter six. Whilst Warrington adopts the position that Jesus healed so that he could teach, scholars such as Pilch argue the opposite – that Jesus healed and that the teaching followed. This latter position is the more radical and fascinating one from the point of view of disabled people, who are more interested in the effect of the healing miracles on themselves than on the audience. Those who witnessed the miracles are taught about disabled people rather than simply being taught about the personhood of Jesus. Whilst the ability to heal and a concern for healing was passed on to the disciples, apostles and all believers, Jesus uniquely used the opportunity of healing to teach. Faith certainly was not a precondition of healing but each story usually produces a pericope, or saying about the faith which was evoked in the onlookers, the person being healed or about the faith which had inspired relatives and friends to bring someone to Jesus. It is clear, he argues, that the Synoptic Gospels, and particularly St Mark, wished to demonstrate the uniqueness of Jesus in relation to his Father. Warrington has a tendency to provide a heading before the exegesis of each miracle which invariably uses the phrase, 'Jesus provides an opportunity to believe in him'. Whether this simplistic ascription of motive to Jesus is justified is a moot point – Jesus was in fact quite secretive about his messianic role in the Gospel of Mark. Warrington is very careful to say that Jesus inspired faith in his *person*, thus avoiding the issue of his true Christological identity.

> The conclusion drawn is that the healing accounts in the Gospels demonstrate that the motive of Jesus in healing was to achieve two main goals, namely to teach his followers concerning his person and mission, and to address their attitudes, particularly in relation to faith and obedience. As such, the healings are to be recognized as having an integrally important pedagogical function, to be borne in mind when considering the beliefs of those who claim to operative a healing ministry based on the teaching and praxis of Jesus.
>
> (Warrington, 2000; p 162)

There are several difficulties with a book which argues for the centrality of faith in healing miracles, albeit that faith is not necessary to meet God's purpose of providing wholeness and redemption to those who were lost to the norms of society and who were called back into fullness of life by the power of Jesus. First, disabled people maybe objectified by such an approach. Are they really simply adjuncts to the ministry of Jesus or are they central? If they are central, Jesus had a greater purpose than rescuing the lost and teaching the meaning of faith to others. Second, when form criticism is examined in the next chapter, it will be possible to see whether the healing miracles come from traditions which were built long after the resurrection, when faith had assumed a greater dynamic in the risen Lord and in the totality not only of the ministry but of the life of Jesus. There are unanswered questions here which Warrington does not have to address from his perspective but which raise faith from the immediacy of witnessing a healing miracle to an existential faith in the totality of Jesus the Christ.

Whenever faith is preached about in the context of healing miracles, there is a potential atmosphere of ambiguity within a church and its congregation. The presence of a disabled person heightens the drama of emotions which can be played out during and after a sermon. Any mention of a miracle begs many questions: Why not now? Does the fact that we cannot bring about improvements in our disabled friend mean that our faith is weak? Is his faith lacking in that our prayers for the sick are not answered? What must our church do to be a place of welcome for disabled people where acceptance can become a mark of faith? All these questions are possible whenever a sermon raises such issues and the presence of one with a disability simply emphasizes the rarefied context of the life of Jesus where cure meant cure and there was no agonizing over the process of healing and of acceptance. Furthermore, churches were certainly not financially embarrassed as they are now with all thoughts turned to survival let alone expensive alterations which might have to be made under the Disabled Discrimination Act. A disabled person is increasingly like the demoniac. If only the congregation could get rid of the problem it would save money, it would save a test of faith and it would save making a leap of faith by making measures of acceptance which may be quite challenging. Faith without acts does not solve the problems of today as it did the theological problems at the time of the Reformation.

Forgiveness of Sin

When Jesus taught of forgiveness there were three components to his teaching. These were not all connected with sin, save that he believed that just as mankind could sin against God, so we could sin against each other. This is most obvious in the Lord's Prayer, '… forgive us our debts, as we also have forgiven our debtors'. He further elaborates this in Matthew 6:12 & 16 as part of the Sermon on the Mount. The agony of being unable to forgive a fellow human being ultimately separates one from God, as bearing a grudge is both tiresome and demeaning. Next, Jesus taught about forgiveness in some of his parables. This is most noticeable in the parable of the unjust servant who so feared his master that he was unable to act creatively with the wealth with which he had been entrusted. He was cast into outer darkness for misdeeds which were not based on his misuse or wrongdoing with money, but on the fact that he feared his master to the point of having all creativity drained from him. Often lack of forgiveness results in this irrational fear and dread of a potential enemy.

Jesus taught about forgiveness in a practical way in his death upon the cross. 'Father, forgive them; for they do not know what they are doing.' (Luke 23:34) is central to everything that Christianity stands for socially. If Jesus could forgive his executioners and those who presided over a sham trial, so as followers of Jesus we must learn to forgive in all circumstances. These strands of Jesus' teaching have a common theme which will be relevant when we come to consider the forgiveness of the alleged sins of people who were sick. Jesus' teaching, both in word and action, demonstrates how lack of forgiveness cuts one off from both God and society in a destructive way. It is inconceivable that Jesus could have been exalted by the resurrection if he had gone to his death filled with hatred and lacking the love which was so powerfully demonstrated in the resurrection. However, the crucifixion was the price of blasphemy which it was believed he had uttered so frequently, not least when he took upon himself the authority to forgive sins, usually those of the sick.

This brings us to the teaching which Jesus offered regarding sin and sickness, or disability, which can easily be taken in isolation but in fact unites the three elements which have gone before. Jesus taught that healing and forgiveness were closely united or even synonymous. As a faithful student of the Old Testament, Jesus would be well aware of the general perception of the time that illness was a misfortune, that it could mean that the sufferer was ritually unclean, or excluded from normal social relationships by economics, fear or prejudice. There seems little doubt that in the Old Testament people thought that God blessed people with good health whilst he cursed those who defied him with illness. Sin could be carried from one generation to the next and this was reflected in attitudes to parents. It was equally true that although disease caused fear in close-knit communities there was an understanding about what constituted sin and what was simply misfortune. Sin was a separation from God and an alienation from the wholesome activities of the Israelite nation. Halakhic traditions and laws offered prescriptions for the compassionate care of disabled people and even allowed the violation of the Sabbath and other such proscriptive laws, but it did so because those who were disabled were potentially fully able members of the Jewish Community. Rabbis wrote commentaries on the Torah, particularly Leviticus and Deuteronomy, after a tradition which became known as Halakhic (Marx, 2002) – a tradition which lasts to this day. Jesus was well aware of the devastating effect of isolation and identified sin with the worst aspects of that isolation. When he forgave sins in the context of illness, he was neither talking of punishment nor of wrong-doing but of the isolation which was being imposed by the community on the sick person. Contrast his treatment of the paralytic whose sins he forgave in a very non-specific way with his treatment of the woman caught in adultery. In this case Jesus was very specific in not forgiving her sins but remitting them because of the failure of the community to live up to the high ideals of the Torah. He told her to sin no more, thus acknowledging that she had been guilty of sin. At no point does he ever suggest a specific transgression on the part of a sick or disabled person. The sin that they are being forgiven of is the sin of isolation, which had become a stigma over decades or centuries. However, with such forgiveness came an identity with blasphemy and ultimately with his own isolation exemplified by the sinner's death on the cross outside the city wall, which was so important to the writer of the Letter to the Hebrews.

> The cross represents the revelation of God's love within the Trinity. The love of God has taken the nature of a man who, in his human frailty, feels both rejected by God and is rejected by men. The love through Christ is exalted on Easter Sunday yet we cannot neglect the rejection of Good Friday. A triumphalistic Christ whose power is all-pervading neglects to show the weakness of Jesus which was God's acceptance of all that is unacceptable in human society. In the cry from the cross, Jesus cried and still cries with the disabled as indeed he does today. This reality must be held together by understanding the triumph of Christ in the light of his sufferings, and by holding the two events so close together that they cannot be accepted into a dogma which holds the triumph as the main facet of Christ's life.
>
> (Monteith, 1987; p 70)

In the tension of the isolation from God on the cross Jesus paid for his acts of forgiveness by experiencing the same process of isolation as many disabled people have experienced themselves. Indeed, Dorothee Sölle (1967) characterized Jesus as the representative of all who are hung on the cross.

It has been argued that the chief characteristic of any 'sin' which might have been associated with illness was isolation from the community of Israel and thus from God. If there are, indeed, 'sins of commission' and 'sins of omission', those of the sick and disabled were the omissions of certain abilities in their lives – the inability to associate with the religious community, to sustain oneself economically and the carrying of stigmas such as unclean flesh which caused fear in the general population. Most adults in this situation turned to begging and it is doubtful whether the population would have responded to their solicitations if they had indeed been grievous sinners. Rather, they were unfortunates who were isolated from the most important aspect of life, God, not through choice but by circumstance. Their sins were not commissions, they were not violations of the ten commandments nor of the statutes which stem from them.

Therefore, the forgiveness of these sins by Jesus was not a monumental rewriting of the laws of God nor was it to be regarded as the forgiveness of identifiable individual sins. But when combined with healing, it became the restoration of full participation in the religious society of Israel, not the civil society of today. Jesus paid for this act of compassion by experiencing a greatly heightened isolation on the cross. This is where disabled theologians have had the opportunity to develop a theology of the cross which deals with both the isolation and the helplessness felt by the sick and disabled in everyday life.

First, the example of Lewis' theology of the 'elephant man' becomes important. Jesus assumed a hideous situation on the cross with which many people can identify and did so because he dared to forgive the lame man who was brought to the house that he was staying in. (Lewis, 1982; *see page 46 above*) Eiesland took this theme a stage further by suggesting that Jesus embodied the entire condition of disabled people when he was paralysed (restrained) on the cross. We have been critical of Eiesland's theology in that it tends to distort the doctrine of the Trinity by overemphasizing Jesus' place in it – a position which was never intended in classical theology. In his ministry and in his death Jesus showed the love of God in his dealings with mankind, whilst he gave his Father rightful praise for the powers which lay behind all the miracles from the creation, through healing, to the resurrection. Yet to be bound by such classical statements is to deny Eiesland a rightful hearing. She acknowledges that her theology stems from the investigations of David Tracy who develops the Catholic use of allegorical language and accords the right of groups within a pluralistic society to find correlations which serve the purposes of the many minorities who now seek answers to their particular problems. (Tracy, 1990) It is perfectly legitimate to find solace in the image of Jesus on the cross as sharing the burdens of disabled people but there is perhaps not enough emphasis, as there is with Lewis, on the connection between Jesus' crucifixion and the forgiveness of sins. There is little point in talking about Jesus' dealings with the sick and disabled unless we realize that it was a costly ministry and not an add-on which may or may not have been central to his death.

At this point, we must leave the synoptic Gospels and digress into Pauline theology in order to continue the theme of isolation as a characteristic of 'sin' which Jesus did so much to dispel. Sᵗ Paul was not specifically concerned with disability and sin but he did develop an inclusive model for the Christian communities with which he was associated and to whom he wrote. The implications of this part of Christology has only recently been developed to help explain the Church's obligations to disabled people and has indeed been omitted from the Christological thought of writers such as Karl Rahner. It is possible to find a system in Paul's theology by considering Robinson's description of the Body of Christ. Paul uses words like 'unity', 'whole' and implies by 'reconciliation' the idea that we all acquire a new, 'rightwised' state with God. We in some way become whole persons so that, as with the Old Testament and the Gospels, it is possible to argue that the new man in Christ is also a unitary whole in faith, hence the idea of the Church as the Body of Christ. J. A. T. Robinson comes close to a holistic theory of the Church when he states, whilst commenting on 1 Cor. 12: 12, that: 'The unity of Christ, as of the human body, is his [Paul's] starting point. He then proceeds to show that the body cannot in fact consist only of 'one member', but must be 'many'... The point of the verses that follow... is *not* that the different members must be united among themselves... but precisely that there must be more than one member if there is to be a body at all.' (Robinson, 1951; p 59) We are not members of the Church, as we might be of a trade union; but are members in the unity of the Body of Christ, which is the Church. The community of Christians does not have a specific aim, it is not functional in some restricted sense but is open to all who accept Jesus Christ. The body of Christ consists of people with many talents and with few, and includes both the 'strong and weak'. The World Council of Churches and other authors all make the point now that disabled people are part of the body of Christ and must be respected as such. Although it can be motivated by sentiment, there is almost an imperative placed upon the Christian community to value and accept all disabled people both in baptism and in inclusion at the Lord's Supper. The uniqueness of the Christian community lies not in its purpose or mission but in its inclusiveness and lack of discrimination against those who can only contribute the love through their presence. This can be contrasted with the Jewish rationale for dealing with disabled people in the Halahkic tradition. Jews share with Christians the consciousness of community and recognize the uniqueness of the call of God to each of these two great religions. However, Marx highlights the difference in attitude to disabled people by discussing their treatment within the Jewish community. Jewish law can be violated in order to tend to the disabled because they are only *potential* members of the Jewish Community, not members by right. Marx discusses the example of a baby boy who cannot be circumcised on the eighth day because of deformities to his sexual organs. This is potentially a source of isolation not only from the male community but from the religious community as a whole. The Rabbis developed elaborate rules to overcome such difficulties. Christians have not got such problems. Disabled people can be accepted easily into the community and baptism should not present an obstacle to inclusion. However, Christians have often been as particular as the Jews in posing barriers to inclusion. In some denominations baptism is made available only to those with a mature understanding of its significance, thus excluding those with learning difficulties. Similarly since the reformed tradition stripped away the emotional aspects of communion, it has been denied to many because of their inability to understand it at an intellectual level.

St Paul's demand that the Christian community be inclusive powerfully extends the idea that Jesus forgave sins by breaking down the barriers of isolation which so beset those whom he healed.

St Paul's doctrine of the body of Christ may be historical and originally addressed to certain groups in the early Church who could not tolerate one another or their divergent practices. But if sin is to be interpreted as isolation from God, then today the imposition of limits on how far a disabled person may participate in the worship of God moves this idea firmly into the present. It therefore needs to be applied to all groups within our pluralistic Church of today. And it needs to be recognized that it is the modern Church which now defines the sin associated with disability – not Leviticus or the Pharisees, but the conscious decision of today's Church in its dealing with disabled people. The Church is deeply involved in debates about issues such as gender, race and sexual orientation, and if it spent as much time discussing disability as it does these other issues, the problems of inclusion for the disabled would have been solved years ago. Unlike questions of sexual orientation, congregations are not polarized into opposing factions when it comes to disability and it may be for this reason that disability equality is not a major issue. Activists in the disability movement have the great advantage of pushing at an open door where the only obstacles are ignorance and financial constraints. It is however the practice of the Church to not tolerate disruptive behaviour or to be prejudiced against disabled ministers whose lack of ability to perform one or two of all the expected functions of the ministry disqualifies them from office. To see the Church as an inclusive community is to challenge it to tackle present-day sins as Paul did the disruptions of his own time. Rowan Williams (2000) uses a quote from a clergywoman talking of race to entitle the last chapter of one of his recent books: 'Nobody knows who I am till judgement morning.' In this church he argues that the body of Christ was and is a 'system of interdependence' (p 285), which is an imperative to all ages. The Church's dealings with people define them in the here and now and by so doing reject or accept them into the body to greater or lesser degrees, but it is only on judgement day that we stand beyond the politics of the Church and of society and can examine ourselves free of all the constraints of membership of the imperfect body of Christ which is the Church.

> The Church has been slow to see how and where it is itself trapped in 'telling people who they are'; it is gradually getting used at least to the *idea* that its institution and decision-makers must learn a new tentativeness in listening to those they have assumed they understood – those they have assumed were 'contained' in the categories they work with. But the concrete redefinition of power – as enabling the stranger to be heard, deciding that the stranger has a gift and a challenge that can change you limps very slowly, in the Church's listening to the voice of women and homosexuals as much as blacks.
>
> (Williams 2000; p 289)

It is a great pity that Williams does not include disabled people in the list in the last sentence quoted. Is it possible that he had no reason to include them because the Church at the highest levels of debate and authority do not see disability in theological terms. Over the years the Church has released women from the burden of being unclean; it debates ferociously whether the acceptance of homosexuals is biblically acceptable or not; and Christians are still recovering from the theological understandings of race which justified apartheid. If theologians understood that Jesus actually suffered because he forgave the sins of disabled people, the issue might become theologized and thus promote debates about practice rather than about providing ramps for wheel chairs. Judgement Day, as Rowan Williams uses it, is for everyone. As such, disabled people deserve to be prepared for it as much as any other group by receiving a foretaste of perfect Christian relationships in this life rather than waiting in hope for the next.

God's Rule Over Demons

Jesus was both a healer and an exorcist but to separate these talents is perhaps a mistake because the outcome of both was that the symptoms of an illness or a disturbance were removed. It is as much a source of offence to disabled people to imply that they are possessed as to say that they are sinners. These two words embody polarities which have caused offence over many years, i.e., sinner/redeemed or possessed/free. Jesus treated the question of demon possession in exactly the way he did sin and suffered criticism for this as well. There are eighteen references to demons in the synoptic Gospels and there are nine references to miracles involving the casting out of demons – what we would call exorcism. The main characteristic of demon possession was the fear it instilled in the population. Epilepsy was, and unfortunately remains, a frightening illness. Today epilepsy, and mental illness generally, instils similar fears as it did to the population of Gadarene who found it hard to live with the 'demoniac' terrorizing their neighbourhood (Matthew 8:28-34, Mark 5:2-20). The common theme which Jesus had to tackle was that of fear and he did so by applying the same commonsense to demons as he did to sin. Most of the references about demons refer to Jesus' discussion of their dominion with the Pharisees who disputed that Jesus could show God's power over the demons through his miracles. The quotation which most vividly illustrates the commonsense argument can be found in Matthew 12:27 – 28.

> And if I drive out demons by Beelzebub, by whom do your
> people drive them out? So then, they will be your judges. But
> if I drive out demons by the Spirit of God, then the kingdom
> of God has come upon you.

This saying comes at the end of a debate as to whether Jesus is the servant of a devil or of God. Jesus had successfully argued that a house could not be divided against itself and that he could only cast out demons in the power of the spirit of God. As with the argument about sin, he makes the point that God alone has control over demons which he is simply releasing by his word and actions, and that if his powers came from different sources they would be weakened beyond use in the same way as 'a household divided against itself will not stand'.(Matthew 12:25) Jesus shows a remarkable consistency in his understanding of his powers from God by rejecting any idea that demons are cast out by extraneous magic or formulas – it is God's power and nothing else. Just as the perceived fear of demons caused people to ostracize the possessed out of fear so it was natural for them to believe that a fearful creature, Beelzebub, should have the power to cast them out. But Jesus' lack of fear led to consistent thinking about the power of God as the only one with complete dominion to dismiss nameless fears personalized into Satan and Beelzebub.

Christian commentators have often talked of the need to have faith so that we can escape the fear of unseen powers. St Paul makes the point eloquently in Romans 8: 38 – 39.

> For I am convinced that neither death nor life, neither angels
> nor demons, neither the present nor the future, nor any
> powers, neither height nor depth, nor anything else in all
> creation, will be able to separate us from the love of God that
> is in Christ Jesus our Lord.

Now the word 'powers' comes from the Greek *dunamis* which in its singular form has been used in 'sign' theology to indicate the power of God; but here it can mean the power of demons or general unseen powers. Through faith, Paul is arguing, we are freed from such terrors as Jesus himself was in his life and through conquering death. The Christian is free from fear and protected from this as much as from bodily deprivations such as hunger or nakedness. We also find that the Council of Nicea in 325 inserted into its creed a specific caveat against the dualism that had arisen from belief in the Demiurge who controlled unseen powers in the world, harmful to man and over which some people believed God had little control. The Nicene Creed reads:

> We believe in one God,
> the Father, the Almighty,
> maker of heaven and earth,
> of all that is seen and unseen.

The Council had been established to counter various heresies, in particular the concern about the dualistic idea that there was a good creator and an evil one, when in fact God was the creator of all. Frances Young describes how convinced the early Christian heretics were that the world was equally formed and created by the evil powers of Satan and was a terrifying place in which to live. The clause attributing the entirety to God was a counter to this belief and was supposed to bring comfort and help to those who found the world so terrifying. (Young, 1991: chap. 2)

And so to modern times – Never has there been such a regeneration of fear in the unknown as is evidenced in today's society. Anthony Giddens (1994) asserts that modern democracy is beset by manufactured fears such as poverty, technological advances and single-issue politics which lay hold of peoples lives. Without denying that there are indeed problems, groups in society develop disproportionate fears of everything from mobile telephone masts to paedophiles and find their fears reinforced by a media which not only feeds these fears but then profits from exploiting them. The scene in terms of disability is slightly less complicated and more subtle. If one is racist, one can dislike a black person safe in the knowledge that you will never be black yourself. The same applies to sexism but it does not apply to prejudice against disabled people. The sad fact is that every member of the population may become disabled either through old age or an accident. Seeing a disabled person reminds each one of us of our vulnerability and of the frailty of our bodies. We are either beset by fear of the future or what we think it may be like to be disabled – 'I would rather die than end up in a wheelchair'. Whilst many writers blame society's obsession with the 'body beautiful' for the prejudice against disabled people, there are too many peripheral issues involved in this theme, such as feminism and the vested interests of the media, to justify this view. The culture which promotes the 'beautiful body' is more likely to be responsible for eating disorders and the cult of dieting. Perhaps it is the fear of becoming disabled which lies behind prejudiced attitudes rather than our concern with the body. Jesus encouraged believers to 'think not of the morrow for the morrow will take care of itself', and the Church has an obligation to show that there is nothing to fear in being disabled, not by isolating disabled people but by welcoming them into the fellowship which is exactly what the Jews of Jesus' time were unable to do.

God's Kingdom Proclaimed

The fifth, and final, element in this analysis of Christology involves considering the extent which Jesus presents himself as the proclaimer of a new age of God's rule, the coming of his kingdom. Eric Eve (2002) examines various commentators' views of passages in the Gospels to provide evidence of Jesus' mission. Two distinct groups of miracles have to be considered – the nature miracles, which include the feeding miracles, and the healing miracles. To what extent do the nature miracles of calming the storm, providing food for the 5,000 and walking on water mirror in any way the great miracles of the Exodus? Is Jesus' food similar to manna landing on the desert or is one person walking on water in any way similar to an entire nation crossing the Red Sea? The miracles of Jesus are a lot less spectacular than those by which God saves the Israelites and may be legitimately considered as pointers towards Jesus' status, but they lack relevance to disabled people because such status has no meaning to those who look to Jesus for help.

Fortunately, Eve points out that other commentators show a greater concern for the emphasis which Jesus placed on the prophecies of Isaiah in general and chapter 35 in particular. Verses five and six in this chapter offer a prophecy about a new age where disability will be no more and different elements of nature will be at peace with one another:

> Then will the eyes of the blind be opened
> and the ears of the deaf unstopped.
> Then will the lame leap like a deer,
> and the mute tongue shout for joy.
> Water will gush forth in the wilderness
> and streams in the desert.

Jesus is recorded as preaching from this text in the synagogue in Capernaum. He added that he had come 'to proclaim the acceptable year of the Lord.' (Luke 4:19) This caused outrage and he was expelled because being a healer was one thing, but to make this proclamation was high above his station as a lowly inhabitant of Galilee. Actually the other occasion that he used this text is perhaps even more convincing as an intimation of his messiahship and the dawning of the kingdom of God. When John the Baptist's followers sought conformation from Jesus that he was the one, the Messiah, he sent them back with what was almost a code, this text from Isaiah. Jesus would have chosen this text for two reasons. First, it would be known to John as a messianic text, and second, the miracles which he was performing were a sign that the new age was dawning and that the obstacles to its reality – disease and disharmony – were being removed. This is not to imply that disabled people were an offence to be overcome but rather that in the kingdom of God they would be restored and loved both by God and by his community of believers. The evidence seems to indicate that the writers of the Gospels valued the vision of the future in Isaiah much more than in Exodus. For instance, in the temptation story, there is a harmony in the desert among wild beasts who were normally opposed which was prophesied in Isaiah. (See also page 194ff.)

If it is the case that Jesus had the restoration of the sick and disabled at the centre of his ministry, though not perhaps of his teaching, there are very important implications for those who read the Gospels today. True followers of Jesus cannot afford to exclude disabled people from their communities because their Lord and Master sought to put them in the centre. Furthermore, they must be honoured as they were honoured by Jesus himself, if the miracles stories are understood correctly. Yes, the healing miracles do affirm the messiahship of Jesus and it is legitimate to use them to highlight his status. But it is equally important to remember that Jesus was dealing with people and offering them dignity and restoration. The objects of the miracles cannot be a matter of indifference when Jesus himself rejected the offer to perform miracles which would change stone to bread and allow him to jump unharmed from the pinnacle of the temple. Such miracles were more relevant to magic even if they might have affirmed his status, than to the scriptural tradition from which Jesus understood his father and the status which had been accorded him.

Summary and Some Principles

Christology is about the nature of Jesus as the Christ. It is principally the study of the teachings and actions in his life which justify a claim to be the Messiah although it also concerns the metaphysical relationship between man and God. The chief evangelical concern of any churchperson must be to glorify God and to explain the pivotal role of Jesus as his Son and as our Saviour and there has been no intentional effort to diminish this concern. But it has to be pointed out that disabled people have been regarded more often as objects of Jesus' purpose and the Church's preaching than subjects who were loved by Jesus and given a central role in the kingdom of God. Thus it becomes necessary to begin to identify principles which both honour Jesus and do justice to disabled people.

It is worth reiterating as a reminder some of the dichotomies which were outlined in the introduction. They apply more to this chapter than to any other, though not exclusively so.

Sinful ←→ Forgiven

    Clean ←→ Unclean

    Impaired ←→ Unimpaired

    Blind ←→ Sighted

    Light ←→ Darkness

Faithful ←→ Lacking faith

Possessed ←→ Free

The dichotomies which are not indented are of chief concern here. Beginning with the middle one, this chapter looked at faith, then considered the meaning of sin and finally at the rule of demons. Jesus undoubtedly hoped that people would have faith as a result of his miracles. Many preachers have given the mistaken impression that Jesus healed only on condition that people had faith. This is emphatically not true. There were occasions when a healed person did confess faith as a result of healing, such as Bartimaeus, and others were prompted by their faith to seek healing like the woman with a haemorrhage. Jesus was moved by people's faith but never demanded it in the context of healing and no preacher should ever put the burden on a sick person to find faith to overcome the illness. It is worth noting that in the letter of James, it is the elders who are to pray in faith for the sick person, not the sick person him or herself. (James 5:14-15)

Second, there is the matter of sin. The association of sin with illness and disability was a tradition stretching way back in the Old Testament, but the essence of it was that sin resulted in disease which resulted in ill people's isolation from the community. Furthermore in many instances they were also excluded from the religious community and could only be restored to it on recovery. Jesus, it has been argued, took a commonsense attitude to sin and realized that those whom he healed were isolated, were unclean or were causing great fear and commotion in their communities. His forgiveness was combined with healing and abated the fear which others had of those who had come to him. In the case of lepers, Jesus sent them right back to the religious community to have their restoration recognized by the local rabbi.

It has been argued that demons existed where fearful souls believed in them, allowing them to breed in people's minds and social habits. Jesus dismissed demons as he would fear and brought freedom to those who had been considered to be possessed.

The principles which we seek to establish are that disabled people can be honoured by discussing and dismissing the dark side of sin and possession by considering the effect Jesus' actions and words had on those who were liberated by his enlightened understanding. So we come to the purpose of Jesus' ministry. Jesus was acutely aware that his father's kingdom had long been prophesied, perhaps most notably in Isaiah, and that he had to show that one of the obstacles or offences to such a kingdom had now been redeemed i.e. disabled people. Just as there are central issues to his teaching and great narratives about love in his death and resurrection, so there is a consistent story about his desire to restore those who were excluded because of the Jewish community's continued belief in sin and demons and their lack of understanding of faith.

Chapter 4

Miracles are Merely ...

Form Criticism

Every community develops its own folklore and received wisdom about disability. It is the aim of scholars to identify the nature of these. New Testament scholars have more recently been concerned to try and characterize the cultural meanings of disability in New Testament times using methods which focus on disabled people rather than upon the theology which the early Church built around disability through its understanding of healing miracles. (See Chapter 5 and the references to John Pilch in particular.) Form criticism has long been a way of looking at the miracle stories as reflecting the culture of the early Church and thus, by implication, its attitude to disabled people. This chapter will examine two developments which come under the heading of form criticism and which greatly influenced the Church in the first half of the twentieth century and, in the case of the second, certain groups in the present day Church. Both have the same roots but subtly different aims.

Rudolf Bultmann became known as the foremost advocate of form criticism and of building a theology of the New Testament on the forms which could be identified within the body of the Gospels. His aim was to show how the writers of the Gospel took the oral tradition surrounding Jesus and formalized them into the Gospels of Matthew, Mark and Luke which are collectively known as the synoptic Gospels, i.e., the Gospels which were seen through roughly the same eye basing the written material on that which was gathered by Mark and supplemented by material which came to be known as Q or *Quelle*. The richness of the material was reflected in the form and strength of the gathered stories and sayings which make up these Gospels. The synoptic Gospels thus represent to Bultmann and his followers the distillation of the gathering tradition of the early Church and they portray the message which they believe is important and to be the essence of Jesus' teaching and acts. The second group of scholars which will be examined here make up the self-styled *Jesus Seminar*, in California, under the leadership of Robert Funk. The Seminar shares similar tools to their predecessors but has a different aim in a different ecclesiastical climate. Bultmann's aim was to identify the tradition behind the Gospels; Funk's aim is to discover the authentic words and acts of Jesus. The difference is considerable in that Bultmann was prepared to accept that the Gospels formed the basis of an evangelical theology; whilst Funk believes that unless we discover the authentic Jesus we remain at the mercy of fundamentalists who offer their own inauthentic interpretation of the true Jesus. When it comes to disability, Bultmann assumes that the early Church had some cultural understanding of it; whilst Funk does not find any compelling evidence of the historicity of the miracles and therefore dismisses both them and the disabled people who are involved, except insofar as they were among the marginalized to whom Jesus sought to minister. However, it seems unlikely that the early Church had any concept of disability that we would recognize in the twenty-first century. They probably had notions of theodicy as outlined in the previous chapter but this does not represent an understanding of disability. This sets our agenda here: first, it must be asked whether it is possible to identify a cultural understanding of disability in the New Testament which has come from the early Church; and second, is it justifiable to ignore disability in an attempt to find the authentic Jesus?

Bultmann sets out to use form criticism as a way of identifying the cultural traditions which influence the writing of the Gospels by the early Church. Form criticism is not about the aesthetic structure of narrative, as is apparent in the denials of Dibelius that this was so, nor in Doty's (1983) studies of stylized writing in the Pauline letters, but is about how diverse units of a story come together to form a unit of narrative. Bultmann's emphasis is on the coming together of tradition but he does dismiss entirely the possibility of some historical background:

> The less the miracle stories as such are truly historical reports the more we need to ask *how they found their way into the Gospel tradition*. And even if some historical events underlie some miracles of healing, it is still true that their narrative form has been the work of the Tradition. And even if the motifs have grown up spontaneously in the early Church, there would be both central and peripheral motifs taken over from popular and even perhaps literary miracle stories.
>
> (Bultmann, 1972:p 228)

The tradition of which Bultmann writes is one that treats disability and illness as phenomena which can be used to emphasize the heroic nature of the miracle worker. Miracles come in the form of legends, typically nature miracles, resuscitations, and less importantly healing miracles. These latter were often associated with exorcism of demons which were supposed to be the cause of many conditions such as epilepsy or madness. (See the healing of an epileptic boy, Matthew.17:14-21, Mark 9:14-29, Luke 9:37-45a; or the Gadarene Demoniac, Matthew. 8:28-34, Mark 5:1-20, Luke 8:24-39.) Jewish and Hellenistic literature is full of examples of healings and other legends which Bultmann claims were assimilated into the form and corpus of the New Testament Gospels. As with Funk, such stories feature the description of an illness, the words and actions of Jesus, the cure and in many cases the acknowledgement of the public. Some of the healing miracles reinforce the teachings of Jesus such as the healing of the man with the withered hand on the Sabbath (Matthew. 12:9-14, Mark 3:1-6, Luke 6:6-11). However, the tradition that comes through time after time is that Jesus forgives sins in the course of healing. This is a tradition that was examined in the previous chapter but which adds a uniqueness to Jesus' ministry compared to the other healers of the time.

It appears that the tradition on which the Gospel writers built was one which made objects out of sickness and impairments by recording miraculous events by diverse healers of the time seeking to cure or alleviate symptoms and suffering. These healers were not dissimilar to many of the exploitative faith healers of today. Indeed in every age people have been able to quote examples of such charlatans either in defence of miracles, or to attack them like Hume. The many facets to the healings of Jesus are dependent upon a theological understanding and interpretation of the gospels which would have been lost if the acts of Jesus had simply been recorded as the acts of another itinerant healer. It is a mark of the richness of Bultmann's thought that his later works reflect his evangelical desire to give theological meaning to the healing miracles in the Gospels.

There is a dangerous logic to magical forms of healing which Jesus could easily have been accused of performing which forms a link between this primitive tradition and the richness of well thought out traditions. The medical model of disability has exhibited a practice over the course of the twentieth century which has harmed many disabled people. The medical profession has objectified disabled people by using them remorselessly in demonstrations in front of medical audiences. The lesser examples which come below are as nothing compared with the treatment of disabled people by Nazis in concentration camps reducing their bodies to interesting specimens with no regard to humanity or dignity. (Disability Rights Advocates, 2002) Disabled people were treated as sub-human in these camps and subjected to horrendous experiments in the name of medicine which was not designed to benefit them in any way at all. The mentality which allows demonstrations has unfortunately pervaded the medical profession in the west until this day. Disabled people are exhibited in front of quite large audiences with little regard for their dignity. Their modesty is seldom protected by clothing and their naked bodies – naked well beyond the abandon of early childhood – show up spastic (*sic*[9]) movements and other deformities without allowing any consideration for the dignity of the 'subject'. The subject is described in magical jargon which is probably only comprehensible to the medical profession and certainly not to the mortified disabled person. Hopefully, as the medical profession learns the need for a more holistic approach to disability, doctors will cease from displaying dehumanized bodies in the way they have done even to this day.

To suggest that form criticism totally dismisses any authenticity in the healing miracles of Jesus would be unfair and would ignore the theological understanding which Bultmann and others had of the New Testament. What they sought to do was to show firstly, how traditions had influenced the way Jesus was portrayed in the Gospels; and secondly, to try to discover and understand Jesus' understanding of God. Dibelius was one of the first form critics and an inspiration for Bultmann. His concern was to show how oral traditions about Jesus became encapsulated in the Gospels and woven into the records of salvation as they had been developed by Jesus.

> ...the most significant of all means...has to do with the interpretation of tradition. The evangelist, in making his collection, strives to do this by setting a number of traditional elements in a particular setting. He knows how and why they must have taken place in accordance with the Divine Plan of Salvation.
>
> (Dibelius, 1934; p. 230)

The deposits of tradition which Jesus left included his teaching about the nature of God, his own relationship to him, and also that of mankind. From Dibelius to Wrede the emphasis was upon understanding the traditions behind the written record of the Gospel and the other material such as Q. The overall message of the synoptic Gospels is built up by Bultmann in Volume 1 of his *Theology of the New Testament.* Jesus' message is one of the end of the age and the dawning of the rule of God – the coming of his kingdom.

> The dominant concept of Jesus' message is the Reign of God. Jesus proclaims its immediately impending irruption, now already making itself felt. Reign of God is an eschatological concept. It means the regime of God which will destroy the present course of the world, wipe out all the contra-divine, Satanic power under which the present world groans – and thereby, terminating all pain and sorrow, bring in salvation for the People of God which awaits the fulfilment of the prophets' promises.
>
> (Bultmann, 1952; p 4)

How was this conception of God to be understood and related to the healing miracles or miracles in general? The first thing that has to be said is that Bultmann's writing has tremendous evangelical potential which his critics have often chosen to ignore and who were confounded by his preaching. The second thing which is worth noting is that the most concise description of the understanding of Jesus and its relation to miracles appears in Chapter 4 of *Jesus and the Word* (1935). In this chapter, Bultmann shows how Jesus was acutely aware of both the remoteness of God and his nearness. Jesus believed that since God ruled over all, everything was providential and everything was a reflection of God's love for his creatures. The psalms often illustrate the remoteness of God as the one who inspires the Old Testament characters with awe and hides his face from them in cloud and mist transforming Moses' face after his encounter with Him on Mount Sinai. Yet his care also extends to ravens and the lilies of the field (Luke 12:27). The nearness of God could be found in the conviction of Jesus that his teachings were the immediate will of the Father brought close to the people, usually disciples, who heard it and who understood the nearness of the reign of God. Miracles came into this category as well – they were entirely the work of God and were performed in intimate ways being disclosed to few. In Mark's Gospel, they are part of the 'messianic secret' which Jesus was reluctant to share. In the healings there is a process, be it the laying on of hands or the naming and expulsion of a demon, which laid bare the work of God to the witnesses who were often hostile either because miracles were performed on the Sabbath or because of the implication that Jesus could forgive sins. The closeness of God's reign puts enormous strains upon people's beliefs and Bultmann illustrates this with reference to the father of the epileptic boy in Mark 9:14-29. Of most concern in this context is verse 24:

> Immediately [after the cure] the father of the child cried out
> and said, 'I believe: help my unbelief!'

It is commonly assumed that the father believed and gained faith after witnessing the miracle, but Bultmann argues differently. More probably, the father did already believe in God and was well aware of his mighty works and providence. But he understood this as the work of a remote God. However in this miracle God had come near, so that now the father believed in God in a totally different way as one whose dawning reign extended to the humble care of his son. This interpretation offers a new richness to the text. Just as God is remote and near at the same time, so it is argued that he is also a God of the past, the present and the future. Miracles in particular offer a future to the person being cured. That person, and at the moment we are thinking literally, is given a future free of illness and of all the attendant social disadvantages. In subsequent chapters this future will be considered in greater detail in the light of other approaches but in the context of miracles it is not one that Bultmann develops to any great degree.

In common with most scholars of form criticism, Bultmann sees miracle stories as ways of emphasizing the choice of faith which was presented to those around Jesus. In most cases, however, it is the faith of the onlooker which is given most importance, as with the father in the miracle story discussed above. Bultmann does not offer compelling explanations of the sick person's reaction to being healed. It is almost as if the miracle is an act of theatre offered to the crowd that they may have faith, in the same way as modern medical demonstration theatres offer knowledge to aspiring physicians. This would be consistent with most Hellenistic healing stories, such as those involving Asclepius, the Greek God of healing.

In the previous chapter, we saw some of the difficulties of

understanding miracles as signs in that they turn all the focus away from the disabled person to God. Now we see the tendency of miracles to be regarded as a signpost to faith. Yet many disabled people have argued that this causes many tensions. First, they are not healed because of their lack of faith. As Nancy Eiesland put it:

> Failure to be healed is often assessed as a personal flaw in the individual, such as unrepentant sin or a selfish desire to remain disabled.

(Eiesland, 1994; p 117)

Second, they are demeaned as simply instruments of God to illustrate his glory that others may have faith (See the previous chapter). Third, Colleen C. Grant has drawn our attention to writers and colleagues who have questioned the need for the Gospels to dwell on people with impairments and thus not whole, perhaps even unwholesome. Furthermore, they question the way in which the Gospels suggest that the only way back into the community is to conform to the norm (1998; p 77f). To be fair to Grant, her solution is to honour the disabled person in her exegesis. In the context of the understanding Jesus had of God these authors' charges are unfounded but embarrassing. It is worth holding on to the idea, which will be developed later, that not only do miracles illustrate the nearness of God but also that they always offer a future – a future not only of faith but of a different social status for the healed person.

The idea that God offers a future to disabled people is an important point which will be gradually developed in many ways. There is one pious meaning, however, that must be avoided which suggests that a disabled person can be comforted by the knowledge that a bright future is mapped out for him or her – disabled people are not offered any more hope in the future than anyone else, *pace* Christopher Reeve who seemed to devote all of his life to the hope for a cure which many similarly disabled people have long abandoned for as full a life as independent living permits. With hope comes faith and Bultmann's understanding of faith must not be dismissed simply because he emphasizes the faith of others rather than the disabled person who has been subject of the Gospel miracle. Bultmann actually cares little about our knowledge of the historical Jesus when it comes to faith. He maintains that we develop faith in Jesus Christ who lives in the traditions of the early Church and every Christian community thereafter. The future lies in finding faith in the living Christ who is encountered in the resurrection, which is to be found in both the past and the present. We have the witness of the historical resurrection stories combined with our personal experience of the Jesus Christ of tradition to give a powerful awareness of a change in our lives brought about by faith. In order to experience this, one must live in the future as well as the present and so meaning must be found in the miracles which offer healing to disabled people. It will take deeper understanding of all that the future held for the disabled people mentioned in the healing miracles before it will be possible to satisfactorily honour their position in the tradition of the healing miracles. Such developments will require the examination of still further theologies but we must grasp the concept of faith located in the future by our understanding of the tradition of the Gospels. The future of any person with a disability must be better than their past if our faith dictates that barriers are forever falling, but if they remain standing all of humanity is left as zombies in limbo rather hopeful, vibrant women and men.

An Excursus into Magic

John M Hull sought to explore the influence of magic on the synoptic Gospels in an early work before turning to an examination of miracles in the light of his own blindness which was a progressive condition. (See Hull, 1990 & 2001) He argues that throughout the Hellenistic world there was a tradition of magic which was also pervaded by sorcery and astrology. In Jewish culture there were several famous 'healers' using magic ritual contemporaneous with Jesus. There were common patterns to the rituals surrounding healing and Hull shows how the Gospel writers used these traditions to frame the healings of Jesus. The evidence of magic is most obvious in the use of angels in Matthew and Luke and in the story of the Magi who are depicted as either wise men or astrologists. He argues that in the realms of healing Mark shows the most typical magical pattern but that this diminishes in the subsequent Gospels. Typical features of a magical episode can involve the saying of spells, the use of spittle and other materials like clay and the use of amulets or charms. Bultmann and others would argue that God is at work in miracles of healing, that the 'finger of God' can be seen to be pointing at the person involved in the miracle. Hull on the other hand points out that a popular amulet throughout the middle East was a 'finger of God' which when combined with spittle was a very powerful tool to be inserted in a deaf man's ear. In the healing of a deaf man Mark 7:31-37, Jesus appears to use all the apparatus of magic – he sticks his fingers in his ear having first used spittle and then he recites a word which was usually in a different language, *Ephphatha*, which meant in Aramaic 'be opened'. According to Hull, as the Gospels were refined such ambiguity surrounding miracles and magic began to disappear. Jesus was not simply a thaumaturge or miracle worker but became recognisable as a Saviour. The writer of the story of the temptations of Jesus was keen to show that he eschewed the spectacular and popular demonstrations of power or talent in favour of what Mark portrays as a low-key approach to healing. But then in the whole Gospel construct of everything miraculous there are so many inconsistencies that a paradoxical conclusion may be the most straightforward. Hull writes:

> We can perhaps venture to suggest however that Jesus did not think of himself as a magician, any more than he thought of himself as pre-existent Logos or as metaphysical Son of God. But to the early Christian the myth of the magus was helpful in various ways; it drew attention to certain aspects of the salvation of Christ in a manner which no other myth was able to do.

(Hull, 1974; p 144f)

Hull illustrates how form critics found ways in which the Gospels had been influenced by, and would remain enriched by, traditions which now seem slightly alien to Christianity with its emphasis on the purity of the Word. Of course, if we were to take magic at its face value we would once again be looking at the charlatans of many ages who have duped disabled people into accepting miracles based upon illusion and trickery. Yet, Jesus often appeared to offer healing to the very people whom successive generations of faith healers have sought to avoid. (See Hull's personal reminiscences in Chapter 1 of *In the Beginning There was Darkness*, 2001, of being at a healing service at a young age.) We have seen that such sentiments have led protestants to reject the whole reality of healing miracles lest their chicanery contaminated the glory of the ultimate miracle, the resurrection. The irony of form criticism is that it argues strongly that the Gospel writers utilized contemporary tradition to stress the uniqueness of Jesus in both his teaching and dealings with people.

More Radical Criticism

The *Jesus Seminar* was founded by Robert Funk in 1985. The fellows meet twice a year at the Westar Institute in California. Their aim is to judge and clarify the authenticity of the words and deeds of Jesus based on rigorous scholarship and study of all the historical sources besides the four Gospels. In this endeavour their work follows on from form criticism as expounded by Bultmann and many others of, but they endeavour to go further by voting on the degree of authenticity of passages. They vote according to a colour scheme where red represents a fairly certain conviction that a historical fact about Jesus is being recorded to black which represents a fictional account. As one might imagine there are very few red passages or even phrases. In this way, the *Jesus Seminar* hopes to give a truer and more lively picture of Jesus compared to the prevalent fundamentalism of America.

Like their predecessors, the fellows draw on contemporary Hellenistic literature but make especial use of the apocryphal gospels which generally have much more graphic descriptions of the healing miracles. This latest quest for the historical Jesus borrows a lot from previous quests but has adopted a much more radical and unique methodology. That radicalism is premised on a non-metaphysical view of God, and thereby considers that God does not intervene in any supernatural way.

> The notion that God interferes with the order of nature from time to time in order to aid or punish is no longer credible, in spite of the fact that most people still believe it. Miracles are an affront to the justice and integrity of God, however understood. Miracles are conceivable only as the inexplicable; otherwise they contradict the regularity of the order of the physical universe.

(Funk, 1998, §4)

The fact that there is no power behind miracle makes Funk's argument one that has not thus far been encountered, although the last sentence of Thesis 4 is reminiscent of Hume's dictum. (*see page 73 above*) Funk denies that miracles can be experienced as fact and that their existence can only be accounted for by people's rationalization of events which they do not understand or have not experienced. Hume argues that miracles may be experienced but that that experience is so isolated and remote from reality that it cannot be regarded as any kind of natural occurrence which follows the normal laws of nature. In a very real sense, Funk denies miracles at a dogmatic level without philosophical justification and goes on to suggest that they are fabrications with the motive of heightening the claims for the divinity of Jesus. This being so, the simplest way of explaining healing miracles is to say that the disease or disability was psychosomatic and that Jesus exercised some kind of psychological pressure on the recipient of the miracle. His argument is actually very common amongst non-believers but falls into the trap which Hume neatly avoids – that of denying God's power completely. Shortly, the 'invisibility' of disabled people will be considered but here Funk is mirroring another common belief about disabled people, which is that they are malingerers, hypochondriacs or have the ability to overcome their disability entirely within their own grasp.

Remus attempts to answer the question, 'Did Jesus really heal?' by dwelling almost exclusively on psychosomatic aspects of recovery. In doing so he depends upon a Fellow of the Jesus Seminar, John Dominic Crossan (1991) to list explanations for healing from spontaneous remission to willed healing. Now we have seen the beneficial effects of self-help groups and the value of investing in complementary therapy in order to find a cure, but it has never been suggested that these were effective for people with severe palsy or paralysis or most types of blindness. To answer the question, 'Did Jesus really heal?' with these types of answers is a form of denial of the severity of the afflictions which Jesus encountered in his ministry. Remus quotes at length the discoveries of social anthropologists in Australia who have encountered shamanism, but these practices do not even correspond to the magic posited by Hull. There is an entire literature, and indeed sector of the Christian Church, which engages in healing based on psychological techniques which will require further exploration in a later chapter.

The myth of Jesus developed over a great number of years commencing in the latter half of the first century with the writing of the Gospels, developed further with the establishment of organized religion and was enriched by the development of creeds following the influence of Paul and the deliberations of Councils like that held in Nicea. (Funk, 1996; p 36ff) The story of this development of myth is common to many scholars but this most radical form of it has peculiar characteristics which have a bearing on the theology of disability.

First, Funk attacks most of the miracles as fictional but with specific purpose. He believes that the young Church wished to exaggerate the importance of Jesus by developing the story of the virgin birth and of the resurrection. In order to prove this point they quote many other examples of infancy narratives and resurrection narratives. Funk goes on to attack the healing miracles in more subtle ways by suggesting that they mirror the classical Greek myths of Asclepius, whose healings were recorded as 'wonders' which is the preferred word to 'miracles'. (Funk, 1998a; p 21) The actual link between classical mythology and Christianity must have been tenuous in the extreme in Palestine at the time of Jesus and the Apostles.

The second technique employed by the *Jesus Seminar* is to outline the form in which these miracles or wonders are couched. They offer a very simple format: the presentation of an illness, the healing and the affirmation by the afflicted of the success of the healing. Such a format is simpler than the form criticism of the 1950s but is noticeable for the lack of concern for the disabled person. His or her role is not really very different from subdued nature or water changed to wine – the disabled person is simply regarded as the instrument of the narrative. This brings us to the third point, what is disease or disability to Funk and his colleagues? Funk tends to see illness in terms of diseases which could credibly be cured without ascribing any external power. He regards the illnesses which Jesus encountered as psychosomatic or, in the case of leprosy, a lesser skin disease. In the case of the latter, he is absolutely correct but the motivation behind his argument is suspect because he is seeking to lessen the severity of the illness. The scholars have voted that Jesus did heal and may even have exorcized but cannot vouch for the historicity of any individual miracle. (Funk, 1998) Nevertheless and in short, Funk betrays his dependence on David Hume when he characterizes Jesus as

> '… [a] wonder worker, or thaumaturge, who temporarily suspends the processes of nature in order to perform something out of the ordinary'.
> (Funk, 1996; p 252)

The objection to Funk's treatment of disabled people in the New Testament is of a different order to arguing that he inadvertently supports the medical model of disability. It is often argued that disabled people become invisible in a crowd. Those who are in wheelchairs are never at the same level as a company's normal eye level and they lack the mobility and agility to manoeuvre into the normal postures of social interaction in a crowd. This invisibility is reinforced by lack of access or care for someone who is blind and is particularly noticed by people who have an invisible disability such as deafness where a degree of social sensitivity is required by an able-bodied person who is interacting with such a person. The factors which cause this invisibility represent true ignorance or denial of the problems associated with disability. This diagnosis can clearly be made of Funk's easy dismissal of disability in the appropriate miracles.

There were a group of heresies in the second century, which were broadly classified as docetic. The perpetrators maintained that Jesus was nothing more than a spirit. His appearance of humanity was caused by God to deceive us and to give the impression of flesh, which was an embarrassment. The 'scandal of the Cross' was overcome by maintaining that Jesus' suffering was purely illusory. Such a heresy undermined the entire doctrine of the Incarnation. What would happen if the same principles were applied to other characters in the gospels? What if disabled people were not really disabled but only gave the appearance of being so. This charge is often levelled at many modern miracle workers who plant stooges in the audience complete with crutches or wheelchairs which can be thrown away on cue and with great alacrity. Other quacks have been noted throughout history, concentrating on vulnerable people with symptoms which are easily manipulated. (Porter, 2000) By suggesting, as do the Fellows of the Jesus Seminar, that Jesus only healed people with psychosomatic illnesses are they not extending the docetic heresy to other players in the gospels by suggesting that the suffering of those who came with impairments and diseases to Jesus were not really suffering with any severity? It seems as if there is a whole group of theologians who are willing undermine the suffering of Jesus' characters in order to afford a rational explanation of his cures.

Furthermore, it seems that all those who offer the psychosomatic explanation of the healing miracles forget that self-healing, hysteria and psychological blockages have only been understood or used as explanations or the basis of therapy for just over a century and were certainly not current theories in the time of Jesus and the Apostles. This is not to say that there are not psychosomatic illnesses that cannot be treated by psychology but rather that it remains a very modern application which in various forms has taken over the search for explanation of miracles.

Our discussion of quantum theory introduced the concept of energy and we will see in a later chapter that this has greatly contributed to the 'psychologizing' of healing and has given rise to many schools of thought which believe in healing powers which are outwith normal medical practice.

Chapter 5

Medical Explanations or Confusions

Disability as a Social Construct

This book has, on the whole, been critical of the way theologians have deliberately or, more often inadvertently, ignored the sensitivities and needs of disabled people as members of congregations. However, this must be balanced by an awareness that disabled people can make unreasonable demands on both theology and congregations and that this book strives to reach a balance. There is a very real question as to whether the Gospels talk about disability at all. If disability is regarded as a social construct, is it a construct which was present in the time of Jesus? It is highly unlikely that this is the case and will make us regard more circumspectly some of the claims which have been made by the disability movement and also by physicians who have looked at the miracles from a medical point of view. Historical records are limited by their perspectives and aims. In the case of the Gospels, the principal aim is evangelical not some forensically accurate description of all Jesus' encounters. The main strength in form criticism is that it seeks to identify hidden meaning in the culturally determined structures of the stories.

In the course of the last chapter or two it has become obvious that it is difficult to decide what to call a disabled person when discussing healings in the context of theology. It is even more difficult to find the appropriate nomenclature when it comes to setting disability in the context of biblical language. One has to admit that non-politically correct language provides a convenient and often more accurate shorthand when discussing the healing miracles. But behind this superficial observation there lies a much deeper question: is it appropriate to talk of disabled people at all in the context of biblical narratives? Disability is a modern social construct which has very little relevance to biblical times. In those days the fact that one was disabled probably had very little political significance beyond the fact that the misfortune of an impairment set people apart from both the political and economic mainstream of society. Such people found themselves certainly excluded from religious office and very probably also from religious observance, but the poor in society probably did not aspire to these in any case. There was no disability movement and probably no theories about disability save those which were recorded in the scriptures of the Old Testament and the very specialized writings of the Rabbis in the Talmud and other repositories of wisdom. There was limited literacy and very little travel between major centres for all but the mercantile classes. Thus the modern corpus of literature about disability would have been unthinkable and even superfluous not only in biblical times but probably up to and well beyond the invention of the Gutenberg Press in the fifteenth century.

It is undoubtedly the case that some of the people who were healed by Jesus would today be regarded as disabled, and further there is evidence that Jesus cured not only disabilities caused by accidents or degeneration, but also congenital impairments. It is highly likely that children with the worst forms of congenital deformities probably lived for a very short time and if the impairment itself did not cause death, complications probably did. Those who lived with a disability probably would not develop what we now regard as a social identity and would not have developed any solidarity with any other disabled people against the system which we now regard as often being hostile to disabled people. Disability was a tragic misfortune which very few had the opportunity to escape from and both the social structure and the religion of the time would emphasize the tragedy of it. Today's disability movement abhors the idea of 'tragic misfortune'. But that is precisely what it was and still is in many parts of the developing world. Whether it be in the first century or the twenty-first century, begging was the only remedy. Alms giving was a religious duty which people would perform without all the sentimental appeals that so blight appeals for funds today. Pilch quotes one scholar who argues that those suffering from 'leprosy' actually did conspire together to involve Jesus in the healing of their particular skin complaint, but this is rather the exception to the rule. (See Chapter 7 below)

If theologians and church people insist, as they must, to address disability in the Gospels they must be conscious of the need to make a decision as to the nature of their interpretation at two levels. The first level involves understanding the nature of the discussion of the healing miracles: and the second level involves the application of principles which will make a hermeneutic acceptable to today's sensitivities. This second level is the subject of this book and will be applied to three healing miracles in the final chapter but the first level requires an explanation before discussing medical matters.

It is necessary to discuss the meaning of two words: 'emic' and 'etic' so that there is a clarity in our understanding of what foundation our interpretation of scripture is based on. Writing of these two terms whilst reviewing the work of Howard (see page 156f), Pilch describes these

> perspectives (which are etic or 'outsider' views) applied to New Testament data (which are emic or 'native' reports) are not 'derived' etic views, as anthropological method requires. They are rather 'imposed' etic interpretation, which is only the first step in working toward a derived etic.

(Pilch, 2003)

Etic simply means taking words at their face value and as understood today through a 20th century thought process. It probably means understanding the Bible in a literal sense to the extent that any interpretation rests upon the linguistic development of the words. An etic interpretation of a healing miracle would be that Jesus cured the lame man or gave sight to the blind with very little critical understanding of what is being suggested as happening. Yes, there might be room to accommodate the theologies so far discussed but only if the words stand on their own merit. An emic interpretation of a story means looking at the symbolic and social process behind the words *in their original context*. Take for instance the raising of Lazarus. An etic interpretation of the story takes the words quite literally from within a perspective of faith – Jesus raised Lazarus from the dead and by doing so not only amazed the crowd but afforded himself the opportunity to make one of the great christological statements, 'I am the Resurrection and the Life'. An emic interpretation of this story would not negate this but might go beyond the words to the process and apply criteria, outwith the *Weltanschauung* (world view) of faith, which rely upon disciplines which cast light on the underlying processes.[10] It is has been argued by some that in Jewish times in the first century death was a process that lasted about a year. (Sawicki, 1994; cited by Pilch, 2003) This means that socially there were many stages which the deceased had to go through and likewise the mourners. If we find this hard to understand, think of the rituals Victorian widows went through with degrees of mourning dress and jewellery which was appropriate to their emotional state and often involved the encapsulation of locks of hair and other relics of the deceased. It was also a way of controlling marriage – remarriage could not be considered for at least a year. If there were similar processes at the time of Jesus, an emic interpretation of raising Lazarus would involve an understanding of what stage death and mourning had reached and meant at the time when Jesus intervened. To answer this is beyond the scope of this book but it is not impossible to look at the social processes facing disabled people who were healed by Jesus. By the end of the final chapter, we may be forced to make a choice between etic (imposed) interpretations and more radical emic (derived) ones – or perhaps not. Meanwhile, the distinctions will divide medical approaches to the healing miracles fairly starkly into those by physicians and those by medical anthropologists.

Having discussed the impossibility of sick people regarding themselves as disabled in the time of the New Testament, the discussion of disability as a social construct must continue with the consideration of two other factors which have at various times helped to build up the construct. The first one is the way in which modern miracles have developed: and the second involves the rise of the modern disability movement. It is this movement that provides a contrast with biblical times and makes it impossible to conceive a disability consciousness in biblical times.

Lourdes provides a good example of how healings or cures became institutionalized in the Church and caused ambiguity towards disabled people. Anecdotally, Lourdes has been described as the Blackpool of the Roman Catholic Church. Many disabled people visit it on a regular basis with no real hope in their hearts of a cure, but they return having had a good holiday and most certainly spiritually refreshed. Lourdes is located in France close to the Pyrenees and came to notice after a peasant girl had a vision there of the Virgin Mary in 1858. There happened to be a spring in the town which fitted well into the peasant tradition of visiting such springs for cures of various ailments. Although the peasants evoked the help of various saints for different ailments, it was a popular movement which did not attract the interests of priests and maybe their disapproval. Scottish saints were supposed to have blessed wells and springs throughout the land endowing them with curative properties, and ministers often recorded their parishioners' interests in this folk healing without being any more than historians or antiquarians in their interest. (Hamilton, 1981; p 84ff, also Beith, 1995) However, in Lourdes with increasing numbers visiting the shrine and alleging cures both the local priests and the Catholic hierarchy began to take an interest in the cures and the quality of spiritual belief which accompanied cures. Gradually, priests had to be present to record all the facts surrounding a cure and attest the faith which accompanied a cure. Unlike Scotland, the Third Republic of France was highly anti-clerical and it was in the interests of these parties to debunk any cures which took place. Thus, not only clerics became involved but sympathetic physicians who examined pilgrims for evidence of cures. There came a time when people actually had to bring documentary evidence of their illness in case a cure was obtained and evidence was required to prove it. This became all the more important when Emile Zola wrote his novel, *Lourdes* (1894), which characterized recipients of cure as hysterics and maladjusted women (in matter of fact most were single women in the latter four decades of the 19th century). This book sparked the debate which anti-clerics wanted – a debate between science and religion which science probably would have won had it not been for the founding of the Medical Bureau in 1883 which tried with relative success to test and sift claims of miracles. Their work goes on to this very day and their relative mainstream status is why they have been chosen in this study as opposed to more charismatic healing movements. Ruth Harris' account (1999) of the early history of Lourdes and the Shrine of Bernadette illustrates two of the issues which are important to the development of this chapter. From this brief history we can see how miracles became appropriated from folk medicine into the structures of the Roman Catholic Church and how disability became exploited by clerics eager to prove miracles. The development of an ecclesiastical <u>corpus</u> of knowledge is another example of how an issue can be made into a social construct to serve the interests of those in power and not the simple peasants who were originally going about a normal activity of finding commonsense remedies to minor ailments. Miraculous cures of today may be blinkered in their aims with the consequent reduction in their significance. In an interesting editorial in a medical journal which mentions Lourdes, Martin argues:

> Acts of healing which are not explicable in terms of our
> current knowledge of medicine are believed to have been
> mediated by God; unfortunately, as research closes the gaps

in medical knowledge so God appears to be 'edged out' or at least to become less active.

(Martin, 1986; p 3)

He cites as an example the behaviour of certain syndromes, which may result in 'miraculous' remissions ('cures') when medical science has not yet documented the natural history of such syndromes. There was a case before the Medical Committee of Lourdes when a woman was declared cured of Budd Chiari syndrome which involves blood-clotting close to the liver. She subsequently relapsed and died in 1970. In other words, many instances which the *International Medical Committee of Lourdes* find to be miraculous are revealed to be medically explicable some years later. The concentration on the single symptom reduces the eventual religious significance of the incident and takes away the holistic understanding which is central to the social model of disability – the social construct of most interest. Harris (1999) mentions blindness but not many impairments which would be classified as disabilities.

In Emile Zola's emphasis on hysteria we also have a premonition of one of the major debates to be covered in this chapter, the debate about functional illness versus psychosomatic illness which is central to texts written even in the 21st century.

Modern Models of Disability

The most important component of the social construction of disability must be its development into a concept which the majority of the medical profession is slowly beginning to accept, and which gives disabled people an identity of which they are proud and around which they can organize themselves in ways which would have been inconceivable up to and including the first half of the 20th century.

The most international constructions and definitions of disability might reasonably be expected to come from the *World Heath Organization* (WHO) but in considering them as a contribution it is worth remembering that they have a medical perspective on the subject. However, a closer examination of their terms concerning impairment, disability and handicap clearly reveals a social dimension to their classifications as well. (WHO, 1980) An 'impairment' is any medical condition which restricts or deprives a person of a function. Blindness is a sight impairment. A 'disability' is understood by the WHO to imply a restriction on normal function as a result of an impairment. 'Handicap' is a word which has become rather politically incorrect in most circles but it was the term used to imply the social restrictions which a disability caused. In these definitions were all the potential trappings of the social model of disability but they lack the urgency which is implied by the model when disabled people use it. Recently, the WHO has moved away from this categorization of disability and has developed a new model entitled the *International Classification of Functioning* (ICF) (2001). This seeks to classify disability in terms of the functions which an individual can perform and although it classifies performance in personal and social terms, at first sight it appears to be a step backwards into the medical model of disability and a reductionist view of the individual. But in actual fact it eliminates terms such as impairment and handicap which can be so ambiguous and introduces the concept of functioning. This is so creatively broad that it allows most illnesses and disabilities to be described in objective terms which will satisfy both the medical profession and disabled people if it is properly understood. Functioning is described as:

> an umbrella term encompassing all body functions, activities and participation; similarly, disability serves as an umbrella term for impairments, activity limitations or participation restrictions. ICF also lists environmental factors that interact with all these constructs. In this way, it enables the user to record useful profiles of individuals' functioning, disability and health in various domains.
>
> (WHO.2001:p 3)

The paper believes that the components of a disability have personal and environment factors which contribute to the loss of function in disabled people. It suggests that the ICF recognizes the dialogue and the tension between the medical model and the social model of disability, but by stressing functions, it obviously is willing to show how the loss of some functions are intrinsic to the individual whilst others are caused by society and will remain in place until there is the political will to alter physical barriers. The WHO summarizes its amended position thus:

> Management of the disability is aimed at cure or the individual's adjustment and behaviour change. Medical care is viewed as the main issue, and at the political level the principal response is that of modifying or reforming health care policy. The social model of disability, on the other hand, sees the issue mainly as a socially created problem, and basically as a matter

of the full integration of individuals into society. Disability is not an attribute of an individual, but rather a complex collection of conditions, many of which are created by the social environment. Hence the management of the problem requires social action, and it is the collective responsibility of society at large to make the environmental modifications necessary for the full participation of people with disabilities in all areas of social life. The issue is therefore an attitudinal or ideological one requiring social change, which at the political level becomes a question of human rights. For this model disability is a political issue.

ICF is based on an integration of these two opposing models. In order to capture the integration of the various perspectives of functioning, a 'biopsychosocial' approach is used. Thus, ICF attempts to achieve a synthesis, in order to provide a coherent view of different perspectives of health from a biological, individual and social perspective

(WHO, 2001; p 20 - §5.2)

It is a credit to the consciousness developed by disabled people that many countries have introduced legislation to combat the barriers facing disabled people. However, it must be added that, even in countries that we consider to be the most advanced, institutions tend to meet only the minimal requirements, thus leaving huge barriers to be overcome by the most severely disabled. Whilst the WHO has cautiously moved towards a radical understanding of the social model other writers have unwittingly adopted models which do not immediately aid disabled people.

One such is Arthur Kleinman, a doctor and psychiatrist, who has written a long series of books on suffering and deprivation amongst his patients. The fact that he is a psychiatrist will feature later in this chapter. In *The Illness Narratives* (1988) he seeks to describe the psychological impact which illness has on an individual and he tends to lump together both illness and disability in the same uncomfortable way as been experienced here. He distinguishes between *disease* and *illness* in a compelling way, although this does not help the social construct or consciousness of disability. Disease is what doctors study – it is a catalogue of symptoms which can or cannot be treated with recognized remedies. The difficulty in his categorization lies in the qualitative difference between a disability and an illness. A disability such as cerebral palsy has many symptoms but few remedies whilst an illness like a stomach complaint has a great assortment of remedies and curable symptoms. In Kleinman's mind there is common ground between these two illnesses when the latter has devastating effects on the individual as, for instance, when the only remedy is a colostomy. The psychological effects of a stoma can be very incapacitating to someone unable to adapt to its use and side-effects. The result may be that the person is just as disabled as someone with cerebral palsy but the extent of the disability will be measured psychologically. The social and psychological effects of a disease constitute the 'illness' and the narrative of how the patient copes is the subject of his book. Kleinman argues that illness can produce many coping mechanisms which are dysfunctional in an individual. He also argues that many narratives are created by patients who are suffering psychosomatic diseases which are designed to help them cope with some episode in their life which has caused trauma. He goes on to assert that illness can also involve shame and stigma, such as the supposed smell and disfigurement accompanying the wearing of a stoma or coping with facial or other body blemishes. The problem with his book is that he is describing psychological processes whereas most disabled people who are active in campaigning for rights have become comfortable with their disability and regard the inconveniences, which Kleinman would consider to be part of the illness narrative, as a deprivation of rights. Illness narratives describe the feelings which chronically sick people have about the symptoms and associated effects on their lifestyle and expectations. As a psychiatrist, Kleinman concentrates upon people who are disturbed by these effects and he seeks through counselling to solve many of the problems they are having. One of the difficulties with the book is that just as rehabilitation therapy may help a person disabled through trauma, so Kleinman seeks to show how others may be helped by counselling to overcome the negative feelings which make life so unpleasant. The problem is that rehabilitation and counselling work towards a medical end, which is an improvement in the overall performance of the sick or disabled person. As we will see later this leads to a particular understanding of the achievement of Jesus through his miracles which are characterized as a form of counselling, dramatic though these miracles may be. Many disabled activists are precisely so active because they do not possess shame, guilt or a feeling of inadequacy. Most will go through such phases and emerge the stronger and often use that strength to fuel a militant consciousness of their position as disabled people in society.

This is where the tension between the medical model and the social model of disability come into conflict most acutely. The WHO and writers like Kleinman have taken many years to recognize the creative tension, the dialectic (WHO, 2002) between the models, which has sometimes been destructive of relationships between different bodies of disabled people and between them and the medical and paramedical services. The social model of disability developed out of the searchings of disabled people to make sense of their disabilities within society. In terms of an illness narrative, disabled people have really not been exempt from feelings of social exclusion and a lack of equality with other people in their lives. But they have sought to view these in a positive sense which acts as a critique of society rather than of their psychological states. Whilst Kleinman tends towards a psychiatrist's understanding of an illness narrative, sociologists and social anthropologists have described the meaning which chronic illness and disability can assume when seen as a personal crisis. Bury (1982) characterizes sudden disability as a 'biographical disruption' that undermines all the assumptions that have been used to build meaning and security in one's life. Building a new life requires resourcefulness beyond our immediate imagination.

Disabled people, however, are not all activists nor even interested in disabled politics. Old people make up a substantial percentage of disabled people and do not in fact regard themselves are being disabled. Disabling conditions like Alzheimer's, arthritis and the after effects of a stroke are often seen as inevitable diseases of old age and those who develop such conditions often need to be persuaded that they are disabled and to accept the psychological consequences which so many disabled people regard as important. The anomaly of old people's attitudes to disability can often lead to frustrations on the part of disabled organizations who find that an entire constituency is missing from their ranks. Actually, there are also many young people missing, and people who just do not regard their disability as a problem, so tending to get on with life without becoming involved in politics or even seeking solidarity through friendship with other disabled people.

The question therefore is: what does disability mean in the context of the social model of disability? In this model disability is a subjective construct, a little like an illness narrative but not identical. All disabled people have at least one objective impairment, be it cerebral palsy, an amputation, deafness or diabetes. The nature of these impairments cannot be changed but may be helped by medicine, rehabilitation or the social assistance which can be put in place to compensate for the impairment. There may also be objective barriers in society which make an impairment less tolerable such as steps with no ramps facing people in wheelchairs, or a lack of understanding of the importance of the regularity of meals even in a busy work schedule. Some people live well with these barriers; most find them intolerable. When this occurs these barriers contribute to a feeling of disablement, of social exclusion and of discrimination of a negative kind. Thus a person begins to feel disabled and begins to understand that many of the problems he or she faces are of society's making rather than a direct result of their impairment. The old WHO model would say that they are handicapped, but the disability movement now finds this term unacceptable and prefers to talk of disability and to politicize the issues surrounding it. They likewise find that although medicine may treat their impairment at considerable cost, this does not effect a cure and does not offer solutions to the disabling effects of society. Thus, medicine is regarded with great suspicion even to the extent of denying its value in dealing with the common ailments which every member of the population may suffer from time to time. Adherence to the social model of disability can at its most militant be extremely destructive of trust between the disabled and their helpers, be they professional or simply carers, as many disabled people tend to mistake the social model of disability for a manifesto for independence and a licence to demand over-compensation on the part of society as it seeks to find ways to accommodate disabled people. The legislation in Britain is deliberately less litigious than its American forerunner which has resulted in bankruptcies in California where disabled people have sued non-accessible firms with a terrifying alacrity.

Although we like to think that American disabled people are more sympathetic to the Church (such a belief may be exaggerated), the disabled movement in Britain has been antipathetic towards the Church. This has been because those disabled people who have had influence have looked at the miracles at Lourdes and other evangelical campaigns offering healing and have decided that the Church's model of disability is almost as bad as that of the medical profession. Cures are offered by both, but seldom with any great success. If disabled people within the Church were willing to allow the social model of disability to dominate their thinking, not only would little progress be made towards a distinctive understanding of disability but also little progress would be made to rectifying the mistakes which can be found in the secular social model of disability. Christianity can offer a difference of interpretation in two ways: one, it can point out that the secular model is Marxist based; and two, it can develop social inclusion by the use of biblical and more recent doctrine.

First, there is a very real sense in which the social model of disability is based on Marxist theory. It is society which causes disability and structures the nature of disability. There is very little difference between this statement and the essence of Marxism which asserts that all major thought and social patterns are the product of the economic structures prevalent in the society. Disability is actually caused by social structures. Second, there is the issue of false consciousness. Marxists claim that people fail to take control of economic forces and social structures because they suffer from 'false consciousness'. People are content with their lot and position in society and do not believe that it is vital to alter their situations. After all, they are not suffering. 'Ah', say the Marxists, 'if they only knew'. The situation is exactly the same with people who have a disability but either live contentedly with it or cannot have an awareness of it because of profound sensory deprivation or learning difficulties. There are also groups of disabled people who recognize and owe their everyday existence to drugs and medical supervision. Such people include the mentally ill and disabled people with a high dependence on life-sustaining equipment such as respirators. They owe their continued existence to what some accept is a version of the medical model of disability. Such people, so the argument goes, are unaware of the profundity of their disability, although they may be aware of their impairments, and so are unwilling or unable to contribute to the activities of the disabled movement.

There is an increasing academic dissatisfaction with the broad brush strokes which are used to depict disabled people either by the medical or the social model of disability. The individuality of people with disabilities has often been overlooked by the paradigms of past research and ideology.

> We believe that existing theories of disability – both radical and mainstream – are no longer adequate. Both the medical model and the social model seek to explain disability universally, and end up creating totalizing, meta-historical narratives that exclude important dimensions of disabled people's lives and of their knowledge. The global experience of disabled people is too complex to be rendered within one unitary model or set of ideas.
>
> (Corker and Shakespeare, 2002; p 15)

What Corker and Shakespeare are pleading for is a greater sensitivity to individual or group characteristics of disabled people with unique viewpoints which deserve recognition. Those disabled people who become part of the Church might be one such group. The Church has a distinctive view of inclusiveness which has already been dealt with in our treatment of the Body of Christ but can now be further expanded by looking at the doctrine of *Imago Dei*, if for no other reason that they belong to a body with a unique understanding of inclusiveness. (See also page 64 above)

At a WCC seminar in Cartigny near Geneva in October 2001 Professor Frances Young raised the question of *Imago Dei* as a doctrine which has implications both for our attitude towards inclusiveness and also towards the different genetic makeup of people who are regarded as having a disability as a result of differences. If we regard all of humanity as being made in the image of God, will it not be the case that a greater respect will emerge for those who are disabled because of genetic difference? People with Down's syndrome, or conditions which are inherited such as haemophilia, Huntington's chorea and certain forms of deafness must surely be created in the image of God despite their different genetic makeup, for it does not affect their common humanity with the rest of mankind. This has a distinct bearing upon miracles. It is unlikely, Young argued, that someone with Down's syndrome could be cured without actually altering their body. Even in divine terms that becomes manipulation and not miraculous intervention. There is no recorded instance of Jesus altering the body other than to relieve symptoms and there is no suggestion that God has any less regard for such people. We, as humans, are challenged to accept the diversity of our genetic makeup; we are further challenged to consider whether we have the right to interfere with the variety of makeup by genetic engineering which may be achieved through the test-tube or abortion. If we take seriously the inclusiveness of God's creation, it is doubtful whether we have any right to try to alter the genetic makeup to conform with some norm which we dream up as humans. If we truly value people with genetic 'syndromes', we must constantly seek to consider the question of including such people in society at the appropriate times in their life cycle: to educate people with Down's syndrome or to continue to keep people active in society when Huntington's chorea strikes in later life.

The point of discussing this here is to pre-empt the attempt by doctors and those of a medical disposition to suggest that God has it within his power to homogenize humanity by miraculously eradicating genetic diversity. They do not have this power themselves and should not expect God to take it upon himself. The fear of diversity is the fear of the body itself as many feminists and others have pointed out. (McFague, 1993) There is some suffering which doctors cannot relieve, such as those mentioned above, by humane and other methods which are acceptable to God. They must learn to accept their limitations and to rejoice in the humanity which results in so many lives. However, it is at this point that theologians can become guilty of placing an undue burden on many who suffer illness narratives as a result of genetic differences. Irenaeus drew upon the biblical formula that God made man in his image and likeness and argued that whilst we are all born in his image we learn through religious devotion to grow into his likeness. Hick (1966) adapted this patristic model to develop the notion that we all live this life in a 'vale of soul-making' where we are gradually brought through our experience and suffering to a greater likeness of God. There was a virtue in suffering which brought with it the reward of a closer likeness to God, reassured by the fact that we have witnessed God's own suffering in the death of his son on the cross. Whilst we may argue that doctors cannot alleviate all suffering it is equally wrong to extol that suffering as a holy process on the way to salvation. Not many disabled people rejoice in being told that their suffering is a blessing, although this has long been a practice of the Church, but they do value the inclusiveness of a church which takes seriously the doctrine of the image of God, *Imago Dei*. The WCC has recently discussed a major document on disability at a plenary session and may have noticed the following paragraph of the document:

We would therefore argue that:

Christian theology needs to interpret the imago Dei from a Christological and soteriological (the saving work of Christ for the world) standpoint, which takes us beyond the usual creationist and anthropological perspectives.

Christian theology needs to embrace a non elitist, inclusive understanding of the Body of Christ as the paradigm for understanding the imago Dei.

Without the full incorporation of persons who can contribute from the experience of disability, the Church falls short of the glory of God, and cannot claim to be in the image of God.

Without the insight of those who have experience of disability, some of the most profound and distinctive elements of Christian theology are easily corrupted or lost.

(WCC, 2003; § 30)

There is an inherent danger in all the foregoing discussion of disabled people as part of the image of God in creation and it centres upon whether we accept creation as something inherently good or something that is marred by the negativity of sin. Young has hinted that the formulators of the Creeds wished to record that the entirety of creation was wrought by God's hand and owned by him and that demonic forces were not the creation of any other god. We saw at an earlier point how Fox (see page 46f above) asserted that it was necessary to have a positive outlook on creation and that this outlook had been apparent in earlier mystics but was lost after the Reformation. He stressed the Incarnation as evidence of the fundamental goodness of creation and an affirmation of the positive. There are many things in creation that we do not like or occasionally abhor, and there are certainly many things which we would rather not have to face. Disability caused by genetic impairment is obviously one of these phenomenon. It commands our sympathy but we are reluctant to regard it as a consequence of God's will. Such sentiment must be corrected with great vigour by a church which is seeking to bring disabled people into its midst. If we accept that God's son was incarnated in the humanity of our kind, we must accept that God regards all of creation as good including those who have been created differently. To regard people with genetic impairments as simply a gift of God without accepting his active understanding of their role in the incarnation is truly to fall into the trap of dividing creation into good and bad where we place ourselves as judges of God's handiwork. The object of our judgement must be to praise everything he creates by acting in an appropriate way to show the justice of his incarnated creation in the body of Christ. This only makes sense if it becomes a reality and so often discrimination within the Church destroys the reality and builds up fear and resentment on all who are involved in the charade of discrimination. It becomes important to understand that medical definitions are only labels which keep disabled people tied to definitions that arise from the medical model of disability and describe them as tragedies, which is precisely the negative attitude to creation which all these theologians and early fathers rejected.

If such a consciousness does enter the Church and into the minds of disabled people who are looking for acceptance within the Church, this construct of their disability as part of God's creation will be a powerful and potent tool in achieving greater acceptance. It also sets the demand of disabled people for acceptance in a different light from the much more popular and vociferous campaign by gays and lesbians who do not wish to argue that they are genetically different but argue on the grounds that they wish their lifestyle to be tolerated. Disabled people do not have this luxury and thus can make a distinction between their demands and those of the other lobby. There is a huge difference between a lifestyle choice and a genetic makeup which comes with birth. This must be the key to anyone who wishes to understand the different merits of totally different people looking for acceptance in the Church. The working party which wrote the WCC document, *A Church of All and for All: An interim statement*, agonized over the title for a long time because 'a Church for all', particularly in America, is code for a church which accepts gays and lesbians both as members and as clergy. This digression into current ecclesiastical politics is not motivated by a desire to enter into the debate but to offer a way in which disabled people can advocate acceptance in the face of evidence that the western Church is much more interested in dealing with sexuality than with disabled people who have always been with them in mind if not physically.

So what would be the salient elements in the disabled consciousness of a committed Christian. Such a person would be conscious that the Church ought to welcome them because of the inclusiveness of the teachings of Jesus and the theology which arose from it. He or she would have an awareness of the miraculous power of Jesus but might well reject the notion that he can directly cure their impairments. They might even think that the Church manipulates its teachings on miracles to try to attract the vulnerable people to faith in the expectations of a cure. If they believed that the social model of disability contains an understanding of disability which is relevant to them, they may well reject the more extreme interpretations of the model in favour of a constructive criticism of that which impedes their progress in society and, in particular, in the Church. This means that when they view the Church they will not only see all the barriers, not just the physical ones, to participation in the activities of the Church at all levels from worshipping in the pew to ministry in the pulpit. If they are critical of the more radical, Marxist social model of disability they may well feel ill at ease with radical criticism of the Church from a secular body of disabled people. Therefore, when they do come to church, they come not only as reformers but also as people who need support because they are as much part of the minority as many other people today find themselves in their circles of friends or colleagues. When they hear of the healing miracles, they may inevitably pay attention to explanations of the types of disabilities of which Jesus was acquainted and the explanations which are now offered by medical people who are theological trained or literate.

Medical Explanations of the Gospel Miracles

At this point we are going to examine the work of physicians who have written possible explanations of the healing miracles which Jesus performed. This is different from those medical practitioners who sit on the medical panel which examines miracles at Lourdes, and any other similar bodies in that they are concentrating on the healing miracles in the Gospels. Besides these medically qualified people there is now a growing body of experts who work in disciplines associated with medicine such as medical anthropologists and archaeologists. Of the latter, we have no competence to comment and their work is quoted by anthropologists who use their findings to supplement their own knowledge. There is one last group which will have to be considered – psychologists and psychiatrists who have developed a very detailed psychological theory of healing out of the teachings and miracles of Jesus. The discussion of this group will take up a separate section because their theories and actions have profound implications for the reactions of disabled people.

Returning now to medical explanations, these tend to come in two different forms. There are doctors who believe that the miracles of Jesus cured people who were functionally ill, in other words, they were unable to do certain tasks and thus the impairment from which they suffered could be looked at in much the same way as the WHO has suggested. The second explanation which is offered tends to be psychosomatic in nature. If illnesses can be explained this way it is actually more credible to believe that Jesus could effect an instant cure by undoing a hysteria or some such mental illness. The first group of explanations tend to be put forward by people who are biblical conservatives, whereas the second group tend to be made up of people of a liberal persuasion. However, these labels will not prove to be very useful and should probably be dropped now. In each instance, a significant representative of the particular genre will be chosen.

Medical Commentaries

Leprosy

All the main authors who are examined in this section agree, more or less, about the nature of leprosy in the Old and New Testaments. Basically, they argue that it is a mis-translation of the Hebrew word *sara'at* which denotes a generalized skin disease characterized by flakiness and discolouration, usually white. Such disease has similarities to psoriasis. It is doubtful whether leprosy, or Hansen's disease, existed in the Middle East in the time of Jesus. This is one of several skin diseases which leaves skeletal evidence which has not been discovered on remains examined by archaeologists. Much of the emphasis in the Gospels is on how Jesus restored sufferers to cleanliness, thus making them acceptable to society again. Wounds were generally considered to be ritually unclean in the Bible and broken skin, raw flesh and flaking debris would all be considered to be signs of uncleanness. Of course there was a fear of contagion but not all skin diseases spread in this way. With the wisdom of modern knowledge we know that leprosy is not contagious, although it can be terrifying to the eye which is unused to it. With the association of leprosy with being unclean, the Church throughout the ages submitted lepers to unwarranted isolation and in most societies where it exists, sufferers have a tendency to live in ghettos.

The translators of the gospel have done sufferers a terrible disservice by setting up a dichotomy between clean and unclean and, by implication, infectious or benign. The Church however has responded by setting up many charities to treat leprosy and whilst earlier charities re-enforce the ghetto mentality, the welfare they offered and the great men who were spawned by working in the field is a tribute to the Church's efforts to right a wrong understanding of the disease.

The gospel stories are set against a religious desire to regulate and control the spread of skin diseases, and Jesus' involvement went beyond the existing priestly regulations for the control and diagnosis of skin diseases. Two out of our three authors (Pilch and Howard) maintained that Jesus' main contribution to the welfare of 'lepers' was the removal of the barriers which isolated them from the rest of society. We will look at their characterization of this later. Wilkinson concentrates on the actual cure or removal of the offending illness which is probably not to be criticized because even today skin diseases are often ameliorated by very simple remedies involving natural products from mud to seawater. The rare agreement of most authors about leprosy in the Bible is, alas, not replicated in the treatment of other illnesses.

Wilkinson's Functional and Moral Diagnoses

John Wilkinson was a medical missionary in Africa for many years prior to being ordained as a minister of the Church of Scotland. He therefore comes to his writings with qualifications in both disciplines. His main interest is in health and the biblical meaning of it. He makes a clear distinction between what we might call everyday health and the miraculous cures of the Bible. He maintains that the Bible puts forward a moral view of health represented in the Old Testament by wholeness and longevity. In the Old Testament ill-health is regarded as a punishment or at the very least a sign of God's displeasure. His commentary is similar to many others but possibly not as expansive because he devotes most of his book to the healing miracles. Wilkinson never strays far from the moral imperatives of Jesus which proves to be quite attractive in Chapter seven.

In the gospels, the mission of Jesus and morality are inextricably linked and he appears to make some distinction between Jesus' teaching and his healing. This division is emphasized by the very specific diagnoses he offers of those who are healed and the general good health to which all followers of Jesus are called or promised. This dichotomy will produce problems when we consider that disabled people may suffer physical impairments but are not morally impaired.

Wilkinson maintains that there are two elements to Jesus' teaching about health and suggests that the first of those has been commonly used by healers over many years. It certainly accords with the WHO definition (on page 52 above). Interestingly the first one is based on the shepherd motif which runs through a number of the parables and extends back to the Old Testament and particularly the image of God tending the wounded sheep and caring for the weaker lambs in Ezekiel 34. This chapter is the high point in shepherd theology and it is undoubtedly the case that Jesus used it when thinking of parables which described the way his Father dealt with humans. Wilkinson quotes in particular John chapter 10 where the good shepherd guards the entrance to the fold in order to keep the wild animals at bay. The reason for doing so is that those within the fold – the followers of Jesus – 'may have life, and have it abundantly'. (Wilkinson,1998; p 28) In other words in the name of Jesus, his followers are given health and protected from the demons which so pervaded the culture of his time. The second strand of Jesus' teaching which Wilkinson considers to be important is the central teaching of the sermon on the mount, those verses which have become to be known as the Beatitudes.

> The Beatitudes represent a complete reversal of our earthly values and standards, and today the person whose blessedness they portray would be regarded as down-trodden, persecuted, under-privileged and even psychologically abnormal. The meaning of the Beatitudes is that blessedness and health come from within and not from without. The important thing is not the human environment but the human heart. As someone has truly said, 'The heart of the human problem is the problem of the human heart'.
>
> (Wilkinson, 1998; 27)

Wilkinson's characterization of health as having a moral dimension poses some of the same problems that have already been discussed, namely that undue pressure is sometimes put on disabled people by unrealistic expectations of their moral worth. After all, there are saints and sinners in the disabled community as in every other. Wilkinson considers that the Beatitudes bestow upon people with unique qualities a health which others lack. These verses in the sermon on the Mount describe the mournful, the meek, the righteous and those who make peace in the world. In the Lukan version the poor are particularly blessed and certain groups are cursed like the rich and idle. There is no doubt that Wilkinson is correct in asserting that Jesus is addressing a particular group of people who are different from the norm and are characterized by a holiness which can be traced back to some of the Psalms, both those of ritual and of lamentation, but it must be asked whether this group of people indicates anything about God's vision of health. The group who are truly blessed in the Beatitudes are those who have been marginalized by misfortune of some description; they have been persecuted or bereaved, looked down upon because of their poverty or ridiculed for their purity of heart. Wilkinson seems to want to say that such people will receive health and very few would disagree with this, yet a question has to be asked whether this is an adequate definition of marginalization? Much of the literature which examines the disability movement in Britain does talk of oppression (Abberley, 1987) and marginalization but this does not mean that the Beatitudes encapsulate such a definition. If they do, they reinforce the pressure stereotype of disabled people, and if they do not, their value in understanding disability is of minimal use in any hermeneutic about disabled people.

When Wilkinson considers the miracles, he begins from the premise that health as discussed above is different from health restored by miraculous intervention. He seems to suggest that man has an overall responsibility for the health that God offers, but that God himself takes responsibility for miracles performed by Jesus. Because Wilkinson allows himself a fairly literalist interpretation of the Bible, he believes that the miracles resulted in the cure of a functional impairment. This means that he ascribes certain illnesses to different recipients of miracles. He understands blindness as congenital, suggests that the 'man with the withered hand' may have had poliomyelitis and that epilepsy was of a type and genre which was incurable then, as it is now. In all these examples, there are modern cures or images but in biblical times they would only be healed by miracles. It is questionable whether Wilkinson, or any other authors considered here, has a warrant to assign a specific diagnosis to a sick person in a miracle story. Of course, there are indications but that is as far as it goes. Wilkinson does not consider in any detail the history of an illness either in relation to its victim or to the history of the time, with the possible exception of skin diseases. There is absolutely no evidence that polio existed at the time of Jesus, and if it had there would surely have been mention of a plague since it is a very contagious illness and would have caused such distress in the community that it would warrant a mention in historical documents and even the Gospels. When he gives his account of the boy who suffered from epilepsy, Wilkinson believes that the cure was effected by the finger of God in a way which can be contrasted with Hull's understanding of the finger of God as connected with a lucky charm of the time and with magic. (Wilkinson, 1998; p 130, Hull, 1974. *See on page 126 above*)

Wilkinson is quite disparaging of psychological interpretations of miracles. He discusses at length the demoniac at Gennesaret and other such interpretations of demonic possession. He believes that psychological diagnoses are little more than descriptions of symptoms and do not in fact describe an illness. He believes that Jesus cured such illnesses by ridding the person of the demon and does not subscribe to the view that Jesus somehow treated them psychologically. This is a problem to which an answer will be offered in the next chapter.

John Wilkinson spent many years as a medical missionary practising as a physician for 30 years in parts of Africa, mainly Kenya, and on his return became associated with the *Edinburgh Medical Missionary Society*. In common with many, this missionary society has as its aim the spread of the Gospel through medical service which brings life abundant to the many folk who suffer minor ailments and who are also beset by impairments which severely restrict their lives. It is little wonder then that he should consider Jesus' mission to bring abundant life as being of great importance in any understanding of the Gospel. A gospel which fails to offer material remedies to hardship is surely a false gospel, or at least one which offers the Word only with no insight into its practical application. In daily practice a physician is mercifully engaged in the cure of treatable illnesses, but they are only able, at best, to ameliorate the symptoms of those illnesses which still perplexingly and frustratingly defy modern medicine. This may be why Wilkinson seems to set up a dualism between the giving of normal health and the receiving of miraculous cures which have come only from Jesus. This dualism may be reflective of Mullin's distinction between the everyday health, 'providential health', we take for granted and that which is not only worthy of prayer but of God's intervention. (See Mullin on page 38 above) The problem is that this dualism does not serve the modern needs of disabled people. It is wrong to give the impression that severe impairments were only the subject of miracles in the Gospels. In fact, this is not the case. Take for instance the woman with the issue of blood. (Mark 5.34) By today's standards she would not be considered to be disabled – ill, yes, under medical supervision as she was at the time; socially restricted, yes in biblical times, but not today. The failure of doctors was an occasion for this miracle but nowhere else in the Gospels are we given such explicit reference to medical intervention by professionals of the time. According to Eve and others Jesus did specialize in certain kinds of miracles. He seemed to have more concern for disabling impairments, certain types of insanity and the misunderstood nature of epilepsy and ritual uncleanliness than other miracle workers of the period. He appears to have been determined to show his Father's commission by his choice of miracles and to show a greater concern than most folk-healers for their religious significance. (Eve, 2002; p 379ff) At root, Jesus had a concern for disabled people made outcasts by their impairments and who were brought into the 'sheepfold' where the Good Shepherd could tend them. This is a very sentimental way of saying it, but the point is that Wilkinson's dualism lacks a coherent link between everyday healing and the healing of those whose cure would have been miraculous at the time of Jesus. The genius of Jesus may have lain in his ability to understand and place his healing talents in the context of contemporary Jewish beliefs; and the brilliance of the four evangelists lay in connecting the two traditions upon which their subject, Jesus, based his ministry. The flock of Jesus is inclusive of all and his method of bringing people to the fold was one which was seamless in his treatment of all who sought or received his salvation directly or indirectly. Wilkinson's description of the work of a medical missionary, which is implied in his writings, would make more sense if miraculous cures were not bracketed off in the purpose of God to offer life in its full abundance.

Howard's Psychological Understanding

J Keir Howard, like Wilkinson, was a doctor and practised medicine for many years in New Zealand. He was also an Anglican priest but his theological journey took him down a different route. He started life in the Brethren in the south of England but eventually left that environment for a more liberal ecclesiastical scene. He was known as a counsellor and in his retirement wrote on healing in the New Testament. Unlike Wilkinson he devotes a great deal of space to 'conversion illnesses', which distinguishes his approach to miracles. A conversion illness or disorder mimics the symptoms and behaviour of a functional illness. Howard cites 'shell shock' as a typical example where soldiers from the first world war exhibited physical symptoms such as tremors which were really the result of their psychological trauma. (Howard, 2001; p 59f) Howard concentrates on psychosomatic illnesses in many of his analyses of miracles, which he defines thus:

> In much the same way, in modern society, one may observe the tendency for people to consult with the various practitioners of 'alternative' healing methods, particularly when struck down with some form of vague illness arising out of a fear of the effects of an outside agency or as the unconscious response to some form of intolerable situation. Something that is outside, or apparently outside, the normal range of conditions that would be dealt with by the standard medical practices of the time is met by the alternative practices, whether this is the exorcist of the first century or the naturopath, faith healer or other 'alternative' practitioner of the twentieth.
>
> (Howard, 2001; p 25f)

His use of conversion disorders can be most dramatically illustrated by his view of the healing of the boy with epilepsy. He maintains that the fit which Jesus witnessed and cured was a lesser type resulting from stress, but which mimicked all the symptoms of a major fit. In other words, the symptoms were relieved but the boy was not cured of epilepsy, as Wilkinson claims. The downgrading of the miracle takes away the intervention of God, which is central to Wilkinson's description. (Howard, 2001: p 121ff) Many authors develop arguments that Jesus only healed psychosomatic illnesses and they quote in evidence the prevalence of a belief in demons in the first century. But they fail to make the all-important link with Jesus' concern with the eschaton. Howard compares such demons to our concern today with environmental pollution. Other anthropologists have compared belief in demons to the beliefs which occur in societies which practice shamanism, for example in parts of Africa and aboriginal Australia. Appiah-Kubi argues that the Church in Africa must take account of traditional medicine and find ways of accommodating it within their orthodox medical establishments. (Appiah-Kubi, 1975) J. V. Taylor plausibly makes the point that Christian missionaries in Africa must interpret the Bible with cosmological implications for healing of relationships and illness within the local society. (Taylor, 1963; see Conclusion) It is, however, incredibly difficult to produce evidence which actually proves that Palestinian society was dominated by thoughts of demons and satanic practices. It is equally difficult anthropologically to compare the impact of demons with the spells of shamans. Howard shows considerable disdain for all alternative medicine and in several passages seems to portray a belief that any illness without a rational base is psychosomatic in origin. This is a variation of the view which is very common in Christian circles about 'new age' therapies, but which sometimes does not bear scrutiny. Certainly, the majority of interested church people have been prepared to enter the debate during the past two decades. 'Holism' has been appropriated by many professionals, particularly those in health care, by practitioners of complementary therapies, by philosophers and by proponents of a 'new age'. Because so much in 'holistic' medicine is drawn from other cultures and categories, there has been an inevitable clash with Christian values – a clash which has had many manifestations. Yet, other Christians, including this writer, have found a considerable measure of good and challenge in the entire debate. There are many approaches to 'wholeness' which are separated, almost to the point of antagonism, by language, categories and tradition. Religious discourse only serves to heighten the debate. Howard appears to define different understandings of therapy in terms of rationality and ascribes this mainly to conventional medicine and psychiatry even when they are dealing with irrational symptoms.

Although psychological factors in disability will be discussed in more detail in the next chapter, the following major issue needs to be considered here. For a disability to be psychosomatic there must be some hidden explanation for it which cannot be described in medical terms. Most writers who have considered the psychosomatic features of a disability have related it to the society in which we live with reference to the shame of some disabilities, or to the need to be dependent on others in order to escape certain pressures, or to recreate feelings of security which have been lost. No doubt such symptoms and causes do exist but the aim of the disability movement is to adapt to society and to encourage society to adapt to disability. Retreating into a psychosomatic state is simply not on the agenda of disabled people who eschew the medical model of disability. And if there is little evidence that disabled people thus retreat today, what evidence exists that they did so at the time of Jesus? It is reasonable to believe that despite demons and so on, biblical times lacked the pressures which are so prevalent in today's society. Furthermore, those who analyse disability by comparing societies separated by centuries, technology and culture fail to recognize that they depend upon a very American or Anglo-Saxon way of looking at their own society to find the pressures which might have applied in Jesus' time. They often forget the robustness of disabled people in the developing world who lack the luxuries of single-issue politics which drives western disabled people forward and which it has been already argued did not exist in society y until very recently. In summary, it is the repeated reference to psychosomatic condition which leaves Howard's work full of medical commentary but devoid of realistic social commentary.

Medical Anthropology

John Pilch has come to explanations about healing from a third and totally different direction. He has written on liturgy and hermeneutics, counselling and medical anthropology. The conclusions he reaches about healing are based on this background and upon his belief that Jesus was a radical critic of and commentator on his society. The nature of this society is central to Pilch's work and requires to be explored at the outset. He characterizes Palestinian society as 'Mediterranean or Middle Eastern' in nature. This is a large geographical swathe which may not convince everyone.

> … I use the words 'Mediterranean' or 'Middle Eastern' precisely to describe the culture of the people who populate, and whose lives are reflected in the Bible. The insights about the culture of this world are derived from contemporary anthropological investigations … It is legitimate anthropological method to retroject contemporary insights over two and three thousand years because, until the advent of colonialism and the discovery of oil and its consequences, the culture of the region remained remarkably unchanged.
>
> (Pilch, 1995: p xiif)

This sudden departure into geography and related matters may seem irrelevant but it is at the foundation of his theories on healing. Pilch argues that Mediterranean society was characterized by an all-pervading culture of honour and shame. This is the first occasion that an author has actually produced a dichotomy of his own to describe aspects of biblical society. In Palestine, there were both honourable professions and those which were despised. Men had greater authority and respect than women and those who were chronically ill often had to resort of begging to survive. Pilch offers this as a hermeneutic tool for preaching from the lectionary, and if one thinks of the lessons set for the ordinary Sundays of the year, this dichotomy can be applied to miracle stories and parables alike.

Language is the stuff of symbolism and our use of it demonstrates our attitudes to many different things. In the area of health, language tends to categorize illnesses and disabilities in groups and in dichotomies. To say that this is a primitive approach would be wrong because the modern medical profession categorizes illnesses by language into different specialisms – women's problems are gynaecological, skeletal problems are orthopaedic and so on. The weakness of such strict classifications is most vividly apparent in the inability of modern medicine to find remedies for those complex disabilities which transcend the boundaries of current compartmentalization. The same was true in the time of Jesus in the most simple and stark terms. Open wounds signified uncleanness and led to dichotomies which left people with skin diseases in a permanent state of ostracism and prevented their integration into society. Anyone with a limb impediment was considered to be inactive and therefore excluded from the economic activities of society. All this, enshrined in language which could be found in scripture, in the Talmud and the codes of the Pharisees, had a profound effect on how people thought. Pilch argues that Jesus uniquely offered new understanding of the old signs of illness and disability in such a way that he developed people's awareness of how to escape the symbolism of the times. Pilch does not make a great use of the linguistic and symbolic thinkers of continental Europe that were valued in the introduction of this book (see page 21 above), but he does develop the symbolism of Mary Douglas and her work on clean and unclean material in some of her writings. Douglas dwells for instance on the symbolic significance for Roman Catholics of eating fish on a Friday and documents the change in this symbolism after Pope John Paul I abolished this practice. In one stroke he took away a tremendous symbol of the solidarity of the Irish in London in much the same way as Jesus may have threatened to take away some of the certainties surrounding the Pharisees' attitudes to the sick and disabled. (Douglas, 1970) In her book on Leviticus, Douglas develops an interesting theory about the significance for the body of unclean food and offensive conditions. She argues that the Jewish religion, which the writer of Leviticus was attempting to reform, was a religion of the covenant not of nature. It was sealed by circumcision and maintained by an awareness of the proper order of things. She writes of 'the house that Jack built' as a suitable way of imagining the order of a covenant society which cannot blame its ills on demons and which seeks to restore order by imposing taboos and rituals to overcome uncleanness and to offer God the correct kind of animal sacrifice. In the Jewish world, disabled people were loved by God but were different and did not readily fit in to the order which God had ordained for a covenant people. It may well be that Jesus helped his contemporaries to understand the true love of God in overcoming some of the signs which had previous ordered society to the detriment of disabled people (Douglas, 1999). This use of semiotics by Pilch could have been developed further but it does lead us to understand his development of a 'healing hermeneutic'.

Since Pilch's main concern is with hermeneutics, he has to compare 'mediterranean' society with contemporary American culture. In relation to illness he argues that because America is a success-oriented society the failure which is concomitant with disability tends to suggest parallels with the society of Jesus. This begs the question as to whether modern disabled people actually feel shame and it is doubtful whether this is so. Many have come to grips with the limitations on their life, which is part of the 'healing narrative', and have adapted well to their circumstances. Others have shown their anger and frustration in their activism towards the society which has erected a 'wheelchair ceiling', to coin a phrase. At least in the west, the shame of begging has been removed and charities have become sensitive to the feelings of disabled people when fundraising. In a word, it is uncertain whether Pilch's comparison really merits great attention. But what does, is the greater emphasis in the west on achieving results, of setting targets and demanding instant results in health care. In the time of Jesus, a cure, for example of an epileptic fit, may well have been considered the relief of symptoms, whereas we now expect such fits to be controlled, monitored and concealed from society as part of a long term strategy to 'eradicate' the disease. Pilch argues that time is regarded differently in both societies – American society demands results almost immediately whilst Palestinian society lived day by day. In Jesus' time today's miracle was not tomorrow's miracle, whereas now we expect a medical 'miracle' to be repeated again and again after its discovery. This hermeneutic works well in the pulpit, but will it succeed in a critical analysis of the healing miracles of Jesus?

Pilch argues that Jesus understood the dynamics of illness in his society and healed people by suggesting ways in which they could overcome the barriers which maintained the power of that illness to destroy lives. Thus Jesus understood the negative power of being unclean with leprosy, of sin and of the double curse of sin which was attributed to past generations. He also was able to overcome demons which had great symbolic significance. This was achieved by offering to people a hermeneutic of contemporary society.

> He did heal those afflicted with this problem by reintegrating them into society. He restored meaning to the lives of these collectivistic persons. Thus the terms and definitions given to us by medical anthropology seem eminently useful for reading narratives about sick people and their illnesses in the Bible with appropriate respect for their culture and their lives long before scientific medicine developed.
>
> (Pilch, 2000; p 142)

One of the key words in the above passage is 'collectivistic'. Pilch is convinced that in 'Mediterranean' society it is the pressure to conform to the norms of that society and to be aware of the negative aspects of their illness in the eyes of the rest of society which sick people feel. The lesions associated with skin disease constantly spoke of ritual uncleanliness and brought disgrace, whilst blindness deprived people of God-given light and left them in a world of darkness which was assumed to be devoid of religious uplift. Pilch suggests that Jesus offered new understandings of the narratives surrounding these illnesses and so brought people back into the midst of society. This argument is perhaps the most persuasive in this entire review until it is recalled that Pilch places all hope of cure or healing on counselling, rather than any physical relief of symptoms.

At the end of his book he remains agnostic about Jesus' actual ability to heal. But he is absolutely convinced that the people, who were given new understanding of their illness and the opportunity to accept this, were able to receive healing from Jesus in the same way that sick and disabled people can receive healing from counsellors ministering in his name today.

Pilch develops an understanding of the healing miracles based upon what he insists is a native understanding of the body and the status of the sick person. These two aspects make up significance parts of the illness narrative of the person who is being confronted by Jesus. Pilch describes this 'native' approach as taking account of the meanings which people of the time of Jesus were likely to ascribe to a sick person. Pilch has researched at length the concept of 'symbolic healing' and believes that it was the ability of Jesus to offer a new symbolism to a sick person which gave him life, by which he probably means 'life and life more abundantly'. He maintains that such an approach is 'emic' in nature in that it tries to understand the miracles stories from the point of view of an insider. As we will see in the final chapter, John Hull (in press) actually offers a different phenomenological approach to blindness which gives an alternative insiders view. However, Pilch maintains that he is offering an 'emic' interpretation of the miracles which stops us from imposing our own understanding of the healing miracles as outsiders.

The type of thing that Pilch looks at is the significance of different parts of the body which have symbolic import in the outcome of a miracle. The body is divided into three zones:

1) The emotional and thinking zone

2) The communication zone and

3) the zone which controls our ability to carry out 'purposeful action'

These zones are represented by heart-eyes, mouth-ears, and hands-feet respectively. (Pilch, 2000; p107) In each of the miracles that Jesus performed, by implication he restored sanity by 'casting out demons', communication skills by restoring hearing or sight, and gave back the opportunity to do meaningful tasks and employment by restoring mobility to the paralysed and the use of a hand when that limb been withered. Pilch maintains that this is what people of the time would see in a miracle and that they would also understand that God's gifts and blessings had been restored by the removal of darkness, social impotence or confusion all of which isolated the sufferer in a world of their own, far from God's rational rule. Eve (2002; p 376ff) also points to many authorities who suggest that the main aim of a first century miracle may have been to put someone right with God, although any parallels with the doctrine of justification would be spurious.

This interpretation by Pilch is central to any alternative reading of the Gospel healings not as cures but as restorations – restoration to full social participation in a society which was incredibly ritualistic and under the influence of the Pharisees who had devised no less that 400 different rituals for people to follow in order to prove their conformity to the traditional Jewish faith. Pilch backs this argument up with a distinction between 'sickness' and 'illness' following the argument of Kleinman. When social inclusion is so important to disabled people and other activists it is attractive to find a model which shows Jesus bringing disabled people back into the middle of the community. The model which is presented actually accords very well with some of the aims of activists who would argue that if people only understood disability they could demolish the disabling barriers which society erects. The question would still remain, is this an interpretation which does justice to the Gospel's call to serve disabled people? The next chapter will consider whether this is so.

Pilch maintains that biomedicine looks at disease from the outside using common categories – that is, categories common to western medicine – whereas medical anthropologists such as Kleinman try to understand illness by looking at the local meaning which symbolically the illness has within a community. This is commonly called ethnomedicine, and it can be applied just as well to biblical studies as to other fields. Biomedicine looks for causes by research or by recording case histories and is well known to anyone who has been admitted to a western hospital. Pilch calls this approach 'etic' and the knowledge which is gained is held communally by the medical professions and not collectively by the people. Ethnomedicine seeks to understand how a community defines and accepts or rejects an illness. It is 'emic' in so far as it relates illness to the specific culture being studied. Thus, it is quite legitimate to accord to the New Testament variant of leprosy the status of being unclean. Such a state condemns the sufferer to living outside the community and being rejected as much for religious reasons as for public health concerns. This is why Pilch can argue that Jesus healed by giving new meaning to people's lives by offering the sufferers or the onlookers, or both, a new insight into the disease. Declaring a person clean who suffered from a skin disease was one example, but a more dramatic example is offered in the way Jesus releases the parents of a boy born blind from the burden of believing that their sins had caused his blindness. (John, chapter 9) According to this argument Jesus is turning the negative symbols of an illness on their head and showing that sin is not the governing factor in the boy's congenital blindness. At the end of the book, Pilch admits that he knows not whether Jesus actually cured those to whom he offered a new hermeneutic of their impairment and he leaves us with the impression that all Jesus offered, and by implication all Christians can now offer, was a sophisticated counselling which brings new life into those who encounter him. This partially explains how Jesus restored disabled people to a new place within society. But it does not offer any more hope beyond counselling, which can be accepted or rejected by the disabled person. This brings us back to the old argument that the only thing that keeps a disabled person disabled is a lack of faith or of co-operation. Kleinman in particular offers dramatic examples of disabled people whose lives are much worse because of prejudice and their anticipated fear of what people may think or feel about their illness. Lack of confidence, or assertiveness, cannot be equated with lack of faith but can be very negative in the way disabled people tackle modern barriers and will be addressed in the next chapter when Joy Lenny's views are considered on page 183.

In the latter pages, three distinct explanations of healing have been offered from a medical standpoint. All three are united in their conviction that Jesus offered life to those whom he encountered and that compassion inspired him to offer healing. 'Compassion' is not a word greatly liked by disabled people, yet the Judeo-Christian tradition gave a high status to such an emotion and demanded it from all, be they Christ or a simple peasant. Compassion is at the heart of the Deuteronomic law and is echoed by almost all the prophets who demand from us a lifestyle which is compatible with offering justice and relief to the poor and to those who are in need. Wilkinson puts it most vividly when he quotes the Good Shepherd of John chapter 10, but he is not alone in such thoughts. However, after this their differences emerge. First, Wilkinson clearly believes in biomedicine and that Jesus sought to cure identifiable diseases in miraculous ways, which are neither to be explained nor questioned. By attempting to give the miracles a special significance by ascribing to each a disease, Wilkinson sincerely believes that God's glory is more greatly revealed by the overcoming of diseases which the modern reader understands. Second, Howard likewise believes that Jesus cured conditions which he met in his daily encounters with those who were seeking a miracle. However, time after time he diagnoses the disease in psychosomatic terms. Wilkinson would argue that this does no more than describe the illness and because it is all in the mind, it is healing which is devoid of drama and a reasonable truth. Howard would respond by arguing that this is the nature of a primitive society with primitive views of illness and of their causes. Third, Pilch offers a real alternative to these two by moving the discussion from biomedicine to ethnomedicine which seeks to explain both how Jesus was likely to understand illness and how his society likewise understood it and was able to accept new symbolic understandings of disability and illness.

None of these three approaches seeks to honour disabled people. Each tends to adopt the medical model of disability and to assume that medicine has the answers either directly or through derivative disciplines. Such a conclusion is totally justified in the case of Wilkinson and Howard, but Pilch deserves a final look. He is basically arguing that Jesus changed how people looked at illness. Is this not what everyone in the disabled movement would like to see happen – a new perception of disability? This is absolutely true and Pilch almost offers a solution which would make this book redundant. However, despite his assertion that Jesus offers new life, it is life which is only offered after the disabled person is questioned either in reality or by implication. He suggests that Jesus offers a new understanding to both the disabled person and to society. But it is reasonable to argue that modern disabled people know who they are, and in accepting the social model of disability they do not actually want to change or feel an obligation to do so. Society is the disabling force; therefore society must change. There is no easy answer to this conundrum but we must look further than Pilch to find it. He argues that we must always try to get inside the mind of the biblical characters, the emic approach, but whether this can be achieved is a problem which has received adequate testimony by the number of approaches to miracles which we have examined.

Even if Wilkinson's actual diagnoses are discounted and it is borne in mind that he had a strong conviction that Jesus did heal complex functional diseases, we are still left with his conviction that healing took place. This is not shared with the others. It is our belief that the conviction that Jesus healed is precious to disabled people and that Eve is correct in arguing that Jesus deliberately chose to heal those for whom God had long had a major concern as was reflected in the words of Isaiah and in Jesus' reading of them in the Synagogue in Capernaum. If the Messiah was indeed to herald the Kingdom of God, he had to show compassion in removing one of the obstacles and offences to that Kingdom, disability. This is not to give disability a dark or sinister meaning but to recognize that in the inclusive and compassionate kingdom which was being proclaimed, unaddressed disability had no place. In the Kingdom of God such matters are addressed and we who are ambassadors for Christ in the Church of today have the same obligation to eradicate disability in ways appropriate to our time and understanding which inevitably involves promoting some version of the social model over the medical model of disability.

Chapter 6

Social and Psychological Hijack

It is not possible to deal with the psychological impact which faith healers have on disabled people in this book. Most faith healers come from outwith the mainstream denominations and have ministries which require special skills of analysis which are not available here. It is well known that some faith healers are charlatans whilst others have both honourable and holy intentions but often fail to deal sensitively with disabled people with the result that many disabled people carry scars from their experiences of either failure or exclusion from healing services.

Research by Monteith (1997) showed that there were three kinds of people interested in healing either on Iona or within the Iona Community. The Iona Community was founded by the Very Rev'd Lord MacLeod of Fuinary in 1938 to rebuild 'the ancient monastic buildings of Iona Abbey'. Ever since the Community has sought 'to bring together work and worship, prayers and politics, the sacred and the secular.' MacLeod based all his activities on the implications of incarnational theology, which asserted the sovereignty of God over all of life, and from the beginning a healing service stressed the importance of health and wholeness. First, there were those who were committed to healing by divine intervention usually during a healing service but not always. Second, there were those who believed that healing was achieved by the atmosphere and community spirituality to which people were exposed on the island of Iona, just off Mull on the west coast of Scotland. This healing was likely to be a combination of psychological release and awareness of the power of collective worship and responsibilities. Last, there was a group which obviously believed that healing could only be achieved through social justice and that the Iona Community had to play a central role in achieving this as well as struggling for peace in a nuclear environment.

Brian Thorne (2003) contrasts the judgmental and achievement-oriented society with the acceptance of both community and counselling:

> In the face of such incontrovertible evidence of human
> resilience and potential, it is perhaps scarcely surprising that

much that characterises our current culture induces in me an
increasing sense of outrage. In the therapy room, I seek to offer
myself to others without pretence and to extend to them an
acceptance and an empathic understanding which is restorative
and points to life and hope. In society at large, however, it is
the absence of precisely these same qualities which permeates
the very fabric of our collective experience. Judgementalism,
litigious aggression, cut-throat competitiveness, fear of failure
are the hallmarks of a society which rides roughshod over the
needs and aspirations of human beings made in the image
of God and given the primacy instead to the achievements
of economic superiority and the maintenance of what is
ironically called a high standard of living.

(Thorne, 2003: p 4)

It is vital to pause at this quotation for a moment for it eloquently
describes the feelings of that third group in Iona and many who are
involved with counselling up and down the land. People who deal quietly
with individuals in the therapy room can be very active and vociferous in
protest against war and our weapons of mass destruction. The Kingdom
of God is not simply about healing and restoring disabled people to their
proper place in society but is about making God so apparent that people
are not under the pressure to seek counselling in the first place. A society
worth living in is a Christ-like society. However, this may well not be the
agenda of disabled people who would love to fit into the perfect society
but have a greater priority to fit into the imperfect present in which we
live. This is the mindset which will be considered in this chapter.

There are however many healing services in the mainstream
churches which claim to be following the encouragement of Jesus to his
disciples to carry on a healing ministry and they reach out to many people
with any variety of unspecified problems of which disability would be
but one. Besides healing services, many churches offer counselling and
increasingly train their ministers in the various types of counselling so
that that they may minister to people in a much more individualistic
way than was characteristic of congregations which concentrated on the
social Gospel. This counselling inevitably involves an understanding of
some school of psychology. The present chapter will focus on the effect
of this concentration on psychology and on a very general, liberal type
of healing service. It will be shown that, quite frankly, healing has been

wrested away from disabled people and normalized as an activity within certain congregations. The importance of this lies in the charge that both charismatic healing and liberal healing have misled disabled people to their detriment as some of the most vulnerable members or potential members of a congregation. They have either been sidelined by a social agenda where society becomes the focus of healing and reconciliation, or where individuals find healing for long-held psychological scars. Salvation becomes equated with wholeness and wholeness becomes far removed from Jesus' prime concern for disabled people. As Kathy Black characterizes the situation, disabled people can find themselves between a rock and a hard place:

> Both the conservatives and liberal ends of the theological spectrum have contributed to the alienation and oppression of persons with disabilities. The conservative perspective tends to look at healing in terms of 'cure'. The healing texts are taken literally, and accordingly, persons with disabilities today need to be 'cured' to be returned to 'wholeness' – to be in a right relationship with God. The homiletical emphasis is on elevating Jesus and pointing out the lowly status of the person being healed. The implication is that if a person is blind, or deaf, or paralyzed, or 'demon possessed', there is something wrong with the person that needs fixing, the person is in sin and requires salvation, or the person's faith is not strong enough and repentance is required.
>
> The liberals take a more psychological approach to healing or avoid the concept of a healing ministry altogether. The healing texts in the Gospels are used metaphorically, or the healing itself is put aside so that more important issues in the text can be dealt with; the author's intent on using the story in the first place, why it was included at that particular place in the Gospel, or what the story contributed to the author's overall goal in writing the Gospel.
>
> (Black, 1996; p 13)

This chapter will look at what mainstream healing services tend to tackle, that is wholeness and balance, guilt and reconciliation, and will show how counselling has been channelled into dealing with these and seeking to achieve an adjustment by an individual to the situation in life which they have to face. It will then consider the potential pitfalls in assuming that counselling can help people with disabilities.

Healing Services and Environments

Mainstream healing services usually have three components: praying for the sick by name, the laying on of hands usually for those who come forward, and the symbolic anointing of those who have chosen to have this rite. This form of service is based almost entirely on the words in the Epistle of James, chapter 5, verses 13-16:

> Is any one of you in trouble? He should pray. Is anyone happy? Let him sing songs of praise. Is any one of you sick? He should call the elders of the church to pray over him and anoint him with oil in the name of the Lord. And the prayer offered in faith will make the sick person well, the Lord will raise him up. If he has sinned, he will be forgiven. Therefore confess yours sins to each other and pray for each other so that you may be healed. The prayer of a righteous man is powerful and effective.

This passage has been central to the Church's teaching on healing, and has also been the centre of much controversy. In the Roman Catholic tradition, it was common for priests to anoint the sick and often to do so with well-founded medical application but gradually it became corrupted into what became known as the 'last rites'. Anointing was reserved only for those who were on the point of death or indeed had just died. This corruption is beginning to be corrected but will remain with the laity for a long time to come. Protestants have traditionally disliked the entirety of the Epistle of James claiming that it deals with works rather than faith. The commentaries of Luther and Calvin reinforced this feeling and many evangelicals of today still have difficulties with it. They claim that it does not imply that today's Church has been given the same gifts to heal as Jesus had from his Father. Also there is a major debate about the significance of the phrase, 'The prayer of a righteous man is powerful and effective'. Who is this individual whose prayer is powerful, and what is the nature of the prayer for the sick? Warrington argues that this prayer is reserved to a person with Christ-like gifts, to which most of us cannot aspire. He concludes his argument thus:

> Healing in the Gospels and Acts should, then, not be made the fundamental basis for our understanding of the healing ministry today. This is not to deny the possibility of divine healing occurring today, but simply to note that it does not achieve the same unique purposes as the ministry of Jesus did.

(Warrington, 2000; p 151)

These controversies and warnings notwithstanding, liberals and charismatic alike have developed their own healing services, and our purpose here is to look at the services of liberal mainstream denominations who have abandoned any doubt that the healing gift of Jesus was not imparted to all Christians and that it is open to all of faith to offer 'the prayer of a righteous man [which] is powerful and effective'.

One of the services which is most emulated in the British denominations of today is the healing service of the Iona Community. The mere fact that the service has been conducted weekly since 1938 is justification for its influence. It is therefore a good example to take as a case study. It must be recognized however that it is not aimed specifically at disabled people, although many have found the atmosphere of the liturgy and the island conducive to healing and restoration. There is a fairly common view that the laying on of hands is an act which helps disabled people, not by offering a cure or even long term healing, but certainly presenting a unique experience of being included in a service where for a few moments the entire focus is upon the person who is receiving it. This inclusion can be very uplifting for someone who undoubtedly has experienced exclusion and discrimination. For a few moments all the difficulties which the Church has with disabled people disappears. It can also be a very relaxing experience and one which can focus the mind of the individual on what she or he feels can be achieved. The Iona Community is not noted for its involvement with disabled people but this author can remember several occasions when a disabled person has benefited from the service. It has probably done as much or more than some to facilitate physical and sensory access, and for most who attend this service it has overtones of reconciliation, freeing from guilt and the liberating experience of inclusion.

There are two activities going on week by week to do with healing; first the healing service on a Tuesday evening; and second, the Iona Prayer Circle which also operates on a Tuesday, although not exclusively.

In examining the liturgy of the service, there are three components that will be briefly examined and one which will simply be noted. First, it is important to understand its prevailing liturgy and, in particular, the most recent developments. Second, individuals have been inspired to write either hymns or liturgical theories in response to the service. Last, there is the Iona Prayer Circle. This was founded and based on certain principles which are still worthy of note, although it is not possible to analyse the intercessions of the Prayer Circle which is a body, wide-flung beyond the shores of Iona, made up of individuals praying on their own and groups meeting in houses.

By way of introduction, it has for a long time been assumed that most residential visitors to Iona intend to spend a week in or around the Abbey. This means that the pattern of worship is structured on a weekly basis, commencing on Saturday evening with a service of welcome and ending with Holy Communion around the table the following Friday. Since 1981, the night of the healing service changed to give a more logical structure to the week. Monday evening celebrates peace and justice; Tuesday, the healing service; Wednesday, after the pilgrimage around the island during the day, the service is more flexible; and on Thursday is the *Act of Commitment* which is more logically placed on this day, before communion around the long table on Friday prior to departure on Saturday morning. Thus, the healing service is part of a rounded theology and religious experience. Most of the services have liturgies laid out in the service book which is normally prepared by the worship committee, although more recently responsibility has tended to rest with the Warden, and with contributions from the Wild Goose Worship Group. It is significant that the service of healing has always been referred to in the Abbey worship books by words of explanation rather than a set liturgy, but recently congregational participation has become really important.

From the beginning the Prayer List was designed to attract names from all over the world. In his notes, George MacLeod was clearly proud of this, and he mentions in particular requests from Canada and South Africa. People making requests from the UK were expected to make weekly reports of progress or needs, whilst people from overseas were required to write every third week. The organization of the intercessions for the Iona Prayer Circle and the healing service works in two ways. Prayer requests can be made in person, by letter or by telephone until five p.m. on the night of the service. This list is used during the service and then left in St. Columba's Chapel until the following service. The Prayer List which is drawn up for the Prayer Circle is circulated throughout the UK and is used after the main service and by intercessors who receive it at regular intervals.

The most outstanding feature of the healing service is its inclusiveness, both in its rubrics, which seek to involve everyone, and in the open-endedness of the situations for which prayer may be offered. There is a story about one service when R. D. Laing, the famous psychiatrist, shouted obscenities throughout! More to the point, Ron Ferguson writes:

> The laying on of hands is not exercised by one person, but by the whole community – and the leader of worship kneels to receive the hands of the community (just as in the Community's morning office the leader of worship confesses his or her sins and hears the absolution pronounced by the whole congregation).

> (Ferguson, 1988; p 192)

Finally, there is good reason to quote part of a sermon by Archbishop, latterly Cardinal, Thomas Winning before his death in 2001. His words were recorded by Ron Ferguson at the healing service during the week of an ecumenical conference which drew together all church leaders in Scotland in 1984. He appropriately chose to make this statement during the healing service and caught at a very early stage the prevailing openness of the service to the healing of even denominational divisions.

> The path to further reconciliation to my mind cannot lie in brooding over our wounds, or in mutual recriminations, but in a continual series of creative experiments born of goodwill and with a vision of the future which we are building together. The churches have therefore above all to be open to the unifying power of the Spirit. If we are static, immobile, motionless, there will be no room for the Spirit. If the Church is static, it will not command the response from the Lord to come to its aid. But against a Church on the move, open to the Spirit, the gates of hell will never prevail.

> (Ferguson, *ibid*)

Much can be written about guilt and here we have Winning introducing it at the centre of the healing service as a call to reconciliation between wounded and divided denominations.

The opening responses of the regular healing service underscore the theme of solidarity of the people with God, and with his world:

Leader	We come in this service to God
ALL	IN OUR NEED, AND BRINGING WITH US THE NEEDS OF THE WORLD.
Leader	We come to God, who has come to us in Jesus
ALL	AND WHO WALKS WITH US THE ROAD OF OUR WORLD'S SUFFERING
Leader	We come with our faith and with our doubts.
ALL	WE COME WITH OUR HOPES AND WITH OUR FEARS.
Leader	We come as we are, because it is God who invites us to come,
ALL	AND GOD HAS PROMISED NEVER TO TURN US AWAY.

(The Iona Community, 1991; p 38)

This major part of the liturgy emphasizes four elements of the Iona Community's present theology of healing: 1) that healing and wholeness concern not only the individual but the world; 2) that God through Jesus Christ is with us and the world in our suffering; 3) that healing is sought through our own volition but granted by the will of God; and 4) that God is always in solidarity with us. Not only is there a summary of the Community's theology of healing but also a summary of incarnational theology. Staff Members of the Community offer personalized case studies rather than theology as discussion starters. Each of these cases always have social issues built into them. Some also exhibit emotional release which resulted in healing. From the evidence of George MacLeod's prayers and his actions in the early years, the healing service was concerned strictly with healing, but within the broader context of incarnational theology. According to Ian Cowie in unpublished correspondence, the first order of service was in fact English. The Community did publish a pamphlet by Bill Aitken which contained a liturgy adapted from the *Guild of Health* in Crowhurst. George Bennett was warden of Crowhurst Home of Healing in Sussex from 1958 to 1969. He reflected upon the experience in *Miracle at Crowhurst.* (Bennett, 1971) In the very early days of 1938 it was reported in *The Coracle*, the organ of the Iona Community, that they 'struggled with the *Book of Common Prayer*' to provide a framework for morning and evening worship, so it is not surprising that they looked for inspiration elsewhere. The service was always conducted by a minister with one assistant and did not offer the congregation much opportunity of participation. The laying on of hands originally took place on kneeling stools laid out in the chancel as an adjunct to the service after those not wishing to participate were given the opportunity to leave. In recent years it has moved to the transept where it can be more inclusive. Candles have also been introduced as a way of marking a space around which a circle of supplicants may kneel for the laying on of hands. With many of the congregation in a circle linking together by various means and the supplicants in a circle also, there is a real sense of inclusiveness and of participation. Individuals are then invited to come forward with concerns for situations in the world, international, national or domestic. As a forerunner to this wider emphasis the hymn *For the Healing of the Nations* by Fred Kaan was introduced as a regular feature in the Worship Book of 1982. It should never be underestimated how burdened people may feel when they absorb into themselves situations which are not of their own making. People are also openly invited to come forward as proxies for friends or individuals for whom they are concerned.

There is also a greater concern with guilt and with negativities. The invitation to the laying on of hands now appears in an appendix towards the back of the Worship Book. It is difficult to say whether the it is an instruction or a suggestion but it is there for all to read and has constituted some trouble on the part of the compilers. It reads thus:

> At the end of the next song those who seek prayer, either
> for personal need or for a need in our world, are invited to
> come and take it in turn to kneel or take a place at one of the
> cushions here in the crossing.
> { .... }
> So come, you who are burdened by regrets and anxieties,
> You who are broken in body or in spirit,
> You who are torn by relationships and by doubt,
> You who feel deeply within yourselves the divisions and
> injustices of our world.

(Iona Community, 1991; p 77)

George MacLeod and many others have commented on the relationship between guilt and the willingness to go forward for the acceptance of touch in the laying on of hands. These lines of invitation seem to echo such a view. The reasons for the invitation are all negative

– 'regrets', 'anxieties', 'broken', 'doubt' etc.. Two features in *The Coracle* point towards this concern. The first is by Kay Carmichael (1989, but cf 2003), a Friend of the Community and a lecturer in social work at Strathclyde University, who wrote of a concern that the Church of Scotland had no power of absolution as did the Roman Catholic Church. It is a theme which she has alluded to in a paper in a later publication. However she says in the earlier paper:

> There is in the Kirk a repeated message that Christ died for our sins and that through that sacrifice we can claim forgiveness but the exposition is often too cerebral to penetrate the powerful self debasement of those who feel guilty and unworthy. 'Not me', is the thought, 'He couldn't have died for me'.

(Carmichael, 1989; p 10)

She goes on to discuss the socialization of children and the adverse effect which blame and guilt has on the developing psyche. The healing service, particularly the laying on of hands, provides an opportunity for absolution which is lacking. Kathy Galloway comments on this in an interesting meditation on the meaning of ceremony. Ceremonies mark our seasons; they heighten our awareness of the sacraments and give meaning and poignancy to rites of passage. Each ceremony in which we participate offers us a new insight into our innermost feelings and we can find ourselves 'transfigured'. In the conclusion reference is made to narrative theology, but here it is introduced as a moving concern for the significance of the laying on of hands, which blends together so many threads in the reality of a service that is now seen as being about the lifting of many sorts of psychological burdens from a great variety of people.

> We have a service every Tuesday night in the Abbey on Iona, in which we pray by name for people who are sick, and lay hands on any who wish to receive this ministry. Over many years of participating in this service, I have been forced to ask questions, and to draw some conclusions. By far the largest number who come to receive the laying on of hands are people who fall into a category which might broadly be termed those in search of spiritual healing. But even then, there are many people who come forward who I know are not troubled in their faith, who are not despondent and cast down beyond what is usual, who are not in mourning or addicts or whatever.

People go forward to receive the laying on of hands to be healed of anger, of greed, of fear, of selfishness and of all the other things that make us all broken people. People in large numbers, perhaps sixty or seventy at a time, and many of them young people, receive the laying on of hands because they are seeking absolution. And a ceremony in which we invoke the presence of God's spirit, and symbolize our care as a church by our touch, makes that absolution real to people. Touch is such a basic human need, and something that is so often alien to our culture, especially for men, that when it is received in a way that is non-threatening, it comes as a real liberation. It is an experience of grace, a moment of making whole. It is, if you like, a sacrament.

(Galloway, 1995)

George MacLeod stressed that it is important that the person being prayed for knows that this is happening and to be aware of the time of the service. He wishes to encourage the sick to pray for others, whilst recognising that illness sometimes prevents a sick person from finding the energy to pray at all. He stresses the need to strengthen their biblical faith, and is keen to discourage negative thoughts of divine punishment, but rather 'to encourage the thought that they are something God has permitted and desires us to fight with His help; even as he permits temptation and desires us to fight it with His help.'[11] His pastoral concern is such that he considers that it is wrong to pray in an anonymous kind of way. There must always be some reference to the progress and nature of the illness: a patient who is not sleeping requires prayers for sleep; a carer who is at his or her wits end requires prayer more than the patient on some occasions.

'Please pray specially for sleep'; 'Please pray also for his widowed mother, he is an only son', are very helpful. (It frequently happens that when intercession is commenced and largely concentrated upon some distressing symptom, such as a lack of sleep or difficulty in digesting food, a change for the better is seen speedily with regard to this symptom; and that this change comes as a great encouragement both to the sick and to the intercessors, to pray on and to pray more earnestly. Sometimes, too, a full healing is built up, step by step, as one symptom after another, or one need after another, is made a matter of special prayer in this way.)[12]

George MacLeod intended to ensure that these principles were safeguarded by insisting firstly that the person seeking intercession either asked for it or was sponsored by a friend or relative. Elsewhere, he makes it clear that regular reports should be expected from the person requesting prayer – every three weeks for a person in Britain, every month for those overseas. When the rules were finally published, a greater flexibility was allowed offering more time for correspondence and responses to both the temporal matter of postage and the spiritual reality of prayer! The problem in the present day is that the pen has been superseded by the mailshot, and much of the thought that the pen can provoke has been lost in the speed and informality of E-mail.

Arguably the greatest contribution which the Iona Community has offered to the Church of Scotland and other mainstream denominations in the UK in recent years has been in the development of liturgy and hymnology, not least in the area of healing. The Rev'd John L. Bell has been a member of the Iona Community since 1980, during which time his musical output has been prodigious, often in collaboration with Graham A. Maule. They have aimed to write hymns with a distinctive Scottish character and have often adapted famous folk tunes to suit their needs. Bell's talent as a choirmaster led to the establishment of the Wild Goose Worship Group which has been used to experiment with and train local congregations in worship and praise.

When *Songs of God's People* was published in 1988 by the Panel on Worship for the Church of Scotland, it became an overnight success which has run to nine reprints of the words edition. As the Supplement's Convenor, John Bell spent much time touring Scotland, demonstrating and lecturing. He repeatedly made the point that the Supplement attempted to be inclusive of the Church's concerns, as these had changed since that publication of the *Church Hymnary Third Edition* in 1973. Issues such as peace and justice had not previously been addressed, nor had the brokenness of society, women's concerns or healing been adequately covered. The deliberate inclusion of South African hymns reflected the Church's long participation in the struggle against apartheid. Twenty-three songs out of 120 came from past or present members of the Iona Community, and at least three of these dealt with brokenness or healing. This illustrates the lead which the Iona Community has given to hymnological reform in Scotland, and to issues of healing and wholeness in particular. Add to this the fact the John Bell went on to convene the Panel on Worship which saw the publication of the new *Book of Common Order of the Church of Scotland* in 1994, and the evidence of Community involvement in Divine Healing increases. This very fertile period of creative ferment, however, did not produce any hymn to serve as a corrective to the disablist language of Wesley's *O for a thousand tongues to sing* on page 16 above.

The Church of Scotland's service of healing is more formal than that of the Iona Community but is clearly based upon it. It uses much the same format and employs the prayer said over each supplicant which was composed for the Iona service a decade earlier. It is not acknowledged, but then the compilers apologized for their inability to acknowledge every source.

The rubric and prayer reads thus:

Laying on of Hands
In turn, hands are laid on each one kneeling or sitting, and
this or similar prayer is said:
May the Spirit of the living God,
present with us now,
heal you of all that harms you, in body, mind, or spirit.
In the name of Jesus Christ.
Amen.
(Church of Scotland, 1994; p 406)

The liturgy of healing in the Iona Community is more than just the compilation and the recitation of a service. It is a vehicle for the expression of many talents. We witness the pastoral concern of George MacLeod, or the creative and innovative thinking of John Bell or the channelling of latent concerns drawn from personal experience by Anna Briggs. The language is always changing and assimilating new ideas and influences. The concept of energy will recur often, as it will be shown that many of the thinkers within the Iona Community have absorbed ideas about energies and their healing powers. For example, Dr Rev'd Margaret Stewart summed up the assimilation of several such concepts in the introduction to a healing service on 30th July, 1996:

For me to understand the significance of healing I do not look
at the drama of miraculous stories, biblical or contemporary.
For me all healing is amazing, miraculous if you like. The
process by which our bodies and minds can be repaired fills
me with awe. The complexity of the process of repair of

even a small cut, a minor upset seems to me so much more wonderful because it happens from within, the potential for wholeness and fullness of life is present within individual cells of our bodies.

[*a propos* the laying on of hands] ...we come forward with concern for our lack of wholeness, for family and friends, for broken community and by our action in asking and accepting the hands of the people who travel alongside us tonight we open ourselves to the power of the healing spirit. Such can *energize the healing process present in our bodies* [my emphasis], our minds and our spirits.

Often often often comes Christ in the stranger's guise.[13]

[line quoted from a Celtic Rune]

Divine Healing was born on Iona out of a crisis, that of the Second World War. To sustain itself for 50 years is no mean achievement when most healing revivals tend to be short-lived and dependant upon the charisma of one central figure and fed by evidence of healing which is apparent to all. The liturgy which has been examined here deliberately makes no reference to a leader, nor does it offer any evidential results. It has its detractors, yet no-one has been sufficiently disillusioned to topple the overriding confidence in the propriety and logicality of the service within the context of a concern for ensuring 'in all things the purpose of our community, [is] that hidden things may be revealed to us and new ways found to touch the hearts of all.'[14] There is a conviction, and a manifest emotional feeling, that for those attending the service, hearts are being touched, and that the service still commands a central place in the overall strategy of the Community.

The interest in this case study is that the Healing Service of the Iona Community complements their social concerns as well as their known interest in the wellbeing of people who are on retreat on the island. The social concerns are mainly to do with peace and with the healing of the damage which men and women inflict on their environment and on the dreadful social conditions of some inner cities. The Healing Service has moved more towards these issues and further away from health over the years, perhaps as the result of a more sceptical constituency. Iona is not a place for disabled people to visit – the Abbey is a historic building which cannot be made easily accessible and the transport and terrain on the island is often prohibitively difficult. Therefore it is not surprising that a direct concern for disabled people in the service is lacking. Nevertheless, the Community has recognized the 'brokenness' and the lack of inclusion on the island as something which requires healing by practical action and this stresses the importance of the social model of disability.

The theme of reconciliation is common to a number of communities and each in their own way translates reconciliation into healing. The purpose in briefly mentioning some of these communities is because of their links with Iona and because they offer examples of how peace and justice have coalesced with healing, making it appear that the modern emphasis on 'ecological healing' within the Iona Community is perhaps an inevitable consequence of expanded horizons of inter-relatedness. Lourdes comes into a category of its own, which is not entirely relevant because it is based on a 'sacred' site, rather than a purpose. The healing of Lourdes follows from the alleged revelations which took place on this site rather than from its aims.

The three communities worthy of mention are: the Taizé Communité in Burgundy, France; Corrymeela, about 55 miles from Belfast; and Riesi in the centre of Sicily. Roger Schutz established Taizé on what was the border between Vichy France and occupied France, and during the war worked with freedom fighters manning escape routes to Switzerland. It was an ideal site for a centre of reconciliation after the war, and the rule of common care, service and devotion soon provided the opportunity for this. In 1962, a German organization called *Aktion Sühnezeichen Friedensdienste*, which literally means Action Reconciliation Service for Peace, built the Church of Reconciliation. They have also helped in many ways in the life of the Corrymeela Community. Established in 1965 by Ray Davey, who had intimate knowledge of the Iona Community and also Taizé, Corrymeela made the common life and reconciliation central to the life of the Community. It was immediately thrust into the conflicts of Northern Ireland and achieved much by its ecumenical family weeks. A reading of McCreary's journalistic account leaves one in no doubt that individual healing was always occurring as traumatized children and widows came to terms with the brutalization of the conflict. Corrymeela was declared open by Pastor Tullio Vinay who firstly established Agape in the Italian Alps and then Riesi in Sicily. I visited Riesi in the early 70s and found it to be a centre which was attempting to reconcile some of the dysfunctions of Sicilian society – the role of women, the use of land and the dominance of the Mafia.

In terms of wholeness, all these centres plus similar communities in Florence have been studied by Ian Fraser of the Iona Community, who believes that wholeness must be found in the inclusiveness of communities. The point of all these communities is that they each have a common theme of reconciliation and, by default, healing and have been intimately connected by their members, one to the other.

There are not many such centres which are accessible either physically or by intent for people with disabilities. Lourdes is probably the outstanding exception but, and it is a big 'but', the care offered appears to display all the paternalistic pastoral concern for the Roman Catholic flock which can be very disabling, and its approach to healing remains embedded in the medical model of disability.

Counselled Adjustments

When it comes to discussing psychological healing, the issues become more complex. It is not simply an issue of choosing to redirect healing in a social direction but to achieve aims and objectives which offer people peace of mind so that they may be receptive to the peace of God. A great many forms of counselling have been developed and given Christian credence by psychiatrists and others who have either had a strong Christian conviction or have been attracted to the symbolism of the Christian year. This would obviously be the case with thinkers such as Jung and Rudolf Steiner. Steiner developed a theory of seven 'levels of evolving consciousness'[15] , and made it clear that consciousness and logic are continuously flowing between these different levels. For our purposes Seddon's conclusion to his *Rudolph Steiner - Essential Readings* is important because it stresses Steiner's view of the uniqueness of the individual:

> Each Human Individuality will have a certain note, and the whole will sound together in a symphony. [Referring to the seventh state of consciousness]
>
> (Seddon, 1988, p 30)

Christian healers themselves have either sought to show how the life of Jesus reflects their school of counselling or believe that people requiring counselling lack a right relation with Jesus which must be restored. In broad terms, what all are trying to achieve is a restoration of the harmony between a saved person and their Saviour. In very many cases this implies that people must make some adaptation to their life in relationship to others and to the Church. It will be shown that disabled people are asked to adapt in ways which feminists would call acquiescence and which caused the author to recant much of an earlier book, *Disability: Faith and Acceptance* (1981), because all the demands were being placed on disabled people to adapt to the Church rather than asking the Church to adapt to their needs.

Disabled people are often considered to be deficient in some respect: they are helpless or cannot adjust to the loss of function or of a limb or whatever. They display unhealthy anger about the fate which has befallen them and young disabled people are reputed to take years to come to terms with their disabilities. Hours are spent wondering if they will ever attract a partner or enjoy sex within or without marriage. Each of these problems seems at first sight to be suitable subjects for counselling in the expectation that normality can be restored by overcoming these deficits. There is however considerable opposition to the idea that disabled people can be counselled into an acceptance of their state. Joy Lenny (1993) argues that there are three types of counselling which assume that disabled people suffer at least one of the privations mentioned above and that counsellors feel compelled to offer support. She rejects firstly the idea of psychological counselling which assumes comfort with a perfect body and sexuality as would be required by Freud and other such schools. She also rejects 'stage' theory – the idea that we are simply passing through phases such as those described by Erikson and that the counsellor must help guide clients through them. Last, she rejects behaviourism because it assumes a model of normality to which disabled people have no desire or need to aspire. She prefaces her analysis with a telling quote about the expectation that disabled people will deny all their privations;-

> The classic psychological response of denial places disabled people in a Catch-22 situation: to deny that adjustment to their disability is a problem for them shows just now great their adjustment problem really is.

> (Lenny, 1993; p 234)

It is in this context that modern culture is discussed, and done so with awareness that Lenny believes that counselling should not be about adjustment but about helping the disabled person to become assertive about his or her rights in society in order to secure a barrier-free environment and access to the choices of independent living. Her analysis is typically rights-driven and secular and thus may not be appealing to every reader. The concept of 'oppression' as an outcome of counselling has been aired by Donna Reeve (2002) and her article is a timely caution which backs up and expands much of Lenny's thesis. That having been said, Reeve defines oppression in terms of the inappropriate way in which non-disabled people talk to and teach people with disabilities. Oppression occurs when there is a clash of cultures between the able bodied world and the disabled world resulting in misunderstandings at best and manipulation at worst in the way a counsellor approaches a disabled person. Her arguments depend upon a solidarity model of disabled people with an identifiable culture and needs which can be easily understood and developed by what she calls 'disability training'. The next author to be examined develops a much softer approach which recognized the minority status of disabled people but avoids the anger and militancy of both Reeve and Lenny.

The rejection of stage theory is also echoed by Rhoda Olkin who has written an encyclopaedic book on psychotherapy and disability in which she places great emphasis on the need to encourage disabled people and their families to 'respond' to disability rather than to adjust to it or to accept it. One of the stages in responding is to have an understanding of the appropriate model of disability. Olkin works with three models of disability: the medical model of disability, the moral model, and the minority model. The latter two have not been introduced before in this book. The moral model suggests that disabled people or their parents are either to blame for the disability or their inappropriate response, or consider that they must shoulder most of the responsibility for dealing with disability which is not really society's concern. She of course rejects this model. She views the minority model of disability as being synonymous with the social model of disability. Although this is understandable and represents slightly more than semantics, it shows how American disability thinkers are much less wedded to the dogmatic collectivism of the social model of disability in the UK. (Olkin, 1999)

Disabled people often need counselling but it is wrong to equate that need with disability. Whilst it is perfectly conceivable that anxieties and depressions arise from a person's perception of their disability, it is wrong to assume that this is always the case. It is also wrong to consider that a disabled person is the best counsellor for a disabled client. It may be so, but not always. Disabled people may want to avail themselves of counselling from different schools as would any one else. Some will seek Jungian analysis or perhaps transactional analysis whilst others will seek more biblically based methods. A secular example might be Transactional Analysis with its emphasis on 'parent', 'adult' and 'child'. Frank Lake's *Dynamic Cycle of Development* (1986) which overtly seeks to witness to Christian values and uses an understanding of Jesus Christ drawn from St John's Gospel is a good example which inspires the Christian application of these terms. Agnes Sanford's book was first published in 1947, and proudly boasts hundreds of reprints, probably mostly in America. She asserts that the 'light of God' is constantly with us as unseen as X-rays, but powerful enough to heal. She flirts with scientific explanations of spiritual healing, but makes it clear that she is primarily concerned with spiritual matters:

> And in the course of our experiments we [scientists] have come to the conclusion that a vibration of very, very high intensity and an extremely fine wavelength, with tremendous healing power, caused by spiritual forces operating through the mind of man, is the next thing science expects to discover.
>
> (Sanford, 1947; p 30f)

Sanford maintains that by prayer and a growing relationship with the Lord it is possible to change harmful memories thus allowing the love of God to enter in. Science, she asserts, has not yet discovered the ways of the Lord but will do so eventually. Dr Kenneth McAll, author of *Healing the Family Tree* (1982), introduces another type of healing service which is based on the Eucharist and a specialized understanding of the Communion of Saints. He believes that injured or hurt relatives from the past can be present at this Eucharist and receive healing along with the living. This is obviously another kind of healing of memories in a liturgical setting.

Perhaps the most popular approach within Christian circles is that of person-centred counselling which has been developed most forcibly by Carl Roger. His methods, which respect the entirety of the individual, have proved popular with Christians and have been taught for many years in most departments of practical theology. It depends upon a profound respect for the individual and a desire to help him to work out problems which impede his development. Interestingly, Lenny approves of Roger and believes that peer counselling based on his methods can produce legitimate results. She quotes a short poem by Lao-Tsze:

If I keep from meddling with people, they take care of
themselves,
If I keep commanding people, they behave themselves,
If I keep from preaching at people, they improve
themselves,
If I keep from imposing on people, they become themselves.

Brian Thorne's (1998) sermons and articles illustrate clearly how
much Christian counsellors, who rely on and are inspired by Carl Roger,
idealize the way Jesus treats people. Jesus is the precursor of the whole
person counsellor and his dealings with people are considered to be
probably more important than his healings. Often the most quoted text
is about the woman taken in adultery (John 8: 3 – 11). The problem
which has to be asked of Christian counsellors is whether their beliefs
assume that people are going to have to make an adjustment to the
morality and expectations of Christianity.

In the past few years, peer counselling has burgeoned within the
disabled movement as disabled people assert their rights to confide
within and between one another. Dr Jean Morrison has both defined and
expressed reservations about the process in personal correspondence:

It is 'peer' because both client and counsellor have some
experience of disability. This experience may be similar or
totally different and both similarities and differences can lead
to misunderstandings that are not picked up.

Peer counselling can be easily organized by disabled organizations
but the demand for high skills and costly supervision makes the
process very expensive. At the time of writing, there is no knowledge
of specifically Christian peer counselling. The problem is that there is
no evidence that disabled people want counselling as a specific tool of
Christian healing. The more important question is whether counselling
can ever be considered an activity which mimics the healing of Jesus.
If Pilch is correct Jesus did change the meanings of the illnesses he
encountered and there is no doubt that counselling can do likewise
today but at the expense of adjustments which may be a denial of their
disabilities.

In order to set 'illness narratives' in context, it is worth considering
the culture in which many disabled people find themselves. We live in a
culture of the perfect and beautiful body. This is portrayed through the
media by a concentration on models with perfect figures and advice to

others who are less fortunate as to how these may be obtained through dieting etc. Cosmetic surgery is not only widely advertised and available but has become a source of entertainment on television in programmes which either deal with disasters or with the most extreme procedures which some would maintain almost verge on pornography. Although this culture is manifestly present for all to see, it is hard to document how many people actually succumb to it. It is doubtful if much of the entertainment actually is regarded as anything other than entertainment or prurient voyeurism. Mike Oliver was quick to denounce the use of Paul McCartney's wife as an example to the disability movement because of her involvement in the modelling business and the fact that she has had her leg amputated. It is hard to believe that people are actually so involved in following these image makers that it affects the desire to conform to the ideal type of life which is conveyed by the media.

There is not a dichotomy which can be characterized as perfect/ imperfect in the sense that both are defined by the media but in terms of disabled peoples' own body image and self awareness there is still a great deal of research to be done. The likes of Professor Oliver would argue that all disabled people conform to a class whilst more sophisticated research examines how individual disabled people build up their own image of themselves. Oliver is probably correct in criticising the then Minister for Disabled People for using popular icons to relate disability to modern culture:

> [Margaret Hodge in her] column for *Disability Now*, the disability newspaper that passes for the disabled version of the *Sun*, … makes no promises to provide fully comprehensive and fully enforceable civil rights legislation but instead promises to permanently change the climate of opinion towards disabled people by fully involving a combination of newspaper moguls, business, the Royal Institutes, one legged models and fading television personalities, many of whom most of us thought were dead. *Haven't we heard all this for the last 50 years and hasn't it proved to be an abject failure?*
>
> [Italics added] (Oliver, http://www.bcodp.org.uk)

There has been a move away from the collectivism of Oliver *et al* to a greater interest in how individual disabled people regard their impairments and disabilities. Thus, research by Watson (1998) focuses on the attitudes that people with multiple sclerosis have of their own situation. This shows that their concerns and worries about their medical situation, family life and general satisfaction is much more important to them then whether they conform to a generalized characterization of disability. Similarly, Shuttleworth (2002) has examined the sexual feelings of men with cerebral palsy in California highlighting their individual concerns, successes and failures rather than making them conform to a general view of what the media regard as acceptable sexuality and what earlier theorists of disability have tended to lump together to make a generic problem rather than an individual response to private feelings. When disability is treated as a class or group of problems with only one social meaning, disabled people have to conform to that; whereas if their individual circumstances are carefully considered conformity is not required. This is where the medical model of disability and the social model of disability share a common dictatorial root; they both can seek to push a disabled person into one mould designed to fit all and demand that they adjust to the expectations either of the medical profession or of the social agencies working on behalf of disabled people. There is a real chance that those who psychologize Jesus' healing into models of meaning may be guilty of exactly the same thing.

Kleinman argues that many illnesses (disabilities) come with shame on both the sufferer and their families. Clearly the most modern example is AIDS which seems to compel people to hide away, to avoid normal contact and gradually to accept that some types of sexual behaviour (both heterosexual and homosexual) are either unacceptable or must be totally modified. We have already mentioned some of the other sources of shame which Klienman so eloquently writes about. He puts forward the case that such people can be helped by counselling to find a true and liberating understanding of their illness. Kleinman believes that the answer to the treatment of chronic sickness is to construct a careful and listening ethnography around the patient's illness noting their experience and concerns:

> These insights become the stuff of his [the physician's] clinical experience and serve to inform theories, generate research reports, and stimulate a robust extraprofessional genre of essays and fiction. Both practitioner and anthropologist, furthermore, are students of hierarchies of practical relevance that concentrate people's lives; the exigency of life difficulties that makes living 'one damn thing after another, …'
>
> (Kleinman, 1988; p 232)

The problem with this model, as with any ethnography, is one of ownership. Are the findings of research owned by the subject or by the researcher? Many disabled people would probably argue that the medical profession squeezes them into their own preconceptions of disability and denies them the freedom to define disability themselves. The problems of dealing with doctors, benefit agencies and day to day physical barriers to access become problems which may not be owned by the disabled person who campaigns to rid society of the worst of these problems. When we begin to apply the arguments of Pilch in a Christian context, to what extent can we argue that Jesus had a grasp of the full complexities of an illness narrative? To carry healing forward into a redefinition of illness may be a modern understanding of the Christian message but was probably lacking at the time of Jesus.

When Pilch develops this idea he places such help in the context of Christian counselling and shows that people can be changed by accepting new meanings of their illness. He shows that in the miracles, Jesus took currently held meanings of illness and dismissed them. For instance, in the case of the healing of the man born blind (John 9;1 – 41) Jesus subtly builds new bridges between his correct understanding of sin and the people's understanding of it. In the Old Testament mind frame sin was a collective activity and therefore it was quite likely that a whole family's history would be taken into account when considering the plight of the man who was blind. Pilch argues that Jesus managed to break down such collectivism and show that their assumptions of sin were mistaken:

> Two explanations were possible. On the basis of Exod. 20-5, some Israelite scribal teachers argued that the sins of the fathers were responsible for the suffering of their children. Hence a child could be born blind because of the misconduct of its parents. Much later in the rabbinic tradition, other teachers argued that it was precisely prenatal sin on the part of the child that brought on such calamities (Genesis Rabbah 63:6.)! How is this possible? If a pregnant woman worshipped an idol, for example, the foetus was said to do the same (*Song of Songs Rabbah 1:41*). In v. 34, then, the opponents assert this connection between sin and the blindness, but in 9:3 Jesus rejects such explanations (compare John 5:1-4).
>
> (Pilch, 2000; p 132f)

The question is whether Jesus actually only 'cured' blindness by removing the stigma of familial sin in a form of counselling and teaching or whether he actually cured the blindness. Whatever conclusion is reached, what is clear is that Jesus was challenging the culture of the time just as modern counsellors will consider challenging today's culture of either perfection or shame in order to make disabled people feel better about themselves. In fact, prenatal 'sin' is rearing its head yet again in modern society with the condemnation of women who smoke or drink excessively during pregnancy. The real challenge of Jesus in the context of modern society is whether he can bring healing to individuals without recourse to dictatorial models of society by which the normality or abnormality of disabled people is measured. In the context of the Church today, there is an obligation upon all to balance the need to have a class called disabled people, and to have individual people with disabilities who bring their unique problems to the scrutiny of the Word of God as it is revealed for them.

Chapter 7

Eschatology and Healing Miracles

The purpose of this final chapter is to show how exegesis of the Gospel miracles can be undertaken in such a way that disabled people can feel included and honoured by the homiletic which results. There are three questions which must be asked. First, why honour disabled people at all? The Gospels are principally about Jesus' message of salvation and would not have survived the test of time if the main subject of them had been God's dealing with disability. To make such an assertion would be a travesty and to interpret this book as such would be a mistake. However, there is evidence that Jesus had a special message for disabled people and more so for society which has often been ignored. Second, what is this message? It will be argued that this message is eschatological in nature and thus is more central to the Gospel than we perhaps realize. Finally, how do we reflect the complexity of the miracles and of their scandalous nature in the religious atmosphere of the time as having more than just a message about Jesus but about disabled people as well?

In the early 1970s, the author heard a sermon by Professor Donald Macleod of the Free Church College in Edinburgh about the healing of the beggar at the golden gate; which has inspired the motive for this book. It became obvious that the sermon honoured the beggar in a fresh and exciting way which I have not found replicated in any of numerous sermons since on this incident. It transpires that the guidance for the sermon came from a book written in 1857 by a professor at Princeton University by the name of Joseph Addison Alexander whose main work was on Isaiah. In his *Acts of the Apostles* he shows a remarkable empathy for the disabled man who was begging. Alexander manages to locate the man's disability in both his (the man's) narrative and in the social position of Jerusalem. It is worth spending a moment considering his commentary as an early, but modern example of a sympathetic account of the miracle.

There are three elements to the commentary which are worthy of consideration. First, Alexander deals with the situation of the beggar. He has been disabled or lame since birth. This is rare but not unique in the New Testament healing miracles. Alexander points out that Luke mentions it in a way that heightens the severity and import of his illness or disability. In the quotations that follow, it is important to remember the date, 1857, and also that there was no question of political correctness – they are quoted because they illustrate an earlier awareness of disability in the healing narratives.

> It was not a case of lameness by disease or accident, but one of congenital infirmity. It was also one with which the people were familiar, from its daily exhibition in one of the most public situations of the city.
>
> (Alexander, 1857/1963: p 99)

Alexander may be forgiven for stressing the congenital infirmity as being an added sign of the greatness of the name of Jesus in effecting a miracle by Peter and John, but the importance of recognising the social nature of this man's illness offers food for thought to the reader of this commentary.

Second, Alexander captures graphically the social situation of this man and recognizes that he cannot escape the tragic predicament of his disability by depending on charity and exploiting society's weakness. He goes on:

> The practice of placing objects of charity at the entrances of temples, both on account of the great concourse and the supposed tendency of devotional feelings to promote those of a charitable kind, was common among Jews and Gentiles, and is still kept up in some parts of the Christian world.
>
> (*ibid*, p 99)

This man was living in a symbiotic but incomplete relationship with the religious institutions of the time. His proximity to the temple allowed him a good income from his begging but he was not allowed to enter the temple because of his disability. Alexander has stressed this uneasy relationship in the centre of his commentary in ways which very few others have done. But when he comes to discuss his cure he completes the integration of the man into the religious community as a result of his cure. He may not do so with an unambiguous motive of showing how disabled people may be restored to wholeness in their relationship to society and religion but the seeds of such an argument are there and were developed by Professor MacLeod in his sermon. Alexander writes:

> We have then a regular gradation in the cure; his limbs were

strengthened; he sprang up; he walked, or in Wiclif's (*sic*) antique English, *wandered._*The mention of the fact, that he entered with them into the temple, reminds the reader that all this occurred between the arrival of the two apostles at the gate of the temple and their passage through it.

(ibid, p 104)

These three elements can be analysed in another way. The miracle begins with the medical remedy and sign of recovery. The miracle emphasizes the demeaning social status of the man and finally that he is restored to a position not only of equality with the religious worshippers but with society in general. Alexander, in common with most who preach about this miracle without truly honouring the disabled man does emphasis this restoration in the final quote from his commentary:

As if he [Peter] had said, 'this miracle was not done in a corner, but in the holy place and in the presence of the people, who distinctly saw, walking about the sacred courts, and loudly praising God for his recovery, the very man whom they had seen for many years lying daily at the entrance of that very enclosure, a cripple and a beggar.'

(ibid, p 104)

What unites this book with both the temple in 1st century Jerusalem and a 19th century commentary is the imperative to admit disabled people into the worship of the Church and to ensure that this is 'not done in a corner' but in an open and transparent way which permanently restores the excluded disabled people to the centre of many religious communities.

Why Honour Disabled People?

Jesus' mission was to proclaim his Father's Kingdom in parable, miracle and deed – deeds, like supping with sinners, which, combined with all the controversy, cost him his life on the Cross. The intellectual suffering, the social criticism and the physical pain of the passion only took on meaning in the Resurrection. Intellectual debate and social criticism may be interesting but they are not the stuff of a new and lasting religion. Therefore anything in the gospel that points towards an understanding of disability must by its very nature be rooted in the messianic message which drove Jesus inexorably towards the Cross. There are two main sources of evidence that this is precisely what the gospels contain, firstly, in the anticipated fulfilment of prophecy and, secondly, in the parables which talk of disability. In particular, the parable which was quoted at the very beginning of this book (Luke 14:15–23) paints an image of the Kingdom of God as a place where disabled people will be welcomed.

Isaiah 35: 1-6

Jesus and the apostles who wrote the gospels made such prominent use of the book of Isaiah that it is impossible to ignore the text. The most famous use of what has come to be known as proto-Isaiah, i.e. the author who wrote Isaiah chapters 1-39, is the prediction of the 'Wonderful Counsellor' in chapter 9. Actually, although chapter 9 is not our concern here it is perhaps one of the keys to the aim of Isaiah. Writing in 740 BCE, Isaiah looked back in his sermons and songs to the golden age of David and forwards to the coming of a king of equal or greater stature. Chapter 9 is broadly interpreted as prophesying the birth of Jesus but it can also be more accurately understood as bringing encouragement to the court of Israel at a time of despondency. The restoration of the perfect kingdom is the central theme of proto-Isaiah but here we have an embedded song which goes beyond the kingdom to an entirely new age where even nature is subdued to God's will as the desert and the wild animals are tamed.

> [35:1] The desert and the parched land will be glad;
> the wilderness will rejoice and blossom.
> Like the crocus, [2] it will burst into bloom;
> it will rejoice greatly and shout for joy.
> The glory of Lebanon will be given to it,
> the splendour of Carmel and Sharon;
> they will see the glory of the LORD,
> the splendour of our God.
>
> [35:3] Strengthen the feeble hands,
> steady the knees that give way;
>
> [35:4] say to those with fearful hearts,
> 'Be strong, do not fear;
> your God will come,
> he will come with vengeance;
> with divine retribution

he will come to save you.'

35:5 Then will the eyes of the blind be opened
and the ears of the deaf unstopped.

35:6 Then will the lame leap like a deer,
and the mute tongue shout for joy.
Water will gush forth in the wilderness
and streams in the desert.

This is a song which departs only briefly from God's dominion
over nature to a prophecy about disabled people in verses 5 & 6a. It
seems odd that this theme has been added to such beautiful poetry about
a completely different subject but if we look more closely we become
aware that Isaiah makes repeated reference to the blind and the deaf in
other chapters. Although it is widely accepted that Jesus understood
these verses literally and expected that in the kingdom of God which he
prophesied, disabled people would literally be cured. However, in Isaiah
all the evidence points to the prophet's liking of metaphor in dealing with
disabled people. John Hull (2001) points out that the Old Testament is
littered with examples of metaphorical allusions and even jokes about
disability. Isaiah was calling for the people to hear and understand the
Word of God and he wrote in Isaiah 29: 18:
> In that day the deaf will hear the words of the scroll,
> and out of gloom and darkness
> the eyes of the blind will see.

Clearly this verse uses deafness as an inability to hear or understand
scripture and the resultant ignorance led to darkness which was akin
to blindness. Hull quotes similar examples from most of the prophets
and from an early instance in Deuteronomy. It is inconceivable that
Jesus chose to preach in the synagogue from this song concentrating
almost entirely upon the verses about disabled people without mention
of the rest of the messianic message of the restoration of the desert.
Jesus was deliberately focussing upon disabled people and was doing
so literally. Any other interpretation of his sermon just does not make
sense. Furthermore, if we credit Jesus with a sound knowledge of all the
prophets, he would be aware that:
An even more dramatic thought is found in Micah, who suggests

that disabled people will not only be included in the community
of the returning exiles; they will be the very heart and soul of that
community.

> In that day, says the Lord,
> I will assemble the lame
> And gather those who have been driven away,
> And those whom I have afflicted.
> The lame I will make the remnant,
> And those who were cast off, a strong nation;
> And the Lord will reign over them in Mount Zion
> Now and for evermore.
> (Mic. 4: 6f)
> To some extent, the idea is that there is no limit to God's
> restoring power.. Perhaps the able-bodied people were a bit
> bothered about the long return journey, but Micah says that
> even if they were disabled, God would bring them back.
> Indeed, God prefers the lame and other people who in
> weakness and disability have been driven out, because in a
> very special way they symbolize the alienated and oppressed
> people whom God delights to deliver.
>
> (Hull, 2001; p 122f)

Here in Micah, Hull argues, God sets out his stall as one who cares
for those who are disabled and weak and brings them back to the centre.
Jesus chose to preach from Isaiah possibly a slightly different agenda from
Micah, yet He chose to extract from Isaiah precisely the same meaning
and to back it up with the ability to heal, which was not always present
in the prophets.

Disabled people are firstly to be honoured because Jesus included
them in his mission to herald his Father's Kingdom and chose to heal
those who came to him, even if it scandalized the Pharisees and others
who could not bear to see him forgive sins or break the Sabbath in order
to exercise compassion. Jesus chose to preach on these verses of Isaiah
because of his conviction that his ministry was complete and perfect in
its treatment of the outcast who at that time was the disabled person with
no opportunity of realising the perfection demanded by the Pharisees.

Reply to John the Baptist

Jesus also quotes proto-Isaiah when he replies to the followers
of John the Baptist as to whether he was the 'one who was to come'

or not. (Luke 7: 20) Jesus' answer is not a reading or sermon but a paraphrase of Isaiah's apocalyptic verses. Luke neatly inserts a summary of Jesus' ministry before his answer. His healing miracles are factually reported, as they are by Matthew and Mark, but Luke also reports on the preaching of the Word. At this point Luke adds that the 'good news is preached to the poor', yet once more stressing his favour to the poor who would naturally include people with disabilities. The words Jesus uses are emphatically not metaphorical, nor code as some commentators have suggested, but seem to describe the entirety of His ministry. Jesus brings his message to John's disciples to an existential climax in verse 23 when he says, 'Blessed is the man who does not fall away on account of me.' His ministry is distinctive from other rabbis in that it is vested in his *persona* and presence. Jesus declares, 'Today this scripture is fulfilled in your hearing' in either an arrogant fashion or as a statement that the priesthood of God's chosen one has arrived. Such a claim demanded a decision then and immediately – without the benefit of hindsight – of the journey to and through the cross. The mention of the 'priesthood' of Jesus moves into the realm of dogmatic interpretation and is reminiscent of Alan Lewis' characterization of how Jesus took it upon himself to forgive sins when the burden of guilt was an impediment to recovery. (See pages 33 and 92 above)

Parables – Luke 14: 15 – 23

When Jesus talks in parables he is trying to encourage people to make a decision – a decision to join him in the pursuit of his father's kingdom and to align themselves with the new teaching and fullness of life which he brought. A very few of the parables are simply descriptive of the Kingdom but the majority are calls to decision. Descriptive parables are those which liken the Kingdom to a mustard seed or yeast (Matthew 13:31-35) or when he likens the effect of discipleship to salt or light (Matthew. 5:13-16). Many of the parables which require a decision teach about the consequences of the wrong decision: the steward who hid his master's wealth away rather than using it in a productive way, or the failure of the builder to choose a suitable site for a sure foundation (Matthew 7:24-27). Jesus teaches in a strange negative kind of way. But then parables have been compared to riddles, and perhaps he is trying to make his audience think of the dire consequences of ignoring his call to the safety of his Kingdom or to the arms of the Good Shepherd. The parable quoted at the start of this book begins with a wrong decision by many – a refusal to accept an invitation to a banquet and the fabrication of excuses for not attending. Perhaps the offence lies in the excuses more than the non-attendance, putting off until tomorrow what is required today. This is a theme of Jesus' apocalyptic in Mark 13 which stresses the suddenness of the end and the necessity to prepare now rather than tomorrow. Having decided to decline the invitation to the banquet those fortunate few who had been invited are ignored whilst those of the 'streets and alleys' are invited and accepted in large numbers. It is interesting that Jesus associates disabled people with the highways and byways (the terms used in some earlier versions). To some this may be offensive, but in actual fact it is nothing more than a reflection of social reality in the time of Jesus. Those who were suffering from leprosy or were economically disadvantaged because of disability were most likely to be found in the streets and odd places where they could beg and make some kind of living. Jesus himself may have felt a solidarity with those who were homeless or transient when he said, 'Foxes have holes and birds of the air have nests, but the Son of Man has no place to lay his head'. (Matthew.8:20 & Luke 9:58)

Here at the heart of the Gospel, in the principal teaching method of Jesus, is the honouring of disabled people not as a metaphor but in reality. The others had no time to come to the banquet so Jesus turns to those who will be receptive. Having announced his mission by quoting from Isaiah chapter 35, Jesus now consummates his mission by parables and by practical healing as an act of compassion and of consistency with his teaching, but never as a bribe to trick people into accepting the Kingdom. Furthermore, there are occasions when parables and miracles intertwine as Jesus teaches when he heals. He teaches about the proper use of the Sabbath when he heals the man with the withered hand. (Matthew 12: 9-10) He teaches about the true meaning of sin when he disassociates it from disability and shows the meaning of faith when such is declared by either the person being healed or by relatives and supporters. There is no way of escaping the conclusion that the good news which Jesus brings to the poor is concealed from the wise and foolish. It is impossible not to acknowledge that Jesus had a concern for disabled people and reflected it in his ministry.

The Gospel Message

If Jesus invited disabled people to the banquet and if he healed them because it was part of the expectation of the work of the Messiah, how much further must we go to justify his choice? There is a great corpus of literature which discusses the bias Jesus had for the poor and how uncomfortable the Gospel is for those who are affluent. This may or may not be the case but whether Jesus had a bias for the poor or disabled people or any other group for that matter still leaves us with the fact that Jesus demanded a decision. He is quite judgemental in his parables about those who make the wrong decision and is quite clear in his teaching that he upholds the Old Testament injunctions to

> Dt 24:18 Remember that you were slaves in Egypt and the LORD your God redeemed you from there. That is why I command you to do this.
> Dt 24:19 When you are harvesting in your field and you overlook a sheaf, do not go back to get it. Leave it for the alien, the fatherless and the widow, so that the LORD your God may bless you in all the work of your hands.
> Dt 24:20 When you beat the olives from your trees, do not go over the branches a second time. Leave what remains for the alien, the fatherless and the widow.
> Dt 24:21 When you harvest the grapes in your vineyard, do not go over the vines again. Leave what remains for the alien, the fatherless and the widow.

(Deut. 24: 18 – 21)

Deuteronomic law demanded that the Jews showed the same respect for the unfortunate and for the stranger as they would have wanted when they were strangers and downtrodden in Egypt before the exodus. Jesus insisted on no less but recognized that the stranger, the poor and by implication disabled people could most effectively be helped if they made a decision to accept it in the fullness of their humanity. Within the matter of choice there is a paradox. Jesus did not require a declaration of faith before healing anyone, practically every commentator is agreed on this. Yet in the parable of the banquet it is fairly obvious that when they were invited disabled people did accept the invitation, but the actual decision was taken by the host to extend that invitation. Therein lies the paradox; disabled people have not chosen to be disabled nor have they any rational reason for welcoming their situation, yet

Jesus expects his followers – the Church – to accommodate them at the banquet which means around the Lord's Table, in Baptism and service. Many believing disabled people have been burdened by the expectation that their faith must be extraordinarily strong in the face of assumed suffering and opposition, yet Jesus is not measuring the quality of their faith but rather the quality of the welcome they receive.

Wilkinson is absolutely correct, despite the reservation we have about his medical interpretations of miracles, in associating Jesus' teaching on healing with the qualities of those mentioned in the Beatitudes and with the parable of the Good Shepherd in the Gospel of John. Jesus suggested in both that the people who had the qualities required for the Kingdom were often unaware of having them but that the cultivation of these qualities was important in a society which was not going to recognize them. To the bad shepherd lost sheep were worthless and he would cut his losses but the Good Shepherd of Jesus searched high and low for them. (See p 152ff above) In Matthew, Jesus twice mentions 'lost sheep' – Matt. 10:4 – 6 and 15:24. Whilst the whole matter takes greater prominence in the parable of the shepherd searching for one lost sheep:

> [4] 'Suppose one of you has a hundred sheep and loses one of them. Does he not leave the ninety-nine in the open country and go after the lost sheep until he finds it? [6] and goes home. Then he calls his friends and neighbours together and says, 'Rejoice with me; I have found my lost sheep.'
>
> (Matt. 15: 4-6)

Pilch describes Jesus as a healer/teacher in the sense that he not only offers healing but he teaches in such a way that people understand their illness and develop a new attitude towards it. This thesis of Pilch can be overplayed and it is more sensible to acknowledge that Jesus healed and that he taught about the significance of his healings. At times these came together when he spoke of disability in his miracles and confronted his audience with a choice either to accept or to reject his call to compassion towards and inclusion of the marginalized in his Father's Kingdom. The idea of a healing narrative is good as long as it is acknowledged that it must come to an end at some time. Pilch seems to suggest that Jesus altered the course of healing narratives rather than offering an end to the sickness (*sic*) of the person towards whom his compassion had been extended.

Three miracles are now going to be examined in order to highlight ways in which the integrity of Jesus can be maintained as the heart of the Gospel whilst presenting a people-centred approach which does not allow us to forget that the disabled person at the centre of the miracle was human with a story of suffering to tell. The position of people-centred approach was illustrated in Figure 1 on page 25 above and gives us guidance as to how to approach the disabled person as a subject and not an object, as Alexander showed in his treatment of the lame beggar at the Golden Gate in the first part of this chapter. The miracles which have been chosen are not the usual ones within disabled literature, not least because of their brevity, but they highlight some of the issues discussed in previous chapters.

Three Miracles

The Man with the Withered Hand

> Mt 12:9 Going on from that place, he went into their synagogue, 10 and a man with a shrivelled hand was there. Looking for a reason to accuse Jesus, they asked him, 'Is it lawful to heal on the Sabbath?'
> Mt 12:11 He said to them, 'If any of you has a sheep and it falls into a pit on the Sabbath, will you not take hold of it and lift it out? 12 How much more valuable is a man than a sheep! Therefore it is lawful to do good on the Sabbath.'
> Mt 12:13 Then he said to the man, 'Stretch out your hand.' So he stretched it out and it was completely restored, just as sound as the other. 14 But the Pharisees went out and plotted how they might kill Jesus.

To most commentators this miracle has been reported to illustrate the lordship of Jesus over everything including the Sabbath. The Pharisees in the synagogue believed fervently in the observance of the Sabbath and would have only broken it under very strict terms to care for the sick in situations of life and death. Marx (2000) has shown how circumscribed the rules for breaking the Sabbath to help disabled people are under Halahkic Law even to this day, and what the consequences are for orthodox Jews when confronted with the problems posed by disability. It is a reasonable assumption that Jesus was doing something quite radical by healing this man. He had broken the Sabbath before, such as when he and his disciples ate grain as they walked through the field. The difference there was that Jesus had a great deal of backing in the Old Testament – in the Torah – for this small act not of defiance but rather for its inconsequence. However, the story is about a man who had lost his status and possibly ability to work because of the paralysis in one hand. Pilch says that this type of impairment was regarded as an activity limiting sickness and along with many others quotes one of the apocryphal Gospels which says that he was a stone mason who had no possibility of working without his right hand. This begins to give humanity to this man and shows how vital a healing was in the circumstances. He had no work, no income and possibly strained relations with his family and with the synagogue. Whilst we may wonder at the courage of Jesus to heal on the Sabbath, we must also wonder at the consequences for this man's future life. He has been found in the synagogue and is therefore probably a man of faith, and he may only have suffered his injury fairly recently because he still remains part of acceptable society. This might explain why Jesus asks if he wishes to be healed.

Very shortly afterwards, almost in the same breath, Jesus starts to teach. The Parable of the Lost Sheep has already been told in this chapter but now in context it is possible to see what Jesus is doing. Fundamentally the parable asks whether people are prepared to make the decision to welcome disabled people into their heart even on the Sabbath during worship. Jesus is asking them to make an extra effort to understand compassion in its proper religious context and also to accept that this man has a right to have his need met now, and not tomorrow or the next day. The sheep might well be dead by tomorrow; this man would not be returning to work tomorrow after the Sabbath. If we look at the parallel versions of this miracle, it becomes obvious that Jesus always reflected upon the situation. In Matthew, he relates his concern in a parable; in Mark his anger is vented on those who wished to trick him or criticize him for this act of compassion on the Sabbath;-

> Mk 3:5 He looked around at them in anger and, deeply distressed at their stubborn hearts, said to the man, 'Stretch out your hand.' He stretched it out, and his hand was completely restored. 6 Then the Pharisees went out and began to plot with the Herodians how they might kill Jesus.

How many times have disabled people been frustrated by the inability of church authorities to accommodate them? All the literature about reforming church practice to make it more accessible to people with disabilities would be unnecessary if the plotters in this miracle had learnt their lesson from Jesus and realized that closed political machinations were not part of God's Will. There is a sense in which the needs of disabled people are exceedingly threatening to churches. The DDA imposes upon them enormous financial obligations which many congregations can scarcely meet. Fabric funds can hardly cover the cost to the repairs to the roof, let alone providing access up steps which the Victorians built confident in the knowledge that their sick and disabled were safe at home and likely to remain so. The politics of gaining access is going to require the same insight as Jesus showed; he did not condemn the Pharisees but was angry. Much of the politics of disabled people is based on anger and negativity and Jesus showed that neither eventually achieve any goal. Out of this one small miracle recorded in a brief text it is possible to draw all these points which give the man a role and personality whilst at the same time giving the onlooker choices – choices as to whether to follow Jesus and the opportunity to make decisions about the future treatment of those less fortunate than themselves.

The Healing of Leprosy

Mt 8:2 A man with leprosy came and knelt before him and said, 'Lord, if you are willing, you can make me clean.'

Mt 8:3 Jesus reached out his hand and touched the man. 'I am willing,' he said. 'Be clean!' Immediately he was cured of his leprosy.

Mt 8:4 Then Jesus said to him, 'See that you don't tell anyone. But go, show yourself to the priest and offer the gift Moses commanded, as a testimony to them.'

People with leprosy or Hansen's disease have suffered greatly over many centuries since they were labelled 'unclean' in the gospels and separated from the rest of society. We now know that leprosy is not contagious in any way, and even if untreated it still takes several years for disfigurements to appear. However, throughout most of the world's lepers live in closed communities and many build their own culture up in opposition to the prevailing norms of society. Almost every commentator, and even the annotations to study Bibles, accept that the word leprosy actually referred to various skin diseases including 'psoriasis, seborrhoeic dermatitis, patchy eczema, tinea, favus, etc..' (Pilch, 2000; p 40) Miracles involving lepers were different from the other miracles in that Jesus was not healing incurable diseases in this instance but was applying understanding to conditions which could either be cured or improved. Some have suggested that this was the only true example of illness. Anyone who has had mild psoriasis will know that salt sea water can work wonders. In the Old Testament we have the example of Naaman being cured by the waters of the Jordan. This may have seemed to be a miracle but it can also be understood in a commonsensical way. (2 Kings 5:9 – 15) Pilch has suggested that people with skin diseases actually conspired to put Jesus on the spot by approaching him so often during his ministry. (Pilch, 2000; p 69)

Many things can be illustrated by studying these healing miracles, but it is worth concentrating on the way Jesus circumvented what we would now call the social model of disability. People were considered 'unclean' whenever they had open wounds, discharges or any sexual fluid upon them. The Book of Numbers prescribes a period of seven days quarantine for most of these defilements. Whatever the reasoning behind the prescriptions, they made a great deal of sense in many instances particularly those prescriptions concerning childbirth and menstruation, which probably provided a natural birth control without people realising. In the case of skin disease, there was no doubt a great fear of it and a desire not only to see it cured but to get rid of the contiguous clothing or matted hair. In a close knit society it was possible to police these regulations although it has been suggested that at the time of Jesus many of the regulations regarding skin diseases had been devolved to Rabbis who then asked the person to report to the Priest. If this is so Matthew 8:4 illustrates this procedure well and legitimates Jesus' role as a Rabbi and makes it clear that he does not exceed his authority beyond the norms of the time. However, other Rabbis may have been reluctant to be come involved in such practices and the text shows that Jesus took the sufferer's hand, which might have had the same effect as Princess Diana's first handshake on camera with the victim of AIDS. The Book of Numbers prescribed rituals which must have been very demanding and time consuming and Jesus appears to have cut that time considerably and lessened the impact of the rituals. There are many disabled people who have gone through innumerable medical tests in order to reach a diagnosis of either their impairment or something related to it. The medical model of disability has sapped the resilience of many a disabled person and has frequently caused them frustration and anger. Many of these tests are associated with different levels of humiliation, with a resentment at the intrusiveness of the procedures and even of the number of doctors and students viewing patients at their most vulnerable. When Jesus healed a 'leper', he showed the same awareness of the frustration of whatever the skin disease might have been as a sensitive doctor of today might show. Numbers prescribe rituals which both had these qualities of humiliation and personal costliness when it came to cleansing men in particular. Feminists might argue that women were likewise humiliated, but in the context of a simple pastoral society they were better protected.

> The man who is clean is to sprinkle the unclean person on the third and seventh days, and on the seventh day he is to purify him. The person being cleansed must wash his clothes and bathe with water, and that evening he will be clean.
> (Numbers 19:19)

Deuteronomy has similar prescriptions but exacerbates the whole issue into a cult by suggesting that people who were 'unclean' were by implication also unholy. Deuteronomy appeared as a book around the same time that Ezra was seeking to purify the Jewish observance of both the law and their religion. His desire was to produce a people whose perfection mirrored in some measure the perfection of God and much of the statutes about health, disfigurement and even divorce stemmed from this period. Sarah Melcher (1998) uses semiotics, or the science of signs, to illustrate how the Deuteronomic code used symbols of opposites to draw up a long series of clean and unclean food, bodily parts or disfigurements of the body. This method was alluded to in the first chapter (*see page 20 above*), and now we can see how Jesus overrode these symbols by showing people with skin diseases how they could be made clean in a society which was regressing into the conservatism of Ezra. Ezra's cry could be characterized as, 'Be ye holy'; the Pharisees were now calling, 'Be ye separate' – separate by observing all the statutes which distinguished a member of the Jewish faith from the morally suspect and inferior Romans.

The main point to come out of these miracles is that Jesus applied commonsense at all times and did not inflict the greater suffering of a cultic society on to people who were suffering enough already. The message which this offers to us is that the Church must now demolish the barriers to disabled people. These have usually been erected by a collective prejudice which can sometimes be cultivated in the narrow confines of a Christian community which does not reach out to people who are different but have no need to be excluded. The treatment of skin diseases was relatively easy but when Jesus came to treat people with lasting impairments the cost to him was even greater and the rewards to those he ministered to were much, much richer.

Familial Carers

Mk 9:17 A man in the crowd answered, "Teacher, I brought you my son, who is possessed by a spirit that has robbed him of speech. 18 Whenever it seizes him, it throws him to the ground. He foams at the mouth, gnashes his teeth and becomes rigid. I asked your disciples to drive out the spirit, but they could not."

Mk 9:19 "O unbelieving generation," Jesus replied, "how long shall I stay with you? How long shall I put up with you? Bring the boy to me."

Mk 9:20 So they brought him. When the spirit saw Jesus, it immediately threw the boy into a convulsion. He fell to the ground and rolled around, foaming at the mouth.

Mk 9:21 Jesus asked the boy's father, "How long has he been like this?" "From childhood," he answered. 22 "It has often thrown him into fire or water to kill him. But if you can do anything, take pity on us and help us."

Mk 9:23 " 'If you can'?" said Jesus. "Everything is possible for him who believes."

Mk 9:24 Immediately the boy's father exclaimed, "I do believe; help me overcome my unbelief!"

Mk 9:25 When Jesus saw that a crowd was running to the scene, he rebuked the evil spirit. "You deaf and mute spirit," he said, "I command you, come out of him and never enter him again."

Mk 9:26 The spirit shrieked, convulsed him violently and came out. The boy looked so much like a corpse that many said, "He's dead." 27 But Jesus took him by the hand and lifted him to his feet, and he stood up.

The relationship between disabled people and their families has always been a complicated one and not least because very often disabled people do not perceive any problem at all. This is perhaps understandable; does any child fully appreciate a parent's problem or concerns? In the case of a family with a disabled child there are many worries which beset parents about that child's future; what care they will receive and what quality of life which they can expect. Many parents worry about the likelihood of improvements and the success of medical intervention to bring about such improvements. Very often they are wedded to the medical model of disability and are convinced that surgery and physiotherapy can produce results which very often the children may not want. As the children grow into adulthood, those who become involved with the disability movement tend to scoff at the medical model of disability and place an unrealistic 'faith' in the social model of disability. That not withstanding, they usually have a more realistic assessment of their needs than their parents. This statement does not apply to people with profound learning difficulties who tend to be neglected by all and the disability movement in particular. These people do not have a voice and rely upon the voice of their parents and family to secure their rights in a society dominated by a vociferous minority of articulate disabled people. In Scotland, such disabled people were recently given rights by the first Act of the new Scottish Parliament, namely *The Adults with Incapacity Act (Scotland)*, which seeks to ensure that every decision made on behalf of such a disabled person will reflect their own interest and wishes as far as they are known. The important point to note in all this discussion is that there is a tension between a person with a disability and those in his family who care for him.

Jesus displayed an awareness of the difference in attitude between someone who was suffering a chronic illness and those who cared for them. This is not to say that he had prior knowledge of the debate around the social model of disability, but that he had different expectations for each group. Jesus healed out of compassion and he never turned anyone away because of lack of faith. Yes, he was disappointed by the 'lepers' who did not return but he did not condemn their lack of faith but rejoiced at the one who returned. (Luke 17:17) He was similarly moved by the faith of friends and carers as when four men lowered a paralytic through the roof into the house into which he was staying. However, on many other occasions he condemned the lack of faith which a carer had and was quite sharp at expressions of doubt. The passage quoted above is a good example. The father had gone out of his way to bring his son who was deaf and mute to be healed by Jesus. In verses 17 – 19 we witness a dialogue between Jesus, the father and the audience of which he may have been considered to be part. Jesus makes it clear that those who brought the boy belonged to a faithless generation and he almost grudgingly took the boy and healed him. This type of relationship to a carer occurs elsewhere in the Gospels. Jesus is short with Martha and Mary when they chide him for not being present when Lazarus died – John may well have built the example in, in order to give context to Jesus' declaration;-

> Jn 11:25 Jesus said to her, "I am the resurrection and the life. He who believes in me will live, even though he dies;
> Jn 11:26 and whoever lives and believes in me will never die. Do you believe this?"

He praised the faith of both the Syrophoenician woman for the humility and realism with which she expressed her care for her daughter who was ill (Matthew. 7:24 – 30); and likewise the Centurion who sought him out to cure his servant (Matthew. 8:5 – 13). In both these cases the mother and the centurion spoke with great humility when describing their faith in rather obtuse ways which touched Jesus greatly. Relatives and carers must therefore be in a different category from those who actually suffer. Jesus is looking for faith and finds it in the responses of the people who come. The faith is in the person of Jesus and in his ministry which puts sin into perspective and gets rid of guilt, makes demons totally submissive and gives a message to society as a whole that those who are oppressed, as disabled people are, are to be welcomed back into the mainstream of society. In the interim, Jesus also demolishes all the rituals which have caused so much trouble to those who are disabled in first century society and earlier.

What can carers learn from Jesus today? The obvious answer is a lot of platitudes which will neither serve the Church nor indeed this author. It does not even behove anyone to quote Jesus' saying about worry – 'Therefore do not worry about tomorrow, for tomorrow will worry about itself. Each day has enough trouble of its own.' (Matthew 6:34) There is another and perhaps wiser interpretation which may be based upon a modern case study, that of the Peto Institute. To this day this institute is hailed as magnificent by parents of children with cerebral palsy and spina bifida and decried by the adult disabled movement. Dr. András Petö established an institute in 1945 in Budapest which by the

1950's became the *András Petö Institute for Conductive Education of the Motor Disabled and Conductors' College.* Since that time it has offered to children the opportunity to gain the four basic skills of walking, dexterity, speech and personal hygiene by offering intensive one-to-one therapy over a sustained number of hours every day, the treatment continuing during the night on specially constructed beds. It offers the prospect of normality to children of parents who believe that these four basic skills are vital to their children's future life. The Peto Institute takes children from all over the world and until Britain established its own centres in Birmingham and in Scotland, parents raised vast sums of money to send their children privately to Budapest. The popularity of the Institute was no doubt enhanced by the refusal of charities such as *Scope* and *Capability Scotland* to place the same emphasis on and to meet the prohibitive costs of training and employing 'conductors' when other techniques could reach the needs of even more disabled children who not only suffered from cerebral palsy but had profound cognitive difficulties as well. The Institute brought hope to parents who began to see their children walking and who were unaware of the fact that evidence now shows that people with cerebral palsy tend to take to a wheelchair in their late forties or fifties in any case. These parents were asking for solutions offered by the medical model of disability which can be equated to the signs and portents which Jesus so readily condemned as signs of a faithless generation. When Vic Finkelstein visited the Institute in 1988 he observed that it was an institute that put the entire onus on the child to adjust to society as it is today – barriers and all, not about making adjustments in society. Finkelstein wrote:

> ...the central philosophy of the institution is so deeply rooted in normative assumptions, it is educational goals that become subverted and medicalized. If schooling is about preparing children for life as adults in society then the way that this world is perceived will influence the character of education. Clearly the assumption behind the 'Peto Institute' is that society is fixed, it is for able-bodied people, and the task of 'conductive education' is to fit disabled children into this world. As I listened to these views I felt increasingly disabled! This was not just an example of the inappropriate application of the medical model of disability corrupting the potential of education to enlighten but a stagnant view of the very nature

of society and human potential. The whole history of human
endeavour to alter and change the world we live in was being
reduced to the goal of 'normality'. What a triumph for the
medical model of disability and what a denial of the right of
disabled people to make their mark on the world that we all
live in.

(Finkelstein, 1990: p 2 [electronic version])

The medical model of disability is characterized by a dependence
on other people to solve problems related to disability. These problems
are usually couched in the language of normality, namely that people
with disabilities should appear and behave as normally as possible.
Sometimes children and adults do show signs of 'cures' in that they
overcome disabilities which might otherwise impede a 'normal' life.
Jesus asked for faith in order that someone with an impairment could
be accepted back into society as they were and offered a new start.
The healing of the woman with a haemorrhage (Matthew 9: 20 – 22)
illustrates the argument well. She had sought the advice of physicians,
and presumably other women, over a long period of time without
success. Doctors practiced at that time purely on a theoretical basis
with no practical examination of the patient or hands-on treatment
and presumably all their deliberations had failed this woman, as indeed
the medical model of disability has failed so many disabled people. But
her faith, or rather her willingness to see the personality of Jesus, gave
her power to overcome the symptoms of her ailment. She was 'cured'
by her proactively seeking Jesus. Whilst parents often want to see their
children overcome tremendously distressing symptoms, their reliance
on the medical profession can sometimes take away the spontaneity of
learning to adapt and to grow with a disability in a society which can
learn to accommodate it.

Christological Principles Revisited

The three miracles which have just been examined, four if you
include the healing at the Golden Gate, have been designed to honour
the disabled person who is featured in the story whilst recognising
that the story is principally about Jesus. He healed on the Sabbath, he
circumvented ancient ritual in the case of 'lepers' and he demanded
that parents showed hope which was inevitably tied up with faith. His
healing was not revolutionary as we would now think of a new cure but

it was based on a clear conviction that the Kingdom has no space for the fears and anxieties which held so many people back from a fuller life. In chapter four, such principles were laid out on page 111ff above in such a way that Jesus remained the central figure in all the healing miracles. But the miracles only took on life and a resonance of truth when it was seen that someone had been freed from the dread of demons or the curse of being unclean by an application of commonsense towards their illness. Jesus met people where they were and by offering a touching hand, which no physician would do, he crossed the barriers which the rest of society had erected. The followers of Jesus today, the Church, has to reach across these barriers now, not simply by building ramps and printing in Braille, but by actually offering an honoured place to disabled people as Jesus did in the heralding of his Father's Kingdom.

Conclusion

Disability is Natural

The purpose of this conclusion is to reflect briefly on the importance of the themes raised in this book.

Every human being represents the pinnacle of God's creation, but we are creatures who are fragile and whilst God allows this fragility he has not automatically taught us how to live with it. The majority of people fear the breakdown of their bodies almost as much as they fear death, perhaps even more so for some. An unshakeable faith in an after-life helps us to come to terms with death but not with disability. Each one of us remains at the mercy of providence as to how we inherit a body and how its complete functioning may be snatched from us by a freak accident, a gene or the bestial violence of war or criminal activity. It is absolutely natural to wish away disability and to seek any remedy which would offer a cure. Throughout the ages we have accepted cures from many sources – physicians, magicians and holy men. Jesus ranks above all these because his healings betray neither self-aggrandizement nor answers which are beyond our understanding. The healing miracles of Jesus are firmly rooted in the traditions of his faith, Judaism, and his conviction that he had a ministry to show how these traditions could be more humanly understood and humanely applied to those who suffered outwith the parameters of the coming Kingdom. Such is our dislike of suffering that we have applied our understanding of the life of Jesus to search for an escape from our fragility. We are led far beyond the miracles themselves to a conviction that the life which Jesus reveals opens the door to a new humanity which might be devoid of the worst aspects of our physical suffering.

Whenever we do not like something we reflect it in our language. This is the essence of swearing, of bad language. There is something satisfying in finding short ways of dismissing unpleasant aspects of life in a short sharp expletive. This becomes much more serious however when we build up whole vocabularies to denigrate subjects or groups of people who cause us to fear or even to hate. This is the essence of disablist language. It allows us to describe our feelings about disability without really thinking about them, as is also the case with racist or sexist language. The easiest way to achieve a map within our minds of something like disability is to symbolize everything in terms of opposites, like normal/abnormal or all the examples that have been offered in the earlier chapters relating to the false inheritance of Christianity. If these patterns cannot be broken, there remains a simplistic misunderstanding of disability which pervades society and likewise the Church. This is why it has been repeatedly stressed that Jesus broke down these patterns and introduced a new understanding. Sin, for instance, is no longer one end of a spectrum where non-disabled people are sinless but Jesus taught that sin had to be dynamically understood as the source of the exclusion of disabled people from society and also from the religious practice of the time. The need to accept the common sense understanding of Jesus still remains at the heart of the Church's proclamation of the Word, but over the centuries theologians and ministers have been trained, in some of the traditions that have been examined, to look, for instance, for normality when it does not exist.

This was the central philosophical issue which faced thinkers like David Hume. Did Jesus not restore normality? If it is claimed that he did, how can we have any credence in miracles which are seldom observed and are contrary to the normal laws of nature. Such philosophical thinking did tremendous harm to religion as a whole and it set back our understanding of disability even further by labelling it 'abnormal'. There is nothing abnormal about disability: it has natural causes, natural remedies and there are natural ways of circumventing the barriers which society erects to emphasize the restrictions facing people with disabilities. It may have seemed odd to digress into modern physics and to risk falling into the same optimistic trap of those who think that there are now no laws of nature and that anything is possible. What was argued was that scientists and philosophers can no longer view the world as a clockwork watch, but must rather recognize that there are powerful and different forces working for good in the world and that disabled people represent one such force. If miracles occur, it is not to rectify an abnormality but to offer a greater opportunity to develop or aspire to the new humanity which Christ offers.

All the rest of the book follows from this dislike of irregularity. If the miracles can be explained away or if they can be shown to be absolutely natural forms of healing, they no longer constitute an embarrassment to the modern mind. This is precisely what form criticism and more radical criticism permitted, and it resulted in a generation of preachers and teachers who could ignore disabled people from the pulpit because the miracles were totally irrelevant compared to the preaching about the underlying kerygma of the Christ who offered a new and exciting interpretation of God's will.

What this book has tried to stress is that the situation is precisely the opposite. Jesus wanted to place disabled people at the heart of his Gospel. They were people who were excluded from God's Kingdom but were most deserving of a place within it. He could survey the whole of Jewish scripture and find that although disabled people had been excluded at all levels of society and of the cult, the prophets looked to their restoration as if they knew of the affront caused by their exclusion. As Jesus approached what he considered to be the last days, he offered them integration into the dawning Kingdom which lesser prophets had failed to realize. Thus, this central message: disability is normal and acceptable to God, but only if an effort is made to overcome the barriers to the integration of those so inflicted.

So is Disability a Gift?

Disability unattended is a curse. There is no possible way of telling someone who is in pain or who feels that life is pointless that the situation is a gift from God. Such an assertion is an insult to God and to the person as well. To God, it suggests that he is cruel and uncaring; to a human being with a disability, it suggests that they should respond to a trite and facile answer. Many a disabled person has cried, 'My God, My God why have you forsaken me?' (Matthew 27: 45) They have cried it in situations of enormous adversity but also in the face of the very tiny frustrations of everyday life. These words were not originally Jesus' but David's. Jesus was reciting the psalms on the cross, showing the same despair as many a disabled person, but David wrote these words in Psalm 22 verse 1 when he was in dark despair himself. He suffered from mental illness and sought comfort in his writing and his music (Hull, 2001). Despite all his good fortune and high rank, David suffered the pangs of unattended disability.

The question of disability as a gift is probably more vexing than any other question in this book. It is simply not possible to believe in a loving God who subjects people to suffering and the indignities of disability, or who subjects parents and families to the burdens and emotional trauma of caring for someone who has been born with a disability or struck down by an inexplicable accident. Disability in this context is emphatically not a gift from God but is a natural occurrence which we would prefer not have to deal with and would either rather ignore or suffer in silence. This is the central tragedy of a church which excludes disabled people not only from their midst but from the heart of their activities. If the healing miracles of Jesus have any meaning at all it is that disabled people can be brought out of their loneliness and despair and offered a richer and more fulfilling future. It is in this sense that disability is a gift from God, because when people are released to offer themselves in service to humanity, or, if they choose, to the church, they bring gifts which have burgeoned forth in the light of a new day. Disability unattended, captive, can be understood by a botanical metaphor just as St Paul used the dying and subsequent germination of a seed in 1st Corinthians 15: 37:

> When you sow, you do not plant the body that will be, but
> just a seed, perhaps of wheat or of something else.

Paul then climaxes his illustration of the death and resurrection of Christ and his believers in 1st Corinthians 15: 42 – 44:

> The body that is sown is perishable, it is raised imperishable;
> 43 it is sown in dishonour [an unfortunate translation of
> ajtimiva which in the next couplet is rendered as 'weakness'],
> it is raised in glory; it is sown in weakness, it is raised in power;
> 44 it is sown a natural body, it is raised a spiritual body.

A bulb kept dry and in the dark over the summer will lie full of energy and nutrition ready to burst forth into leaves and a flower if given water and soil to allow it to grow. The gift of God is there in its latent state but it remains absolutely hopeless and helpless. It is only with tender planting and care that it comes to its full glory and fully illustrates God's gifts for all to see. The same holds for disabled people who can grow and offer their skills if they are afforded the opportunity as they were by Jesus in Palestine, or as they should by society and by the Church today. That is when the true miracle of healing becomes a reality in today's society.

Did Jesus Really Heal?

Most books on miracles end with this obligatory question and this will be no exception. The journey of this author is from agnosticism to belief that Jesus did cure, but that the method of that curing remains clouded in mystery because we do not have the means to understand the true nature of the illnesses or disabilities that he encountered, nor do we have any warrant to impose our own understanding on the miracles which we can read of in the gospels. However, within these restrictions it is possible to believe that Jesus was a healer and that he had a genius for illustrating the religious and social significance of the healings which he undertook. Two books where particularly interesting in leading to this conclusion.

Whilst researching healing on Iona, I came across a book by a journalist from Canada who had become an Anglican priest. The book was riveting like few others which made up the research. Its inclusion was an accident – Tom Harpur had included a biographical chapter on a healer who had influenced George Macleod in the 1930s. Godfrey Mowatt had had psychic experiences, in common with many healers, which led him to become convinced that he had the power to heal and that he should devote his talents to the service of the Church of England and beyond. Thus, he came to Iona. He was blind and was therefore a disabled person but he never appeared to offer great help to disabled people. Harpur ends his book by affirming that Jesus was a healer and that he employed a talent which all but the few like Mowatt have forgotten in their ministry. The upshot of all the reading of his book was that I inherited an unshakeable belief that Jesus was a healer and that no amount of analysis of the Gospels could detract from this fact. In the course of this book it has become obvious that very few scholars can emphatically deny the healings of Jesus, with the possible exception of David Hume who did so after much agonising and very timidly. All the other scholars who have been examined have shown little desire to label the healings as a falsehood although many have qualified their positions until they have suffered 'death by a thousand qualifications'. It is safer and better simply to acknowledge that Jesus was a healer and to develop from that starting position. This may be done in many ways but here the conviction that Jesus had a concern for those who were outcast or marginalized is proven beyond doubt. It is at this point that his healing power becomes relevant to people with disabilities and transforms interesting stories of healing into a mandate for the Church in the 21st century.

Jesus appreciated that people who were sick were excluded from his society. It is safer to talk of his concerns about inclusion rather than his concern with disability because it has been shown that disability is a very modern social construct which could not possibly have been understood at the time of Jesus. But what was understood was that people were excluded from intimacy, religion and the opportunity to make a living by their disabilities, which almost certainly caused offence to the Jewish religion of the time. Jesus took it upon himself to teach about inclusion whilst he healed in an attempt to show that the hope of the Jewish people was not vain that sickness and illness could be eradicated from God's coming kingdom. It had been vital in an earlier age to rid society of everything that was different – everything from mixed marriages to race, and from food to bodies which carried marks of difference. None of these could be tolerated in Jewish society, particularly at the time of Ezra. Now Jesus was restoring the balance, as St Paul would with regard to other differences.

A second book has been of seminal importance in developing a picture of Jesus as the healer who had a vision of God's inclusion kingdom. Consider the following from Eric Eve:

> Firstly, healing and exorcism were, perhaps, the only type of miracles available to Jesus. Secondly, he was nevertheless an extraordinary gifted healer and exorcist who, even more than Pedrito Jaramillo, excelled among the folk-healers of his time. Thirdly, he understood this gift as an even greater empowerment by God's spirit than that of the great prophets of old. This experience of divine empowerment (coupled with a special sense of a close relationship with God) prompted Jesus to reinterpret, combine and transform Jewish traditions. He then understood his individual acts of healing and exorcism as prophetic signs, not only of the imminence of the Kingdom of God, but of its nature.
>
> (Eve, 2002:p 380)

Healing miracles around the time of Jesus tended to be characterized by maliciousness or vindictiveness, self-aggrandizing magic, or were concerned with very narrow and easily handled problems. Jesus chose to tackle difficult problems which had meanings far beyond the sufferings of the individual and went to the heart of the narrow religion of the Pharisees who were clinging to past traditions in much the same way as many resist modernization today. Jesus performed healing miracles with humility and a deep concern for the individual before him. He did so with risk to himself because by tackling the issues of demon possession and sin he inevitably offended the Pharisees and others who were content with what they had and to which they could cling. Jesus said 'no' to their conformity and 'yes' to the inclusion of others at the centre of lives developing around the growing number of synagogues. Is not the situation just described somewhat like the Church of today? It is a Church which is under threat, in the UK at least, by growing secularism and new standards which demand responses which are sometimes unpalatable. The call still goes out for an understanding of healing but very often it is not combined with a call to make social inclusion a major issue. The Gospels make it plain that the teaching of Jesus and the acts of Jesus are inseparable, and that those who believe and preach about healing miracles must also consider the marvellous opportunities Jesus gave to people to regain inclusion whose lives may well have been blighted by the exclusion which others imposed.

References

Abberley, P., 1987, The Concept of Oppression and the Development of a Social Theory of Disability, *Disability, Handicap and Society*, Vol. 2 No. 1.

Adams, M. M., 1999, *What Sort of Human Nature? : Medieval Philosophy & the Systematics of Christology,* Marquette University Press, Milwaukee.

Alexander, J. A., 1857/1963, *The Acts of the Apostles,* Banner of Truth, London.

Allen, E. A., 1995, Wholeness, salvation and the Christian health professional, *Ram (Ed) op cit,* Ch. 1.

Appiah-Kubi, K., 1975, The Church's Healing Ministry in Africa, *Ecumenical Review*, Vol. 27, July.

Ash, M., 1987, *New Renaissance,* Green Books, Bideford.

Barnes (Ed), C., 1999, *Exploring disability : a sociological introduction,* Polity, Oxford.

Barr, J., 1961, *The Semantics of Biblical Language,* OUP, London.

Beith, M., 1995, *Healing Threads,* Polygon, Edinburgh.

Belkin, D., 2004, Religions beginning to embrace disabled, *Boston Globe*, 23 May.

Black, K., 1996, *A Healing Homiletic,* Abington Press, Nashville.

Block, J. W., 2002, *Copious Hosting,* Continuum, New York.

Bohm, D., 1996, *Wholeness and the Implicate Order,* Routledge, London.

Bornkamm, H., 1958, *Luther's world of thought,* Concordia Pub. House, Saint Louis.

Boyer, M. W., 1958, *Luther in Protestantism today,* Association Press, New York.

Bradley (Ed), B., 1990, *Penguin Book of Hymns,* Penguin, London.

Broadie, A., 2000, *Why Scottish Philosophy Matters,* The Saltire Society, Edinburgh.

Broadie, A., 2001a, *The Scottish Enlightenment,* Birlinn, Edinburgh.

Brohn, P., 1986, *Gentle Giants,* Century Publishing, London.

Brown, M. L., 1995, *Israel's Divine Healer,* Paternoster Press, Carlisle.

Bultmann, R., 1935, *Jesus and the Word,* Ivor Nicholson and Watson, London.

Bultmann, R., 1955, *Theology of the New Testament - Vols I & II,* SCM Press, London.

Bultmann, R., 1972, *The History of the Synoptic Tradition,* Basil Blackwell, Oxford.

Burns, R. M., 1981, *The Great Debate on Miracles,* Bucknell University Press, Lewisburg.

Bury, M., 1982, Chronic illness as biographical disruption, *Sociology of Health and Illness,* No. 4.

Calvin, J., 1953, *Institutes of the Christian Religion - Volumes I & II,* James Clarke & Co., London.

Campbell and Oliver, J. & M., 1996, *Disability Politics,* Routledge, London.

Capra, F., 1975, *The Tao of Physics,* Wildwood House, London.

Capra, F., 1982, *The Turning Point,* Wildwood House, London.

Carmichael, K., 1989, Guilt and Forgiveness, *The Coracle,* Spring.

Carmichael, K., 2003, *Sin and Forgiveness,* Ashgate, Aldershot.

Cassidy, D. C., 1991, *Uncertainty,* W. H. Freeman & Co., New York.

Church of Scotland, 1994, *Book of Common Order of the Church of Scotland,* St Andrew Press, Edinburgh.

Clark, R. W., 1973, *Einstein,* Hodder and Stoughton, London.

Collins, G. Sj., 1995, *Christology: A Biblical, Historical, and Systematic Study of Jesus,* Oxford University Press, Oxford.

Corker & Shakespeare, M. & T., 2002, *Disability/Postmodernity,* Continuum, London.

Corker & Shakespeare, M. & T., 2002, Mapping the Terrain, *Corker & Shakespeare (eds), op cit.*

Costen, M., 1993, The Pilgrimage to Santiago de Compostela in Medieval Europe, *Reader & Walter (eds) op cit.*

Crossan, J. D., 1991, *The Historical Jesus: The Life of a Mediterranean Peasant,* Harper Collins, San Francisco.

Darton, R., 1968, *Mesmerism and the End of the Enlightenment in France,* Harvard U.P, Harvard.

Davidson, I., 1991, *Here and Now: An Approach to Christian Healing through Gestalt,* DLT, London.

Davidson, M. B., 1977, *"You Tell Me"*, Scottish Council for Spastics (*sic*), Edinburgh.

Davis, P., 1983, *God and the New Physics,* Penguin Books, London.

Dibelius, M., 1934, *From tradition to gospel,* Ivor Nicholson and Watson, London.

Disability Rights Advocates, 2001, *Forgotten Crimes,* Disability Rights Advocates, Oakland California.

Swain, Finkelstein, French & Oliver J., V., S. & M., *Disabling Barriers - Enabling Environments,* Sage, London.

Doty, W. G., 1983, *Letters in Primitive Christianity,* Fortress Press, Philadelphia.

Douglas, M., 1999, *Leviticus as Literature,* OUP, Oxford.

Drake, R.F., 1999, *Understanding Disability Policies,* Macmillan Press, London.

Duncan, D., 1988, *Health and Healing: A Ministry to Wholeness,* St. Andrew Press, Edinburgh.

Eareckson Tada, J., 1991, *Joni,* Marshall Pickering, London.

Early, E., 1982, The Logic of Well-Being - Therapeutic Narratives in Cairo, Egypt, *Social Science & Medicine,* 16.

Eiesland, N. L., 1994, *The disabled God : toward a liberatory theology of disability,* Abingdon Press, Nashville.

Eisland and Saliers, N. L. & D. E., 1998, *Human Disability and the Service of God,* Abington Press, Nashville.

Eve, E., 2002, *The Jewish Context of Jesus' Miracles,* Sheffield Academic Press, Sheffield.

Ferguson, R., 1988, *Chasing the Wild Goose,* Fount, Glasgow.

Ferngren, G. B., 1992, Early Christianity as a Religion of Healing, *Bulletin of the History of Medicine,* Vol. 66, No. 1.

Finkelstein, V., 1990, Conductive Education - A Tale of Two Cities, *Therapy Weekly,* Vol. 22 March.

Flanagan, S., 1989, *Hildegard of Bingen - A Visionary Life,* Routledge, London.

Flew, A., 1961, *Hume's Theory of Belief,* Routledge and Kegan Paul, London.

Foster, J., 1991, *The Immaterial Self,* Routledge, London.

Fox, M., 1985, *Illuminations of Hildegard of Bingen,* N. M. Bear & Co., Santa Fe.

Fox, M., 1993, *Original Blessing,* Bear & Co, Santa Fe.

Fraser, I. M., 1990, *Living A Countersign,* Wild Goose, Glasgow.

Frayn, M., 1998, *Copenhagen,* Methuen Drama, London.

Fritzson & Kabue, 2004, *Interpreting Disability: A Church of All and For All,* World Council of Churches, Geneva.

Fuller, R. H., 1963, *Interpreting the Miracles,* SCM, London.

Funk, R. W., 1988, The Coming Radical Reformation, *The Fourth R,* Vol. 11, No. 4.

Funk, R. W., 1996, *Honest to Jesus,* Harper Collins, San Francisco.

Funk, R. W., 1998, *The Acts of Jesus,* Harper Collins, New York.

Galloway, K., 1991, Transfigured by Ceremony, *The Coracle,* Winter.

Giddens, A., 1994, *Beyond Left and Right,* Polity, Cambridge.

Goffman, E., 1961, *Asylums,* Doubleday, Garden City, N.Y.

Graham, R., 2004, *The Great Infidel,* Tuckwell Press, East Lothian, Scotland.

Grant, C. C., 1998, Reinterpreting the Healing Narratives, *Eisland and Saliers (eds), op cit.*

Greer, P., 1995, The Aquarian Connection: Conflicting Theologies of the New Age, *Journal of Contemporary Religion,* Vol. 10, No. 2.

Griffiths, T. N., 1988, Healthy Spirituality and the Trinity-Unity Model of Man, *Holistic Medicine,* No. 3.

Haggis, T., 1994, *The Spirituality of Taizé,* Grove Books, Nottingham.

Hamilton, D., 1981, *The Healers - A History of Medicine in Scotland,* Canongate, Edinburgh.

Hancock, W. K., 1968, *Smuts: The Fields of Force 1919 -1950,* Cambridge UP, Cambridge.

Harpur, T., 1994, *The Uncommon Touch: An Investigation of Spiritual Healing,* McClelland and Stewart, Toronto.

Harris, M., 1976, History and Significance of the Emic/Etic Distinction, *Annual Review of Anthropology,* Vol. 5.

Harris, R., 1999, *Lourdes - Body and Spirit in the Secular Age,* Allen Lane, The Penguin Press, Harmondsworth.

Hauerwas, S., 1990, *Naming the Silences,* Mich : Eerdmans, Grand Rapids.

Hick, J., 1977, E*vil and the God of love,* Macmillan, London.

Horne, S., 1998, "Those Who Are Blind See", *Eisland and Saliers (eds), op cit.*

Howard, J. K., 2001, *Disease and Healing in the New Testament,* University Press of America, Lanham, Maryland.

Hufford, D. J., 1993, Epistemologies in Religious Healing, *Journal of Medicine and Philosophy,* Vol. 18, No. 2.

Hull, J. M., 1974, *Hellenistic Magic and the Synoptic Tradition,* SCM Press, London.

Hull, J. M., 1990, *Touching the Rock,* Arrow Books, London.

Hull, J. M., 2001, *In the Beginning There was Darkness,* SCM Press, London.

Hull, J. M., 2002, 'Sight to the Inly blind'? Attitudes to Blindness in the Hymnbooks, *Theology* Vol CV, no.827, September/October.

Hume, D., 1777/1902, *Enquiries concerning the Human Understanding & concerning the Principles of Morals,* Clarendon Press, Oxford.

Iona Community, 1991, *The Iona Community Worship Book,* Wild Goose Publications, Glasgow.

Jain & Tribhuwan, N. & R. D., 1996, *Mirage of Health and Development,* Vidya Nidhu, Pune, India.

John, J., 2001, *The Meaning in the Miracles,* SCM Press, London.

Keller & Keller, E. & M-L., 1969, *Miracles in Dispute,* SCM, London.

Kelsey, M. T, 1995, *Healing and Christianity,* Augsburg, Minneapolis.

Kenny (trans.), A., 1970, *Descartes: Philosophical Letters,* OUP, Oxford.

Kerr, Shakespeare & Varty, A., T. & S., 2002, *Genetic politics : from eugenics to genome,* New Clarion, Cheltenham.

Kleinman, A., 1998, *The Illness Narratives,* Basic Books, New York.

Kolbe, F.C., 1928, *A Catholic View of Holism,* MacMillan, London.

Lake, F, 1986, *Clinical Theology,* DLT, London.

Lambourne, R. A., 1963, *Community, Church and Healing,* Darton, Longman & Todd.

Lenny, J., 1993, Do Disabled People Need Counselling?, *Swain et al, op cit.*

Levin & Vanderpool, J. S. & H. Y., 1989, Is Religion Therapeutically Significant for Hypertension?, *Social Science & Medicine,* Vol. 29, No. 1.

Levin, J. S., 1994, Religion & Health: is there an association, is it valid and is it causal?, *Social Science & Medicine,* Vol. 38, No. 11.

Lewis, A., 1982, God as Cripple: Disability, Personhood and the Reign of God, *Pacific Theological Review,* Vol. XVI, No 1.

Lewis, C. S., 1947, *Miracles,* Centenary Press, London.

Lodge, D., 1995, *Therapy,* Penguin, London.

Lovelock, J., 1988, *The Ages of Gaia,* OUP, Oxford.

MacIntyre, A., 1977, Epistemological Crises, Dramatic Narrative, and the Philosophy of Science, *The Monist,* No. 60.

Mackey, J. P., 1979, *Jesus : the man and the myth,* SCM, London.

Mackie, J. L., 1982, *The Miracle of Theism,* Clarendon Press, Oxford.

MacManaway & Turcan, B. & J., 1983, *Healing: The Energy that Can Restore Health,* Thorsons, Wellingborough.

Marks, D., 1999, *Disability,* Routledge, London.

Martin, E., 1986, Divine Healing: the Christian View (Editorial), *Journal of Royal Coll. of General Practitioners,* January.

Marx, T. C., 2002, *Disability in Jewish Law,* Routledge, London.

McAll, K., 1982, *Healing the Family Tree,* SPCK, London.

McCloughry & Morris, R. & W., 2002, *Making a World of Difference,* SPCK, London.

McCreary, A., 1975, *Corrymeela - The Search for Peace,* Christian Journals, Belfast.

McFague, S., 1993, *The Body of God,* SCM, London.

McGilvray, J. C, 1981, *The Quest for Health and Wholeness,* German Institute for Medical Missions, Tübingen.

McGrath, A. E., 1990, *The Genesis of Doctrine,* Wm B Eerdmans, Grand Rapids.

McGrath, A. E., 1997, *Historical Theology,* Blackwell, Oxford.

McGrath, J. F., 2001, *John's Apologetic Christology,* Cambridge University Press, Cambridge.

Melcher, S. J., 1998, Visualising the Perfect Cult: The Priestly Rationale for Exclusion, *Eisland and Saliers (eds), op cit.*

Melinsky, M. A. H., 1968, *Healing Miracles*, Mowbray, London.

Monteith, W. G., 1987, *Disability: Faith and Acceptance*, St Andrew Press, Edinburgh.

Monteith, W. G., 1997, *Paths to Wholeness*, Unpublished PhD Thesis, University of Edinburgh.

Monteith, W. G., 2002, "Disability Movement Agendas: What's in a Word?", *Contact*, No. 136.

Mullin, R. B., 1996, *Miracles & the Modern Religious Imagination*, Yale University Press, New Haven.

Nave, O. J., c1979, *Topical Bible*, T. Nelson, Nashville.

Nolan, C., 1987, *Under the eye of the clock*, Weidenfeld and Nicolson, London.

Norris, C., 1987, *Derrida*, Fontana Press, London.

Oliver, M. J., 1999. "Capitalism, disability and ideology: A materialist critique of the Normalization principle.", First published in Flynn, R. J. and Raymond A. L., *A Quarter-Century of Normalization and Social Role Valorization: Evolution and Impact*, 1999. Internet publication URL: *http://www.independentliving.org/docs3/oliver99.pdf* .

Olkin, R., 1999, *What Psychotherapists Should Know About Disability*, Guildford Press, New York.

Pannenberg, W., 1993, *Toward a Theology of Nature*, Westminster/J. Knox Press, Louisville, KY.

Peacocke, A., 2001, *Paths from Science towards God*, Oneworld, Oxford.

Penton, J., 2001, *Widening the eye of the needle -2nd edition*, Church House Publishing, London.

Percy, M., 1992, "How to Win Congregations and Influence Them", *Modern Churchman*, Vol. VI, No. 34.

Percy, M., 1996, *Words, Wonders and Power - Understanding Contemporary Christian Fundamentalism and Revivalism*, SPCK, London.

Pilch, J. J., 1995, *The Cultural World of Jesus*, Liturgical Press, Collegeville, Min..

Pilch, J. J., 2000, *Healing in the New Testament*, Fortress Press, Minneapolis.

Pilch, J. J., 2003, J Keir Howard - *www.bookreviews.org/pdf/1502_3268.pdf, Review of Biblical Literature*.

Porter, R., 2001, *Quacks,* Tempus, Stroud.

Poynton, J. C., 1987, Smuts's Holism and Evolution Sixty Years On, *Transactions of the Royal Society of South Africa,* Vol. 46.

Rahner, K., 1975, *Theological investigations. - Vol.13,* Darton, Longman and Todd, London.

Ram (Ed), E., 1995, *Transforming Health: Christian Approaches to Healing and Wholeness,* MARC World Vision, Monrovia.

Reader & Walter (eds), I. & T., 1993, *Pilgrimage in Popular Culture,* MacMillan, London.

Reeve, D., 2002, Oppression within the counselling room, *Counselling and Psychotherapy Research,* Vol. 2, No. 1.

Remus, H., 1997, *Jesus as Healer,* Cambridge University Press, Cambridge.

Robinson, J. A. T., 1952, *The body : a study in Pauline theology,* SCM Press, London.

Russell et al (eds), R. J., 1996, *Quantum Cosmology and the Laws of Nature,* Vatican Observatory Foundation, Notre Dame, Indiana.

Sanford, A., 1947, *The Healing Light,* Arthur James, Evesham.

Sawicki, M., 1994, *Seeing the Lord,* Fortress, Minneapolis.

Schleiermacher, F., 1928, *Christian Faith,* T&T Clark, Edinburgh.

Seddon, R (ed.), 1988, *Rudolph Steiner - Essential Readings,* Crucible, Wellingborough.

Shakespeare, (ed.), T., 1998, *The Disability Reader,* Cassel, London.

Shuttleworth, R. P., 2002, Defusing the Adverse Context of Disability, *Corker & Shakespeare (eds), op cit.*

Smuts, J. C., 1927, *Holism and Evolution,* MacMillan, London.

Sölle, D., 1967, *Christ the representative,* SCM, London.

Southgate (Ed), C., 1999, *God, Humanity and the Cosmos,* T & T Clark, London.

Speck, P., 1988, *Being There - Pastoral Care in Times of Illness,* SPCK, London.

Swain, Finkelstein, French & Oliver, J., V., S. & M., 1993, *Disabling Barriers - Enabling Environments,* Sage, London.

Swinburne (ed), R., 1989, *Miracles,* Macmillan, London.

Swinburne, R., 1970, *The Concept of Miracle,* Macmillan, London.

Taylor, J. V., 1963, *The primal vision Christian presence amid African religion,* SCM, London.

Thatcher, A., 1990, *Truly a Person, Truly God,* SPCK, London.

Thorne, B., 1998, *Person-Centred Counselling and Christian Spirituality,* Whurr Publishers, London.

Thorne, B., 2003, *Infinitely Beloved,* DLT, London.

Thuillier, J., 1988, *Franz Anton Mesmer ou l'extase magnétique,* Editions Robert Laffont, Paris.

Tiffany & Ringe, F. C. & S. H., 1996, *Biblical Interpretation: A Roadmap,* Abington Press, Nashville.

Tracy, D., 1975, *Blessed Rage for Order,* Seabury Press, New York.

Tracy, D., 1990, God, Dialogue and Solidarity: A Theologian's Refrain, *The Christian Century,* No. 10.

Ulrich, I., 1990, *Hildegard of Bingen - Mystic, Healer, Companion of the Angels,* Liturgical Press.

UPIAS, 1976, *Fundamental Principles of Disability,* UPIAS, London.

Vaux, K.L., 1984, *Health & Medicine in the Reformed Tradition,* Crossroad, New York.

Wallis, R., 1992, Encounter With Healing, *I J of Alternative & Complementary Medicine,* April.

Ward, K., 1996, God as a Principle of Cosmological Explanation, *Russell et al, op cit.*

Warrington, K., 2000, *Jesus the Healer,* Paternoster Press, Carlisle.

Watson, N., 1998, Enabling Identity: Disability, Self and Citizenship, *Shakespeare (ed), op cit.*

Wilkinson, J., 1998, *The Bible and Healing,* Handsel Press Ltd, Edinburgh.

Williams, R., 2000, *On Christian Theology,* Blackwell, Oxford.

Wilson, M., 1966, *The Church is Healing,* SCM - Religious Book Club, London.

Wilson, M., 1988, *A Coat of Many Colours,* Epworth, London.

Woodcock, S., 1989, The Holistic Approach to Health, *unpublished MSc. Thesis,* Swansea University.

World Health Organization, 1948, *Basic Documents,* WHO, Geneva.

World Health Organization, 1980, International Classification of Impairments, Disabilities, and Handicaps, *WHO Papers,* Geneva.

World Health Organization, 2001, *International classification of functioning, disability, and health,* World Health Organization, Geneva.

Young, F. M., 1991, *The Making of the Creeds,* SCM Press, London.

Young, F., 1990, *Face to Face,* T & T Clark, Edinburgh.

Zola, E., 1894, *Lourdes,* Bibliothèque-Charpentier, Paris

Notes

[1] More virulent and specific opposition comes from homeopaths who believe that ailments should be treated with greatly diluted medications that mimic the symptoms.

[2] Denis Duncan was editor of the *British Weekly* for many years.

[3] The pilgrimage was in fact to Santiago de Compostela. (Costen, 1993)

[4] In the UK, the term "carers" denotes people who offer care because of an emotional bond usually for little or no financial recompense. There are, in fact, national associations of carers which offer mutual support and encouragement. Professional care-givers are distinguished by a variety of nomenclatures. This may contrast with other cultures which may use terms like familial care-givers etc.

[5] Such a statement was politically correct in the 1950's.

[6] Mozart satirises mesmerism towards the end of Act I of *Cosi Fan Tutti* and makes it more poignant by putting the mesmeric powers in the hands of a servant, Despina, rather than the rich bourgeoisie.

[7] McGrath bases his model of legitimation on that of Berger & Luckmann in their book *The Social Construction of Reality* (1967).

[8] "Nave's topics were originally published in the early 1900's, and consists of 20,000+ topics and subtopics, and 100,000 references to the Scriptures." (Crosswalk.com)

[9] Besides being a pejorative term, "spastic" is also a legitimate medical description of certain categories of movement associated with a range of medical conditions and muscle tone. It is also one of the three main types of cerebral palsy.

[10] Etic and emic are essentially terms used in social anthropology (See Harris, 1976; p 329ff)

[11] *Practical Suggestions for Intercession for the Sick*, GM&ICP, NLS, Acc9084/337[M].

[12]*ibid.*

[13] Abstracted from Margaret Stewart's notes in preparation for the healing service on 30th July 1996.

[14] Iona Community, *Prayer for the Iona Community, Miles Christi.*

[15] The Seven Levels of Consciousness are:

1 'deep trance consciousness'
2 'sleep consciousness'
3 'picture consciousness'
4 'waking day consciousness'
5 'object consciousness'
6 'psychic consciousness' or Imagination (to be achieved in the near future)
7 'spiritual consciousness' or Intuition (final unifying consciousness). (Seddon, 1988, p 26ff)

Index

A

Healing Service. *See* Iona Community
Health Narrative 56, 57
Heisenberg 86
Holism 46, 48, 51
Holistic medicine 49
Holocaust 122
Hull, John 19, 26, 30, 32, 100, 126, 127, 129, 154, 162, 195, 196, 214
Hume, David 20, 26, 33, 44, 71, 72, 73, 74, 75, 76, 77, 78, 79, 84, 87, 88,
        121, 128, 129, 130, 213, 216
    Definition of Miracle 73

I

Imago Dei 29, 48, 64, 65, 145, 147
Incarnational Theology 47, 48
Irrationality & Enlightenment 77
Isaiah 17, 18, 19, 20, 92, 98, 114, 117, 166, 191, 194, 195, 196, 198
    Ch. 35 114, 194, 195, 198

J

Jesus Seminar 119. *See* Funk, R
John the Baptist 115, 196

K

Kleinman, Arthur. *See* Illness narratives

L

Lambourne, Bob 45
Laying on of hands 87, 180
Lazarus 93, 135, 208
Lewis, A 26, 30, 46, 66, 67, 107, 108, 197, 224

M

MacIntyre, A. 57
Medical demonstrations of disabled people 122
Medical model of disability 24, 29, 33, 63, 72, 86, 87, 88, 121, 130, 139,
        144, 148, 158, 165, 166, 182, 188, 205, 207, 209, 210

N

Nave's Topical Bible 98

Printed in the United Kingdom
by Lightning Source UK Ltd.
105486UKS00001B/301-306